D0875053

Quality
of Life

Quality of Life

Perspectives and Issues

EDITED BY

ROBERT L. SCHALOCK
Hastings College
and
Mid-Nebraska Mental Retardation Services, Inc.

MICHAEL J. BEGAB
Editor, AAMR Special Publications

AMERICAN ASSOCIATION ON MENTAL RETARDATION

Library of Congress Cataloging-in-Publication Data

Quality of life: perspectives and issues / edited by Robert L. Schalock.
    p. cm.—(AAMR special publications)
    Includes bibliographical references.
    ISBN 0-940898-23-3: $32.50 (est.)
    1. Mentally handicapped—Services for—United States.   2. Mental retardation—United States.
I. Schalock, Robert L.   II. Series.
HV3006.A4Q35   1990   90-33651
362.3'8'0973—dc20   CIP

Printed in the United States of America

Contents

v

Preface

This book deals with the concept of quality of life for persons with mental retardation and closely related developmental disabilities. There has been a long history of interest in the concept of, and quest for, a life of quality. Ever since the ancient Greeks, people have tried to find out how to implement the conditions of the "good life." Plato's *Republic*, for example, reflects the age-old quest for the means of insuring a high quality of life not only for a few chosen individuals, but for society as a whole.

The concept of quality of life (QOL) has recently become an important issue in the field of mental retardation and developmental disabilities. There are a number of reasons for this interest, including concern that many feel about the quality of life of community-placed disabled persons (Baker & Intagliata, 1982; Bradley & Clarke, 1976; Emerson, 1985; Landesman, 1986; Schalock, Keith, Hoffman, & Karan, 1989; Schalock & Lilley, 1986; Schalock & Thornton, 1988; Zautra, 1983); the demonstration that social environments have considerable impact on an individual's way of life; the fact that complex programs require complex outcome measures; the reemergence of the holistic health perspective; and the concern that many people have about how others find satisfaction and life quality in a rapidly changing world. In addition, Campbell and Converse (1972) pointed to the need for an understanding of how social conditions are perceived and evaluated. Commenting on the evaluation of rising expectations, they wrote:

> Discontent with objective conditions has appeared to be increasing over exactly the same period that those conditions have at most points and by almost all criteria been improving—a discrepancy with portentous social and political implications. (p. 9)

Thus, to many consumers and practitioners alike, conditions of quality in the living, work, and community integration lives of persons with mental retardation and closely related developmental disabilities are not changing fast enough to keep up with the rapid and wide-scale changes in people's attitudes, aspirations, and values. As W. R. Shea (1976) suggested in an essay entitled "The Quest For A High Quality of Life":

> What lends a sense of urgency to the quest . . . is the pervasive feeling that time is running out, not only for philosophers, political scientists, and sociologists, but on politicians [and practitioners] as well. (p. 1)

Developing a book on *Quality of Life: Perspectives and Issues* is not a simple task, because quality of life itself is inherently within the private, not the public, realm of understanding. Additionally, the term itself refers to significantly different phenomena. For example, in 1978, C.E. Meyers edited the first American Association on Mental Deficiency QOL publication entitled, *Quality of Life in Severely and Profoundly Mentally Retarded People: Research Foundations for Improvement*. That monograph focused on behavioral research dealing with stereotyped behavior and communication skills in severely and profoundly impaired people. Conversely, the 1986 President's Committee on Mental Retardation Report to the President was entitled *Twentieth Anniversary Symposium: Maximizing the Quality of Life for Individuals with Mental Retardation and Other Developmental Disabilities*. Major sections of this report focused on "rights, responsibilities and responsiveness," "programmatic trends," "prevention and research," and "economics of disability."

The reader of this volume will find a much different perspective on the concept of *quality of life*. Specifically, the contributors have focused their presentations on personal perspectives (Part I), service delivery issues (Part II), assessment and measurement issues (Part III), and the future of quality of life as a concept and principle (Part IV).

Throughout this book, authors use and define the concept of QOL quite differently. Despite their differences, the following four premises regarding QOL apply (Goode, 1988):

1. QOL is essentially the same for persons with and without disabilities. Persons with and without disabilities want the same things in their lives, have the same needs, and want to fulfill responsibilities in the same way other persons in society do.
2. QOL is basically a social phenomenon and a product primarily of interactions with others. This requires a social ecological definition of QOL for the individual that also incorporates the QOL of significant others in the setting.
3. QOL is the outcome of individuals meeting basic needs and fulfilling basic responsibilities in community settings (family, recreational, school, and work). Individuals who are able to meet needs and fulfill responsibilities in ways satisfactory to themselves and to significant others in community settings experience a high QOL in those settings.
4. QOL is a matter of consumer rather that professional definition. QOL issues should be defined by consumers and other citizens rather than by professionals in the field. Ultimately, it is how the individual perceives and evaluates his own situation rather than how others see him that determines the QOL he or she experiences.

As I have mentioned elsewhere (Schalock et al., 1989), the concept of quality of life will probably replace deinstitutionalization, normalization, and community adjustment as *the* issue of the 1990s. As we begin to integrate the perspectives and resolve the important issues regarding its measurement and use, we will have to become even more sensitive to the consumers of programmatic services who are increasingly concerned about answers to questions such as:

- What futures can we look forward to?
- What are our dreams and aspirations?
- What is our economic income, and what impact does my economic situation have on my life?
- What roles do people have in their community?
- What significant relationships are there in my life?
- Do I have meaningful contact with family, spouse, or friends?
- What would have to change for me to benefit more?
- What are we waiting for?

It was pointed out in a recent editorial by Sharon Landesman (1986) that, "The new buzz words in mental retardation are quality of life and personal life satisfaction" (p. 14). She also proposed in the same editorial that the following four questions be addressed: What does quality of life mean? How can the concept be operationally defined? What strategies are likely to be effective in monitoring the quality of life of individuals and groups? What sets of environmental variables are most likely to enhance the quality of life for different types of individuals at different times of their lives?

These are important questions that must be answered based on advances in consumer satisfaction research, program evaluation methodology, assessment of quality of life and life satisfaction, social ecology, and theories of personal-environmental transactions. It is a large task and one that each of the authors hopes will be aided by this book.

At a personal level, I want to thank all of the persons who contributed so well to the anticipated success of this book. It has been a pleasure to work with each contributor and to learn so much in the process. Even though the last section focuses on the future, a statement in the first chapter by Connie Martinez holds even more true . . . . "you can never have a good life if nobody ever has a dream for you, unless you learn to have a dream for yourself."

Robert L. Schalock

REFERENCES

Baker, F., & Intagliata, J. (1982). Quality of life in the evaluation of community support services. *Evaluation and Program Planning, 5,* 69–79.

Bradley, V., & Clarke, G. (Eds.). (1976). *Paper victories and hard realities: The implementation of the legal and constitutional rights of the mentally disabled.* Washington, DC: Health Policy Center.

Campbell, A., & Converse, P.E. (Eds.). (1972). *The human meaning of social change*. New York: Russell Sage Foundation.
Emerson, E. R. (1985). Evaluating the impact of deinstitutionalization on the lives of mentally retarded people. *American Journal of Mental Deficiency, 90*(3), 277–288.
Goode, D. A. (1988). Quality of life for persons with disabilities: A look at the issues. Final report for a conference held in Washington, DC. April 30–May 1, 1988. Valhalla, NY: The Mental Retardation Institute, Westchester County Medical Center and New York Medical College.
Landesman, S. (1986). Quality of life and personal satisfaction: Definition and measurement issues. *Mental Retardation. 24*(3), 141–143.
Meyers, C. E. (Ed.). (1978). *Quality of life in severely and profoundly mentally retarded people: Research foundations for improvement.* Washington, DC: American Association on Mental Deficiency.
President's Committee on Mental Retardation (1986). *Report to the President: Maximizing the QOL for individuals with mental retardation and other developmental disabilities.* Washington, DC: U.S. Department of Health and Human Services, Office of Human Development Services.
Schalock, R. L., Keith, K. D., Hoffman, K., & Karan, O. C. (1989). Quality of life: Its measurement and use in human service programs. *Mental Retardation, 27*(1), 25–31.
Schalock, R. L., & Lilley, M. A. (1986). Placement from community-based mental retardation programs: How well do clients do after 8–10 years? *American Journal of Mental Deficiency, 90*, 669–676.
Schalock, R. L., & Thornton, C. V. D. (1988). *Program evaluation: A field guide for administrators.* New York: Plenum Publishing.
Shea, W. R. (1976). The quest for a high quality of life. In J. Farlow & W. R. Shea (Eds.), *Values and the quality of life* (pp. 1–5). New York: Science History Publications.
Zautra, A. (1983). The measurement of quality in community life: Introduction to the special issue. *Journal of Community Psychology, 11*, 83–87.

Part I
Quality of Life: Personal Perspectives

One of the common themes presented throughout this book is the subjective nature of quality of life and the necessity of asking persons to describe what influences and impacts their life of quality. We are fortunate to have the contributions of a number of persons who are or have been closely related to the service delivery system and feel strongly about what is important in a life of quality.

The reader should note that this first section presents several persons' subjective impressions of quality of life. By their very nature, these chapters introduce you to the subjective approach to the quality of life issue, which is an evasive concept that is not yet well developed. Thus, the following six chapters are not meant to be empirically or research based, but rather subjective and personal. The authors share their informed opinions to assist us in understanding better the complexity of the service delivery, assessment, and policy issues discussed in subsequent chapters.

1
A Dream for Myself

Connie Martinez
People First Capital Group

I'd like to say a few things about the quality of life of people like me. We can have—and now I *do* have—a good quality of life, but we still have to fight for it. We have to take back control of our lives from the KEEPERS, from the professionals.

Most of the people I've met who work in this field don't believe that I could have a good quality of life or that I could even live on my own. When I was little, the doctor told my parents that I would never be able to take care of myself and that they could put me away. Even though they didn't do that to me, I always wondered why every day my father would come home from work and look at me with anger, like I did something wrong. Mostly I didn't know what I did wrong, and I was hurt. And I started to feel I AM BAD, because I really made my parents unhappy. So I became angry at myself. Now I understand that my father was angry because he thought he was going to be stuck all his life taking care of me like I was a child. But you know what? Just before I was going to graduate from independent living (I was still living with my parents) my father reached out and touched my face like he finally forgave me. Or maybe it was his way of asking me to forgive him. I'll never know, because he died of a heart attack just when I graduated.

But even to this very day, my mother doesn't believe that I have control of my life. I don't know what she thinks when I tell her I am going to Washington, DC, to talk to the professors, but she sure doesn't believe me. I'll always be "pobrecita Connie" to her. She'll always pity me and always be angry at me because she still believes the doctor even when she sees different.

Note. The changes that Connie went through in Santa Cruz didn't get a chance to make her truly independent for 20 years. She sat home and watched TV for years. Then a social welfare agency heard about her, intervened, and placed her in a series of sheltered workshops, culminating in placement in a segregated adult school. It wasn't until a program of training for independent living was started in Sacramento in 1981, and almost immediately after that a self advocacy group was formed, with Connie becoming a charter member of both, that she began to take genuine control of her life.

3

My parents didn't put me away, and finally I'm taking back my life, after losing years of it to the wrong information. But I wonder how many people are under lock and key because that doctor thought he could play God?

So, when I was growing up everybody either thought they had to take care of me, like my parents and my brothers and sisters, or they pushed me away, like some of my relatives and like most of the teachers who stuck me out of the way in a corner of the room and passed me to get rid of me, but humiliated me when they could.

My parents always had a dream for my brothers and sister for when they grew up, but nobody ever had a dream for me, so I never had a dream for myself. You can never have a good life if nobody ever has a dream for you unless you learn to have a dream for yourself. That's what I had to do, and now I have a dream for myself: a little casa, a garden with flowers and peppers and tomatoes, a loved one to share my life with—and more. Even if I don't get all those things, I know I'm alive now. And I believe my dreams will come true.

Quality of life would make a mother support her daughter. That is very important. In my case, there was no support. When I was a child, the doctor said to my parents, "You may have a dream for a perfect child but forget about that. You parented a broken child." And that was Connie. Thus, there was no dream for this child. There was no support. The child was not supposed to feel pain. Growing up, I didn't have the support from school. I didn't have support from family because the doctor was sort of the God. He was telling the parents that the child had nothing; no pain, would be retarded, no dream, no hope.

When you grow up as a child you don't know about handicaps or what being retarded is. But you learn how people treat you different. A child can be cruel. You learn that you get sent to another school because "it is best for you." And you find out that what you learn is making things with your hands (potholders, windchimes, etc.). That's why I hate to do certain things with my hands—because I wanted to use my brain, even though I cannot read. I have dyslexia and I also have trouble saying certain words. And I have a lot of trouble remembering things. They always told me I couldn't get along in life if I couldn't read. But I *can* get along, and I could have a long time ago if they didn't always make me feel bad and dumb.

So, the first thing for the professionals and the parents to understand is that we can have a good quality of life if we have control over our own lives and if we have the help we need to keep that control and independence in our own lives. We don't need KEEPERS, we need TEACHERS.

In junior high I was OK. But then in high school things were different. I had to learn things about the presidents. They knew I had a learning disability, but they sent me to a political science class anyway. I said fine. I want to be with everyone, not just my brothers and sisters with mental disabilities. I want to be in the community. I want people to know I exist. At that time report cards were a competition. I got tired of having Fs. So I lied—and I think I overdid it. One of the girls in the back (she never really spoke to me) asked what did I have? I said "A + ." She went over to the teacher, said to the teacher, "I can't figure it out; how did Connie get A?" And that teacher said loud enough for everyone to hear, "Connie did not get A, she got F." All those young people were laughing at me.

Did you ever see a bird with a long neck that sticks its head in the sand? I was that bird with my head in the sand. Until that moment I didn't know the word HATE. But I began to have a hate for intelligent people. Here was a teacher who had gone to college and learned about everything you have to about teaching, but he missed the point about himself. He forgot that the other person has feelings and wants to be a part of the community. And he didn't care about my feelings. So I started feeling hate.

But then there was another teacher, and she cared for me. When I was in pain and she saw me cry she would hold me. I would cry on her shoulder.

And I remember our high school trip [to Santa Cruz]. A friend asked me why I didn't sign up to go. I said I knew what my mother would say. My mother was very overprotective. But she said, "You have nothing to lose. Why don't you sign up anyway?" And I said to myself, "She's right. I have nothing to lose." So I went and signed my name, Connie Martinez. I went home and told my mom, "Mom, there is going to be a high school trip to the ocean. I have never been there before and I want to go." I said, "Mother, I want to be with people, and with nature." And my mother said, "No, you're going to get lost. You're not going out by yourself. We'd be too concerned and worried."

I used to always accept what my mother said because she knew best for me. But this time I couldn't. I was SICK (. . . enough to have to go to bed). Then the teacher came. The doorbell rang and my mother answered. It was the teacher. I wish I could remember her name but I can't. She had flowers and a card from the other students and a list of names of people who wanted me to be able to go on the trip. She told my mother she wanted me to come on the trip. She said she would take responsibility for me. At first, my mother said, "No, no." And then the teacher came back again, and she convinced my mom to let me go. And I got better real fast.

My mother took me shopping to get new clothes for the trip. The day [of the trip] I got up early. I would never get up early, but I did this time. My mom fixed my lunch and she and my father took me to the school and watched me get on the bus. They called my name on the the bus. I figured the teacher was going to babysit me like they always did at church and wherever else I went; but it was better than not to go to the trip. Even if they watched over this little retarded girl, I would be happy. So half of me was happy, half was not.

And then we started to get near and I saw gorgeous things I'd never seen before in my life—mountains and big trees and everything green, green, green. And the sky was so blue! I just enjoyed it all and my heart was beating fast. And we finally got there. And the door to the bus opened and the teacher said, "Connie, the door is opened. Go enjoy yourself and be with your friends." I thought she was going to watch over me and instead she said go out there. So I jumped into the sand and ran in the sand and just felt good. I took off my shoes. I forgot my lunch.

Did you ever see a bird in the cage? I was that bird. That teacher opened the door to the cage and I flew—it was the first time I was free. No people to watch over me. I wasn't in a cage any more. I was free. And when I came home to Sacramento I wasn't the same anymore. I was still Connie, but I was different. I had changed. There was something inside me hungry to be free.

I couldn't accept that my mom would watch over me, that they were going to watch over me, that they knew best for me. I couldn't accept that any more. I tried to fight it, but it was too strong, and it got stronger and stronger. I'm not saying that my mom didn't love me, but I couldn't live the negative. I knew I had to be on my own, to fall down on my face if I had to (and I have, plenty, and yes, I've been hurt), but I knew I would get up and start over again. And I've done that.

Now all I have is different. But I see that things are not working right for my disabled brothers and sisters, my *familia* I call them, like in the workshops. I don't like how they are being used. The keepers say they know best for us. That is a JOKE! They are making a living off me and my familia. Many mistreat people who can't defend themselves. And nobody listens to the consumers. Who would listen to me if a keeper said I was lying?

After being in such places, I got into independent living. And I decided I had nothing to lose to be in People First. We have civil rights for blacks, chicanos, and women. You know how some people are against blacks? Well, some people are against retarded, too. I see injustice and pain.

How many times do we have to show that we feel pain? How many times do we have to show that we suffer enough? I never had the support of my [biological] family. I wish to heaven that I did, but I never did. They didn't have a dream for me, so I didn't have a dream for myself.

But now I control my own life, and I know I can have my own dream for me. And I DO have a dream. I want to share my life with someone who cares for me. To have a casa to share with him—a home. A family.

A big yard with chilis and peppers and tomatoes. To cook for him, and make tortillas. And even to put the slippers on his feet—that's OK in a dream.

I also have a dream for my disabled brothers and sisters. To change the injustice that is going on.

2
Reflections on My Quality of Life: Then and Now

Nancy Ward
People First

I have my own condominium which I'm really excited about because now I have something to show for putting my money into, plus I don't have anybody telling me what to do, like putting my stuff up on the walls or if I can hang my tapestries and all that kind of stuff where I want to. As far as work goes, I work for a Lincoln Lancaster Drug Project. I really like my job a lot, I'm learning how to do this job. I work with nine teenagers, which can be a handful sometimes. I work with different programs such as teaching them how to get along with their families so that they feel they can work out their problems; in addition, they feel they can work out their problems in a different way than by using drugs.

Q. Does your experience help you be better at that job?

A. I think so. I think I was sort of an outcast, because when I was growing up everyone was calling me retarded. It was hard for me to deal with.

Q. Does your job at this point make you feel important?

A. Yes, because I feel I have something to offer people by my own experiences, what I've learned in how to deal with my problems. Also, it gives me a lot of rewards beside money. I think it's important to the kids also, because they in turn get to learn how to deal with their problems and don't get into more trouble than they already have.

Q. Is your job more important than other jobs you've done or jobs you see some of your friends doing?

A. I feel [this job] is like my previous ones because I was working with people and I was helping people. So I compare with the other jobs I had, such as working in the deli at Leons and working at the laundry at the Villager, and they're not as important.

Q. Why do you think they're not as important?

A. Because they're not what I wanted to do. And I like working with people, I like giving a lot, you know, getting a lot out of what I do.

Q. Is it important just to be able to do what you want to do? Is that in itself why you like the job?

A. Yes, because I think you have to like your job and if you don't like your job, then you're not able to perform up to your highest potential.

Q. Do you live alone?

A. Yes.

Q. Have you always lived alone?

A. No.

Q. Have you had roommates in the past?

A. Yes, I've gone through the whole system.

Q. Of the things that you've experienced in the whole system, is what you're doing now the best option you've had?

A. Yes, it really is because I like to go where I can, have my own space. When I lived in the group home, I had to share my room, so I mean there was no place in the whole house that you could actually call yours.

Q. What about socially. Does living alone present any social problems?

A. I could see where it could present social problems if I wasn't as active in other things.

Q. So you're active in social groups, clubs; what kinds of things do you do?

A. Like, I am a member of People First and also a member of Advocacy First of Lincoln, which is the local chapter of People First. I go around doing speaking engagements and still work with Region V teaching people how to advocate for themselves.

Q. Do you do any social kinds of things that are not directed toward volunteer work for people with disabilities or related kinds of things?

A. Yes and no, because the way to answer your question is that I'll go out with my friends or just do things with my friends. My friends happen to have disabilities.

Q. What are some of the things you like to do?

A. We go to movies, we'll just go out and have dinner, go downtown and go shopping, things like that.

Q. Have you ever been lonely living alone?

A. A couple of times.

Q. How do you deal with that?

A. I go out and ride my bike or do something where I don't have to feel lonely.

Q. On the whole, even though that happens sometimes, do you think living alone in your own place is a better option?

A. Definitely because like I say, I can have my own space, if I want to. I can leave my clothes in the middle of the room. Who's going to tell me I have to pick them up?

Q. How independent do you consider yourself?

A. Extremely independent.

Q. Have you always been extremely independent?

A. No.

Q. Could you talk a little about, how/where you started out and how you got to where you are now in terms of independence?

A. Well, when I became an adult, of course the natural thing to want to do was to move away from home so this is what I wanted to do, but my parents wouldn't let me move away until I was 25, and then I had to move into the system, but the system taught me things like how to make my bed, how to set the table, how to do my wash and all the basic kind of things which I already knew. And I couldn't understand why my parents were telling me I needed to be in this kind of structured setting, when I knew all this stuff they were supposed to be teaching me.

Q. So how'd you deal with it?

A. I got mad and didn't deal with my feelings then and so I got mad and would talk to my parents about it and I think by getting mad every time I talked to them, I knew what their response was going to be. Finally, I decided that if I wanted my parents to treat me as an adult, I'd better start acting like an adult.

Q. One of the things, Nancy, that people worry about, when family members or friends of theirs want to be independent in the community is whether they'll take good care of themselves, be physically well and safe, and that sort of thing. Could you talk a little bit about that issue?

A. Well, I think that's definitely true, because I feel that I was raised differently than my brothers and sisters were raised and by that I mean, my sister would be allowed to go out on dates when she was like 16 and I wasn't allowed to start dating until I was like 18. She was also allowed to stay out later than I. That's just one example. Also, I think that until all my brothers and sisters and I became adults my role with my brothers and sisters was different as they saw me as being retarded and they were going to have to show me how to do all these different things in my lifetime. Now, since we've become adults and I've learned how to act differently than I was then, my brothers and sisters see me as an adult and treat me as such. For example, when I wanted to go to college, my parents were really scared about me doing this and didn't want me to do it. I just had to prove to them as well as to myself that I could do it. After getting my GED I think my parents have let up a lot on me and see that there are some things that I can do.

Q. What would you say is your current relationship with your parents?

A. I like them a lot better, now. I really do. I know how to deal with my feelings now and so I am being treated as an adult, whereas when I was growing up I didn't know how to express myself other than by getting mad or running off or crying or something.

Q. Do you think that's the main reason why you have a better relationship with your family or are there other things, too?

A. I think there's other things in it, too, because I think my brothers and sisters now that they are adults can understand me as a person a lot better than they could when we were growing up.

Q. You talked a minute ago about getting your GED and wanting to go to college. Can you say just a bit about the things you've done living on your own in the community to improve your learning and skills?

A. Ever since I've been a little kid, I've loved working with people so I wanted to become a nurse. So I went out to Southeast Community College and explained to them I was going to need extra classes because of being in special ed; so they worked with me to get the extra classes that I needed and then I took the entrance exam for nursing and missed it by one point. (I about died.) So then I went back to them and explained to them and asked them how was I going to get my grades up and that's when they told me I was going to get my GED and it made me mad, because here I'd been up front with them and explained that, you know, I was in special ed. So why are they telling me 5 years later that I need to get my GED? So that's just one example. But I guess I should finish that. I went ahead and got my GED and I love it (this isn't nice) but the highest I got was 62 and the lowest I got was 49—which gave me an average of 54.2, which was above normal so I went and pushed it in some people's faces. (I couldn't help that.)

Q. How did your history as a student in special ed influence the quality of your life—good or bad?

A. Well see, I had it both ways because I was in regular classes until the time I was in sixth grade. So when I started junior and senior high was when I went into special ed. So I think that gave me an advantage and disadvantage. For example, we had my fifth grade social study book when I was a senior in high school and how's that supposed to make you feel when you are a senior in high school, and you are getting a fifth grade social studies book? But the way it helped me was that I got the attention that I needed and so that helped, but it was also hard in that when I was in special ed it was when special ed was first starting and it was in the corner but it was still in the school building and was called the *dummy room*. So even though it was still labeled it wasn't mainstreamed like it is now.

Q. You seem to resent the fact that when you finished high school in special ed, actually you didn't really have a diploma?

A. Yah, I do because that's what they told me it was. I mean, I would think that they were being honest with us, tell us what we were getting, not just a piece of paper. I mean, I didn't see why we had to be treated any different than anyone else who was graduating. We took the same classes basically and had the same credits and stuff. So why should we be treated any differently?

Q. Living where you do now and doing the things you do now, are you still treated differently? Or are you treated pretty much the same as everyone else these days?

A. The other day when I got home from going to Ohio and our Board meeting, I had this letter from the Police Department and I had gotten a ticket and had paid the fine for the ticket in April and my court date was in May and they hadn't gotten the money so they put a warrant out for me. When I got home and opened this up, it really scared me so I talked it over with my parents and Mom wanted to go down and take care of it for me. I don't want to be treated just because I have a disability different than any of my brothers and sisters would be treated. I wanted Mom to go with me, yes, but [to] give me support, not to do it for me. So we went down there the next day to pay the fine and they told me that I needed to go talk to the city attorney. So I go to do this, because if I would have paid the whole charges now, I would have also admitted to the fact of being guilty without them getting their check and I didn't think that was fair, and so when I went to this city attorney office, Mom was the one who went in, I mean, she was the one who went in, she wasn't going to let me go in. It just so upset me, so I explained to her how I felt about that and then we both went in and I explained to them (but it was hard for me to explain to them), and Mom was getting upset with me for not being calm. Finally, I just told Mom (I shouldn't say this) but finally I just told Mom to shut up. I never told my mom that before. And so the city attorney could see that I had tried to pay for my ticket, that I had to get it in on time, so they dropped the warrant and they dropped the extra court charges, then we went back and paid for my ticket.

Q. Are there other ways you sometimes are treated differently by other people?

A. Like, when we have board meetings and stuff, it's real hard for me to understand big words and to read as fast as other people and we were doing our goals and objectives the other day. Finally I was getting so frustrated I just told them, "I don't understand the big words, I can't read as fast as you guys are reading, can you go slower?" Warren said there wasn't enough time to go slower, but somebody came over and helped me so that could be seen as a time where I would have been treated differently.

Q. Are there other times you don't want to be treated differently?

A. It's like (I don't know how to explain this) because of the experiences I've had with my life, and all the different kinds of problems I've had. It's like at work I have to be a role model all the time for the kids, as to how they have to act and deal with their problems and that's real hard to deal with. And so finally I've just got to the point where I couldn't, you know I don't see myself as perfect, so I just fool people.

Q. You referred several times to your bike, and by your bike you mean your motor scooter. Could you talk a little bit how you came to have a motor scooter and how that has changed the quality of your life?

A. Well, my bike is one of the examples of "I'm not dealing very well with my parents." Because my parents didn't want me to have one and I went ahead and got it, even though they didn't want me to have one. But the freedom that my bike has given me is amazing because I always had to stand and wait for the bus, take the bus wherever I went. I can't describe the amount of freedom because I don't have to stand there for like half an hour to get some place I want to go. It's also given me a lot of freedom in that's how I deal with my problems. Whenever I get frustrated and want to think, I just go out riding, that's how I think.

Q. Did getting a license to drive a motor bike present any problems?

A. Well, it presented special problems in being able to understand what I was supposed to do. I had to have things explained to me and that's one time I'm asking for it and it makes me mad that I need that. Anyway, I got my driver's license, and that was a big step for me. It took me a lot of courage and confidence of myself to go and get it. I wasn't sure I was going to get it. It was just one more example that showed me I could do something I didn't think I could do.

Q. You talked about your problems with the ticket and legal system. Has having a motor bike added some responsibilities that cause you to worry or other kinds of problems?

A. Yah, it has because to learn the laws, this is another place where I was treated differently, don't necessarily like it, but I'd have to have people explain them to me and sometimes, for example, how I got the ticket that I talked about, is that I didn't see a stop sign and didn't stop. Normally, you have stop signs over here and the stop sign was over here. So yah, it's given me some added responsibilities and another way it's taught me I can do some things and it gives me that much more confidence and I'm that much more excited about it, so I think it's neat, actually.

Q. I'm also interested in asking you to talk about how you deal with things like dental and medical services. Do you choose your own doctors and get yourself to your own appointments? Do you take care of that independently, or do you have special help with that sort of thing?

A. No, that's one of the other things I like. I deal with it just like any of my brothers and sisters would deal with it. I have my own doctor.

Q. Did you choose your own doctor?

A. Yah, which again is just something neat that I'm learning how to do.

Q. When did you, at what point, as you came through the system, did you make those decisions to take care of those things on your own?

A. When I learned about self-advocacy. When I developed the self-advocacy skills that I have, I saw myself as a person. I didn't see myself as being retarded, and that's what I was. I saw myself as a person—yes, I have a disability but that's okay. The most important part of me is that I'm a person and like when I go out, do the speaking and stuff that I do, I mean, it took me four years to learn and get confidence in myself before I [could] go and do that. I tell people, no, I'm not going to go out front.

Q. How old are you now, do you mind saying?

A. No, I'm almost 38.

Q. If you could identify two things that are most important to you in the quality of life in the community, what would those things be?

A. Becoming a self-advocate and learning to see myself as a person. Because in seeing myself as a person that started me to start questioning things that were going on in my life and to develop a better life for myself, and then to have my own place would be the second thing.

Q. Besides having your own place, could you pick out one main thing that is different about your current independence from when you were part of the system?

A. When I was living in the system, it made me real frustrated. You had to fit to the system; the system wasn't made for you so that would be one thing I think that the system be made to gear towards individuals as to where they are at. As I've said, some people may know Steps 1–5, so why teach them that?

Q. If you could change one thing in your life, what would you change?

A. I don't know whether I'll make sense out of this. All the anger and not knowing how to direct my feelings in a positive way and my feelings that I've had about my family. Also, to be able to reach more people than I already have reached.

Q. What do you mean, reach more people?

A. People who have disabilities and to show them what life could be as learning how to advocate for themselves, see themselves as a person, as I still think there are a lot of people that are in the services and they're oppressed. Does that make sense?

Q. How are they oppressed?

A. I don't think that professionals listen to what we're trying to tell them. I think that people are now starting to say that we don't like the system the way it is, so why do we have to have [it] that way? Why is it that when we're the ones that know how we feel that we're not being listened to in where we want to live, for example?

Q. At this point in your life, can you go to the movies, or to the store, or to church, or to the park, and be treated just like anybody else and have nobody know that there's anything different about your life?

A. It's a great feeling, in that people see me that way, but even greater feeling that I can see myself as being able to do those things.

Q. Is there anything else you think influences the quality of your life or the lives of other people?

A. Yah, I wish for a lot of my friends—they happen to have physical disabilities which you can see—that they would be able to be treated just as everybody else, you know, also or because that they're harder to understand because they have a speech impediment, for example. I don't see why society in general can't take the time to listen to them. I mean, they got a lot to worry about how they're treated, how they want to be treated, about things that would be an interest to everybody.

Q. What do you think would help?

A. To have society not so fast paced, to have society be able to listen to people, to have society not have to be afraid of people, so I think there's a lot of public education that has to be [done]. I can understand why it's important for people who have a disability to be given a chance to make friends within the community. I mean I really do think that's important, but if they choose to have other people that have disabilities or to somehow have friends connected with the field, then I don't see why that's not okay, too.

A Final Thought: I just want everybody to treat people as they want to be treated. I don't think because we have a disability makes us any different than anybody else. We're more alike than we are different.

3
Quality of Life Versus Quality of Life Judgments: A Parent's Perspective

Diane M. Crutcher
National Down Syndrome Congress

The issue of the need for a book on the quality of life of persons with disabilities disenchants me because I live daily with someone whose quality of life would never be questioned if you only knew her. I have a fear that too many people truly never *get to know* someone with a disability and their respective families and therefore cannot separate the person from the disability. This, then, results in *quality of life* questions.

In order to provide a parent's perspective on the concept of quality of life, I have chosen to distinguish between *quality of life* and *quality of life judgments*. The former unjustly lays guilt at the feet of those with disabilities, the latter places responsibility on the more skilled, intelligent, beautiful, and biased others who superimpose certain factors onto those with disabilities and thereby apply the all-damaging *quality of life judgments*.

To provide some insight into the impact on the family of quality of life judgments, I would like to cite Emily Perl Kingsley's analogy[1] of how it feels to find out that your child has a handicap.

> When you're going to have a baby, it's like you're planning a vacation to Italy. You are all excited. Seeing the Coliseum . . . the Michelangelo . . . the gondolas of Venice. You get a whole bunch of guidebooks. You learn a few phrases in Italian so you can order in restaurants and get around. When it comes time, you excitedly pack your bags, head for the airport and take off for Italy . . . only when you land, the stewardess announces 'Welcome to Holland'.
>
> You look at one another in disbelief and shock saying, Holland? What are you talking about—Holland? I signed up for Italy!! But they explain that there's been a change of plans and the plane has landed in Holland—and there you must stay.
>
> "But I don't know anything about Holland! I don't want to stay here," you say. "I never wanted to come to Holland!" "I don't know what you do in Holland and I don't want to learn!!" But, you do stay, you

---

[1]Kingsley, E.P. (1987). *Kids like these*. CBS TV Movie.

> go out and buy some new guidebooks. You learn some new phrases in a whole new language and you meet people you never knew existed.
>
> But the important thing is that you are not in a filthy, plague-infested slum full of pestilence and famine. You are simply in another place . . . a different place than you had planned. It's slower-paced than Italy; less flashy than Italy; but after you've been there a little while and have had a chance to catch your breath, you begin to discover that Holland has windmills . . . Holland has tulips . . . and Holland even has Rembrandts.
>
> But everyone else you know is busy coming and going from Italy. And they're all bragging about what a great time they had there. And for the rest of your life you will say, "Yes, that's where I was going . . . . that's where I was supposed to go . . . that's what I had planned." And the pain of that will never, ever go away.
>
> And you have to accept that pain because the loss of that dream, the loss of that plan is a very, very significant loss. But . . . . if you spend your life mourning the fact that you didn't get to Italy, you will never be free to enjoy the very special, the very lovely things about Holland.

Let's review this profound statement for the gravity of quality of life judgments present in it—the disbelief and shock at the diagnosis; the desperate quest for normalcy; the questioning of one's own ability; and then the reality that disability is not a " . . . filthy, plague-infested slum full of pestilence and famine . . . [it is] . . another place . . . a different place than you had planned . . . . [but it] has windmills . . . . tulips . . . and even Rembrandts."

Indeed, it is what you make it once you get over society's misconceptions about disability—those with which you have been nurtured and now find significantly difficult to shake. My daughter is 16 years old and has Down syndrome; but that is secondary to her worth as a viable, competitive, proud, and dignified person. In reflecting on her birth and subsequent diagnosis of Down syndrome in light of quality of life judgments, I am amazed that we were able to overcome all of them and provide her with an undeniable sense of dignity that she carries forever with her.

Within 12 hours of her birth, her pediatrician came to my hospital room to tell me in a most antiquated and despairing fashion that she had Down syndrome—would never walk, talk, run, or play, or know that I was her mother. The nearest he ever got to me was to throw the papers for institutionalization on the bed and recommend that I not see her so that I would not get "attached." Sending her away forever so that she did not ruin our lives and going home to "really have another baby" were his final parting suggestions. Needless to say, there were numerous quality of life judgments present within the doctor's prognosis. It then fell to me to tell my husband about our new daughter. We had no background in disabilities but were amongst the fortunate to have a strong marriage. After I delivered the message and we cried together for hours, he went home that evening and pulled down our new and reputable reference journal to gain further insight. He was shocked to see the disability listed under *Monster*—another quality of life judgment?

Is it any wonder that families who are already rocked to the core by a circumstance that they know only happens to other people are further questioning their own ability to parent this child effectively and to maintain other current and future aspects of their lives? What most of us parents didn't realize as we were still reeling from the shock of the diagnosis was that we were being overwhelmed with quality of life judgments and not necessarily facts. It is inherent in our society to respect and adhere to the suggestions of those better educated than ourselves, particularly with regard to the medical profession.

What we were not cognizant of was that all persons, higher educated or not, can be biased, particularly when it comes to what they can and cannot "fix." There seems to be a higher frustration level with professionals when they face a situation that cannot be cured as they have been educated to handle. That frustration then passes itself along to the family in the context of quality of life judgments.

I remember receiving sympathy cards at our daughter's birth and subsequent diagnosis as well as holiday cards a few months later to all members of our family except the one with Down syndrome—as if she did not exist. Quality of life judgments? But there have been some excellent old friends who didn't care that she had Down syndrome; if we loved her, so did they. And there were new ones who accepted us for the family unit we are. The latter have the opportunity of our years of growth and ridding ourselves of quality of life judgments.

Literature abounds with information on the psychological impact of a child with a disability on the family. Much of this literature points to many contradictory findings and is replete with quality of life judgments. But many, many families report to us that the actuality of it is "the rich get richer and the poor get poorer." If the marriage was stable and strong before, if communication was full, if there are not overwhelming other concerns like finances and health, then the child with a disability presents a new challenge, but not one that is necessarily devastating to the unit. The contrary side is that a marriage already in difficulty may see this as the "straw that breaks the camel's back." Something was likely to disrupt the marriage, and this may serve as the catalyst; this is not really the cause of the disruption, but rather poor timing.

As with any family, balance is the key to success. The child with a disability should not be the focal point any more than any other one family member should. The focus must change over time as family needs change—and that is the ultimate quality of life: when the focal point of the family moves from person to person because everyone has an equal quality of life. This is the family's way of acknowledging quality of life judgments and defusing them; but they need professional and lay public support in establishing this attitude and maintaining it.

It is only fair to point out that prior to the birth of my daughter who has Down syndrome, I was not cognizant of quality of life judgments and so no doubt applied them freely as I unconsciously deemed appropriate. It then becomes our enormous job to call that frequent practice to the attention of parents, professionals, and the lay public, because it is quite difficult to change something we don't recognize as a problem.

When my husband and I did realize the quality of life judgments being handed down to our 4 lb. 9 oz. newborn, we came out fighting. We were certain that we were her only true advocates in correcting the misconceptions about her as a person. This then carried over to the service-provision field—no one was free of criticism. As our start in this world of disability had been such a jolting one because of the extremely negative method by which the diagnosis and prognosis regarding the disability were delivered, we began employing that human practice of generalizing to all professionals our perception of their biased attitudes. Therefore, all professionals were automatically suspect and had to prove themselves to us. We did not realize that we were literally impossible to reach and could not be convinced of the true interest of service-providers in our child. So much wasted time passed in learning to trust one another.

But there is now a new generation of professionals and parents forging a more positive path toward acceptance and moving away from quality of life judgments. We are raising our children in the community to live there as productive adults. Parents are talking, sharing, and trusting, as are professionals. Our quality of life is balancing; but we still have a long way to go because quality of life judgments go beyond the person with the disability and impact the family, too.

It is for this reason that parents find themselves demoted to "parent as patient." When my first daughter was born, my husband and I were still teenagers. He was in Viet Nam and I was working to make ends meet. Despite all of these negatives for a good life for our baby daughter, no one at the hospital suggested that I was not equipped to parent her. No one projected her life as an adult from the moment of her birth, and no one predicted her quality of life based on mine. But when her younger sister was born several years later, after we were financially stable, living together in our own home and to a great extent living the "American Dream," we found ourselves viewed as ill-equipped to parent our second child. Her life was projected through adulthood and quite negative quality of life judgments applied to her and, therefore, to us.

All parents have as their goal to live and die in peace, knowing that our children are all right, safe, happy, and living productive lives full of opportunity. That is no different if your child happens to have a disability. We then as parents of children with disabilities have a newfound quality of life ourselves in ridding the world of quality of life judgments. We will no longer be patronized. We will earn and retain our positions as partners within the realm of helping our child. We are members of the team and without us there is no true joint effort.

I do admit that ultimate quality of life is earned and reearned, person by person. But I also insist that that is tantamount to opportunity, and opportunity is accessible only when society decides it shall be. Therein lies our problem, and the one I sincerely hope is addressed within the confines of this book. How do we change society's view of persons who have mental retardation and other disabilities so that they can have opportunities to be the best they can be?

One of the first steps, it seems to me, is in the act of relaying the initial diagnosis. Whoever that professional is should take caution in the preparation and delivery of the message:

- Hold the baby while delivering the message. This implies acceptance on the part of the professional.
- Call the child by name.
- The place of meeting should be private, with the message being delivered as soon as possible following suspicion and tentative diagnosis.
- Accurate information should be on hand, not in overwhelming amounts, but just enough to begin the parents' venture into this new world, with bibliographies available so that they may obtain more information as they are ready for it.
- Refer the family to support systems, including local parent groups. Offer to make the calls for them.
- Avoid prognoses unless they are medically based. Be supportive.
- Do not pity the child nor the family.

Parents do not need or want pity; rather, they want respect—they are earning it monumentally! When the parents start off on as positive a note as possible in this situation, it is better for all involved both in the short-term and in the long-run.

To close, I would like to share some anecdotes from my personal life to emphasize the quality of life within a family who has a member with mental retardation. When we told our older daughter about her new sister shortly after the latter's birth and diagnosis, we stumbled trying to find the right words to relay our commitment and yet allow our older daughter the opportunity to find out how she now fit into our new life. We told her that it was nothing anyone had done wrong and that her new sister would need our help to achieve. Her response (at age four years) was, "But

Mommy, if something happened to me, you'd try, wouldn't you? We have to try for Mindie." No quality of life judgment there.

Some 11 years later, our daughter with Down syndrome was climbing a blacktopped incline covered with frost. She had on new school shoes still slick on the bottom and she fell over and over trying to reach the top of the hill where all of the other neighborhood children were waiting to catch the school bus. I watched from the door wondering if I should assist and finally decided that she had to do it on her own. She deserved and had earned the privilege of trying, falling, and trying again. I don't know which of us struggled more that morning, but eventually Mindie made it to the top of the hill and she turned, victoriously waving to the door, knowing that I would be there watching. Knowing that we will always be there— somewhat removed, perhaps, but with her nonetheless.

She had made it to the top herself—with guts and determination. She took a slightly different route; it took her longer to get there and with more bumps and bruises, but she reached the top nonetheless and there was no one more proud than she. Quality of life? We should all be so well endowed.

4
My Sister Angie: A Sibling's Perspective

Jeff Jacoby

Hastings College

Angela Marie Jacoby was born November 13, 1970, weighing approximately 5½ pounds with a height of 18 inches. She was born with spina bifida with myelomeningocele, which is the area the bifida or tumor was located. Thus, Angie had a obvious lump or cyst-like lesion on the back, covered with a thin membrane, making it actually possible to look into the tumor. The day after she was born she had the bifida surgically enclosed. This was the first of 36 surgeries and revisions Angela would have over the next 16 years. Because of the spina bifida, there were many serious symptoms, such as sensory loss and muscle weakness in the lower hip area, hydrocephalus, and inability to use the bladder.

Hydrocephalus developed right after the bifida was enclosed. After the fluid was drained, a shunt was placed into the side of the head that extended to the heart valve. The shunt had to be revised because of growth, which meant the tube coming from the shunt was placed into the stomach. This created a soft spot just above the shunt that had to be pumped manually instead of having the heart do the same work as in the first shunt surgery. As she got older, the number of times her shunt had to be pumped decreased, until finally there was no need for it except in certain situtations. An example of this would be in the case of a seizure where the pumping of her shunt would be necessary.

Paralysis was evident after the first three weeks following delivery. This was attributable to muscle deterioration and involved complete sensory loss from the knees down. She claims she still has feeling in the lower hip area, but physicians believe there is 90% sensory loss in the lower hip. Along with this symptom, she developed scoliosis. Luque rods were used to straighten her back, with later revisions using Harrington rods that she still has today. She will never be able to walk and she will be wheelchair bound for the rest of her life.

An ileoconduit or urinary bypass was performed because of her inability to use her bladder efficiently. This meant that the ureters were detached from the bladder and inserted into one end of the small intestine; urine is tranferred through the stomach into a plastic bag cemented or glued to the skin. This stoma is an opening of the abdominal wall where urine may

pass through freely. Because of growth, it had to be enlarged, which ac-
counted for five revisions.

EXPENSES

When dealing with total money spent on Angela, one can estimate
approximately $1 million. This can be shown by the following: medical
(hospitalization/surgery)—$800,000; travel and living expenses—$10,000;
physician—$70,000; other expenses (drugs, appliances, wheelchairs, van,
modifications)—$55,000.

Insurance paid for a large share of these expenses, but for young parents
to accept this large a responsibility, they had to turn to family members
for temporary help. As far as outside organizations willing to help meet
financial needs, the March of Dimes was the only organization to contribute. It gave $2,000 for her first surgery and that was to be the last financial
contribution. My parents became very smart money managers because of
Angela, so I never really felt the financial burdens that one might suspect.
We lived very well for as long as I can remember, which means there was
always enough money for essentials plus the little things that every normal
kid desires while growing up.

MOBILITY

Paralysis has meant that Angie has had to become adjusted to many
different forms of mobility or transportation. Because of the increased size
of her head, she was not able to sit up at the age a normal child would
have been able to. She crawled at the age of four mainly by pulling her
body with her forearms. This led to scooting, which lasted until the age
of eight, at which point she was transferred to a wheelchair. The reason
she was not put into a wheelchair sooner is because my parents didn't
want to accept that she would never walk. However, because of her increased size and weight, they had no choice but to put her into a wheelchair.
As far as transportation to school, my mother took her to school until she
was nine years old, when she began to be transported by bus. When the
time comes for her to live independently, she will be transported by bus
at no charge.

As any child would, I had problems dealing with my sister being in a
wheelchair. At an early age, I would be embarrassed to even be seen with
her. For example, if I were in the mall with her, I would not push her and
would do my best to disassociate myself from her as much as possible. As
I got older, I saw her for who she was, not as she was; but when we went

to the same high school, it took me some time to be seen talking with her or pushing her down the hall. The most difficulty I had came from my peers, because I felt that if they knew that my sister was handicapped I would be made fun of or not accepted. I realize that sounds very childish now (a college sophomore).

EDUCATION

Angie was diagnosed as borderline mentally retarded at birth, but no evaluation was given until she was four years old. When given a standardized test, she had an IQ of 67, which labeled her as EMH (Educable Mentally Handicapped). She was placed in a preschool for two years and then she attended an elementary school that placed her in an EMR (Educable Mentally Retarded) program for two more years. In junior high, she was involved with EMH for two years, and DTP (Developmental Training Program) for one year. Today, she attends Hastings Senior High and is still in the DTP program. She will graduate the May before her 21st birthday. Angie also attended summer school for three summers.

I don't see my sister as being classified as EMH, because she talks and acts so much differently than those whom I consider as EMH. It really upsets me when I hear someone talking about Angie and describing her as "retarded." I don't consider her retarded and I never will.

GOALS

Angie has many goals that affect her everyday attitude and activities. She wants to become a doctor and of course this is impossible for various reasons already explained; but there is no reason she should be *told* she can't become one. She must realize this herself and deal with it in her own manner. That's just part of growing up and maturing into adulthood. She, as every 16 year old does, wants to drive. She takes Driver's Education in school and even though the probability is low, there is a small chance that with the right equipment she would be able to drive a car. But even more than those two, she wants to be a mother. The doctors believe that this is highly impossible because even if she were to get pregnant, she would not be able to carry a full term pregnancy.

I mainly feel sorry for Angie because I was given the chance to do almost everything she can't. I would give everything I have for her to live as normal a life as I have lived, but I have grown out of that stage of feeling sorry for her. I now push myself twice as hard because I believe whatever I'm trying to accomplish for myself, I'm accomplishing it for her as well.

ACTIVITIES AND ATTITUDES

Angie is involved in numerous activities. At a younger age, she attended church and Sunday school, while later becoming a member of the First United Methodist Church. She also is involved in Special Olympics. She has won numerous ribbons and trophies for competing in bowling, swimming, basketball, and track and field. This directly affects her attitude because Special Olympics has given her a sense of self-worth and a feeling that she is capable of accomplishing something on her own. But on the other hand, it seems the older she gets, the more frustrated she gets. She's not able to do some things with her friends because of her handicap. Thus, she turns to younger kids who will spend more time with her, doing what she is more capable of doing. I am amazed at how strong spirited she is. She gives 100% in everything she does, and I admire her for that. Also, I have and always will consider her the best athlete in the family.

FUTURE

The future is still some time away, but after graduation she will live independently in living arrangements suited for her specific needs. This is what scares me the most. Even though she is a very strong-willed individual, I don't know if she will be mature enough to take care of herself without me or my family there to help her. I still consider her very reliant on others, and not yet very self-sufficient.

In conclusion, I believe it is not only important to learn about and try to understand someone like Angie and her situation, but to know also a brother or sister's point of view about that individual. There is a question that comes up every once in awhile that interests me the most. "If you had to do it all over again, would you want Angie to be born?" I take that question two ways. First I would say maybe not, because of all the hard times my family has gone through and all the surgeries; but there is no way I would ever want Angie not to be born. I consider her an inspiration not only to me, but to everybody she has ever met. She has been a blessing in disguise.

5
Quality of Life and the Individual's Perspective

Steven J. Taylor and Robert Bogdan

The Center on Human Policy

Quality of Life (QOL) is an illusive concept, especially when applied to people with mental retardation. We do not have an agreed upon standard for determining anyone's QOL. In fact, we seldom make inquiries into the QOL of people who are not disabled or disadvantaged in some way. It is ironic that we usually examine QOL only when we know or suspect that people are suffering. Herein lie both the importance and the danger of studying the QOL of people with mental retardation.

On the one hand, the concept of QOL directs attention to the human needs of people who have developmental disabilities. While it is important that service systems and schools help children and adults with mental retardation to learn and develop, it is more important that they contribute to the QOL of the people they serve. The strongest indictment of institutions and segregated schools is not that they fail to teach people, although this case could be made, but that they deny people respect and dignity. The increasing interest in QOL marks our recognition of the assaults to the dignity of people with mental retardation, very often done in the name of humanity (Blatt, Ozolins, & McNally, 1980).

On the other hand, because we do not ordinarily study the QOL of nondisabled people, the study of the QOL of people with mental retardation runs the risk that these people will be singled out further as different from the rest of us or even dehumanized. As the most extreme example of this danger, QOL has been cited as a justification for euthanasia and withholding medical treatment from infants with severe disabilities (The Association for Persons with Severe Handicaps, 1984; Hentoff, 1985). In an infamous experiment carried out at the University of Oklahoma Health

Acknowledgments. Preparation of this chapter was supported through the Research and Training Center on Community Integration, funded by the National Institute on Disability and Rehabilitation Research, U.S. Department of Education (Cooperation Agreement No. G0085C03503). The opinions expressed herein are solely those of the authors and no official endorsement by the U.S. Department of Education should be inferred.

27

Sciences Center, medical researchers employed a quality of life formula to assist in medical decisionmaking regarding treatment for infants with spina bifida:

> QL = NE × (H + S), QL is quality of life, NE represents the patient's natural endowment, both physical and intellectual, H is the contribution from home and family, and S is the contribution from society. (Gross, Cox, Tatyrek, Pollay, & Barnes, 1983, p. 456)

Even when QOL is not used to justify outright discrimination, formulations of QOL for people with mental retardation run the risk of applying standards to these people's lives that nondisabled people would not accept. Although this danger is real, it is not inevitable. The challenge is to study the lives of people who have developmental disabilities in a way that emphasizes our common humanity.

This chapter looks at QOL from the perspective of the individual labelled "mentally retarded" and argues that the concept of QOL has no meaning apart from the experience of individuals. Because the focus is on the individual's perspective, we start with the stories of three individuals.

LISTENING TO PEOPLE'S STORIES

The following excerpts contain parts of the life histories of three people: Ed, Pattie, and August. (The names of Ed and Pattie are pseudonyms; because August was a plaintiff in a law suit and his circumstances were made public, his real name is used.)

Ed's and Pattie's stories are told in their own words and were constructed from the edited transcripts of indepth interviews (Taylor & Bogdan, 1984). These excerpts are taken from detailed life histories published elsewhere (Bogdan & Taylor, 1982). Both Ed and Pattie had been labelled mentally retarded, although a reading of their stories calls into question the meaningfulness of the label. In contrast to Ed's and Pattie's stories, the excerpt on August is not presented in his own words and is based on an extensive review of case records and, to a lesser extent, on first-hand observations; hence, this is not August's story, but the story of August.

Ed's Story[1]

"What is retardation? It's hard to say. I guess it's having problems thinking. Some people think that you can tell if a person is retarded by looking at them. If you think that way you don't give people the benefit

---

[1]Excerpted from Bogdan and Taylor (1982).

of the doubt. You judge a person by how they look or how they talk or what the tests show, but you can never really tell what is inside the person.

"Take a couple of friends of mine. Tommy McCan and P.J. Tommy was a guy who was really nice to be with. You could sit down with him and have a nice conversation and enjoy yourself. He was a mongoloid. The trouble was, people couldn't see beyond that. If he didn't look that way it would have been different, but there he was locked into what the other people thought he was. Now P.J. was really something else. I've watched that guy and I can see in his eyes that he is aware. He knows what's going on. He can only crawl and he doesn't talk, but you don't know what's inside. When I was with him and I touched him, I know that he knows.

"It's a struggle. I'll tell you it's a constant struggle as long as I can remember. You want your brain to function correctly and you try and try. You're at war with your brain. You want your brain to function but you have got to watch it. Like the other day in the cafeteria at work. I took a coffee pot and began walking out of the dining room with it. I was just walking without thinking. I looked down and there it was. I said to myself, 'What the hell are you doing?' and turned around and put it back. Your mind has to keep struggling. You can't give in to that mental-retardation image. You strive to be extra careful. You struggle to be not what the image of the retarded is. You can't look the way they say you are if they call you retarded. Some people can be real smart, but look and act the way a retarded person is supposed to.

"Sometimes being handicapped has its advantages. You can go slower. Living has always been a struggle to get from the bottom to the top—trying to keep up with everybody. I could never get up. There are no short cuts for me—only the hard way. The way I see it now is that the only thing in life isn't just getting up the pole.

"I think I've come a long way, but I've got a way to go. I've gotten to the point where I can accept certain things. Once in a while I go out now and I have a good time—I'll do different things. It's hard though. Like you can't go out and join clubs and things. A lot of ex-residents would like to join the Y. That would be something that I could enjoy. I could go and take a swim. I've had to adjust more to a point where I can just relax. I've learned to relax in certain ways, but in others I haven't. I'm still nervous. There are fears for people coming from a place like Empire [State School].

"What I am basically trying to say is that for the majority of people, a retarded person is someone to be stared at. You don't want to be seen in a public place. It hurts to watch those people being retarded. And don't talk to anyone unless you know who they are. It's rough and you can't take on the whole world. You try to make the best of your situation and try to think that the world maybe is saying, 'He doesn't look all that retarded.' There are people you just can't talk to. They are responsible if they see it and then make fun of it. People are really ignorant. People consider themselves normal and they put a stigma on people who aren't. They do it out of ignorance. I don't expect people to understand the whole problem. I know that handicapped people are people. They feel and they have a lot to give.

"It is very hard to go through life with a label. You have to fight constantly. 'Retarded' is just a word. We have to separate individuals from the word. We use words like 'retarded' because of habit—just like going shopping every week and getting up in the morning. The word 'retarded' has to be there if you are going to have people help, but what the hell is the sense of calling someone retarded and not giving them anything?

"I don't know. Maybe I used to be retarded. That's what they say anyway. I wish they could see me now. I wonder what they'd say if they could see me holding down a regular job and doing all kinds of things. I bet they wouldn't believe it."

Pattie's Story[2]

"At Empire State School, G Building was for real severely retarded older women. They messed their pants and wet themselves. They would have strings around their fingers and they would whirl the string and look at it. Some of them had bald heads. They would send us over there when we were punished. That was really a sad case when I went over there. They would throw up after they ate and we had to clean it. That was our punishment—cleaning those people in the shower wasn't any fun, either, because they would hit you and pull your hair and stuff.

"I don't know how many times I was sent to G Building. It was quite frequently. The first time I was there I didn't know too much about it. I must have been 12 when I first went on to G. The other girls didn't tell me much. They wanted me to find out for myself, I guess. Once the doctor said that I was going, they didn't waste any time. They sent your papers along with you. The attendant took me down. They said, 'This is Pattie. This is the one that is being punished. Don't give her an easy time. Make her work.' After the first time I was sent there, I started watching other people being punished over there. We would walk through that area when I had to go to church, and I would say 'Hi' to who was there. I would ask how they were and how they were doing. They would

---

[2]Excerpted from Bogdan and Taylor (1982).

be scrubbing floors and I would say, 'You poor girl.' I know because I was there too. I would start crying when everybody went past me when I was there.

"When you were sent to G the only thing you were allowed was what was right there. We were there with the low grades. That's what they called them, 'low grades.' It was another name for severely retarded people. The attendants called them that.

"The first thing they had me do when I first arrived was to clean out the toilets. Then I had to shower some of the girls and dress them. We had to scrub the floors on our hands and knees.

"When I first arrived there and saw all the people, I thought, 'Oh, no. What am I getting into now? What's going to happen?' There are all these people just sitting around and rocking back and forth and back and forth. Some of them were pulling their hair and eating it. One was in a strait-jacket.

"Whenever we had medication they would line us up and they gave it to us down there too. They took us down to the cafeteria with them, and part of the punishment was we had to eat their ground food. They ground your meat and everything. They piled the stuff right up too. That was what they ate, so you had to, too. I got sick and threw up. It was awful, it was nasty tasting stuff. They asked me what was wrong. I told them that I didn't like it. They told me that I had to eat it because I was being punished. One time the attendant turned her back and I slopped the ground meat into one of the low grade's trays and told her to eat it. I thought that was funny. She just gobbled it right down.

"We had a lot of messers on that ward. Mostly they would do it in their clothes and then we had to clean them. I hated to do that. We had to clean the mess if they went on the floor. I hated it. Who wants to clean someone's rear end at that age? I wouldn't mind cleaning a baby's behind, but not them.

"I started treating them kind of mean because I felt if it wasn't for them I wouldn't be there cleaning them. I would throw them on the toilet. I would say, 'Sit there,' and when I got them in the shower I would turn the cold right on them. Sometimes they would start squealing and the attendant would come running and ask what I was doing. I would say, 'Oh, nothing. She caught her toe in the drain.' I was mad. I said, 'If it wasn't for you I wouldn't be here doing this junk.'

"I didn't think about them low grades being in the same institution as me. I really didn't think about anything. I just knew I was there and I was going to live there for a while. Maybe never get out. I thought I was going to be there until I was in my rocking chair. Maybe die there—but it didn't happen."

The Story of August[3]

I first met August in March, 1979. He was living then at Craig "developmental center," an institution for the so-called "mentally retarded" in Sonyea, New York. August had lived at Craig since 1941.

August was one of the most retarded people I had ever met. He couldn't speak, use the toilet, dress himself, or do much of anything. He also had quite a few troubling behaviors. Staff at the institution variously described him as "aggressive," "regressive," the "worst case," and "the most severe behavior problem." He attacked others, resisted directions, and shunned any form of social interaction.

We will probably never know August's side of the story. But the institution's side is well documented in volumes of case records, ward logs, and professional evaluations maintained over the past 40 years.

Born in New York City in October, 1936, August's early years had been far from trouble free. Doctors suspected that he had suffered brain injury at birth and at 9 months of age he incurred a severe head injury in a fall from his crib. In the fall of 1940, his 26-year-old mother was killed as she attempted to rescue August from the path of an oncoming truck. One year later, August, scarcely six now, found himself at what was then Craig State School, hundreds of miles away from his New York City home.

August's first several months at the institution were rather uneventful, at least from the institution's perspective. An entry from the Ward Notes on October 31, 1941, reads: "On ward in good condition. Gets along well with other boys."

By mid-January of 1942, August was striking out at his peers on the ward. "This fellow had been quite well behaved. Lately he attacked other boys who do not fight back." By 1948, he was digging his rectum and smearing feces, and by 1949 he was continually ripping off his clothes.

Throughout the 1950s and '60s, August received a panoply of behavior control drugs: ". . . he is constantly under heavy sedation." At one time or another, he received thorazine, trilafon, prolixin, haldol, quide, ritalin, stelazine, serentil, dexedrine, mellaril, valium, chloryl hydrate, dalmane, and more.

The drugs took their toll. By 1958, August began to experience "extrapyramidal disorders," a drug-induced pseudo-Parkinson's disease involving twitches, tremors, difficulty ambulating, and a loss of balance. To this day, August walks with an unsteady gait.

---

[3]This is a revised version of an article (Taylor, 1984) originally published in *Institutions, Etc.*

Yet the drugs did not control his behavior, reduce his aggression, or eliminate his untidy personal habits. The doctors recognized this as early as 1961. But as late as 1979, they continued to prescribe drugs such as haldol, even though it seemed "to be ineffective as far as controlling extreme aggressive behavior."

August spent the '50s and '60s in restraint: ". . . has to be in camisole most of the time . . ." ". . . Occasionally, patient has days and short periods of time out of restraint."

By the early 1970s, August had lost weight, looked "emaciated and run down," had become "dull and lethargic," and had begun "falling frequently." He still occasionally assaulted his fellow inmates and staff.

They extracted August's teeth around this time. And he lost one ear to the surgeon's knife. His ear was injured somehow and he just kept picking at it. The records do not say much more about this. What is it about institutions that we can find out more about a man's bowel habits than how he lost his ear?

Sometime around the spring of 1972, August started living in a shower room on his ward. The records do not say a lot about this either. Three months worth of ward notes for this period are missing completely.

August spent the next seven years of his life in that shower room. Staff members said they did all they could to coax him out of there. His program plans for the period contain a goal of keeping August out of the shower room.

One staff member recalls that during the three years he worked on the ward, August was locked in the room by the staff. Tears came to this large man's eyes as he described how August did not see the light of day for several long years.

The day I first met August was his second day out of the shower room. August lay on the floor, grunting and groaning, with an agonized look on his face. He did not seem too interested in having visitors—no greeting, no eye contact, no sign of recognition.

As a result of a law suit, August was moved out of the institution. The last time I saw him he was living in a house with six other people. The house was located not far from Craig and formerly was the groundkeeper's residence. It was not part of the community, but it was not the institution either.

August spent his days at a Medicaid-funded "day treatment center." He sat at a table sorting blue and yellow pieces of paper, putting pegs in a pegboard. For doing this day in and day out, August got oyster crackers and some kind words.

August was a changed man. I knew this when he reached out his hand to shake mine.

August had developed some skills and never caused any trouble. He was toilet trained, ate with a fork and spoon, and not only kept his clothes on, but dressed himself.

Perhaps the biggest change in August was his sociability. He never used to smile at anyone else. Now he thrived on human contact. This wild man, this aggressive and then asocial individual, spent the better part of an hour holding my hand, patting me on the back, and taking my hand and stroking the side of his head with it. The supervisor of August's home said that everyone liked working with August. As she described him, ". . . he's loving, kind, and gentle."

THE INDIVIDUAL'S PERSPECTIVE

What does quality of life mean for people with mental retardation, people like Ed, Pattie, and August, or for anyone for that matter? While there are many ways to define and study QOL, the position taken here is that QOL must be studied from the perspective of the individual. The following are propositions to guide inquiries into the QOL of people with mental retardation.

1. QOL Must Be Understood in Terms of People's Subjective Experience

QOL is a matter of subjective experience. That is to say, the concept has no meaning apart from what a person feels and experiences. It is a question of how people view or what they feel about their lives and situations and not what others attribute to them. While we might make assumptions about Ed's, Pattie's, and August's quality of life based on where they lived, what is important is how they experienced their lives.

QOL refers to one's satisfaction with one's lot in life, an inner sense of contentment or fulfillment with one's experience in the world. As a subjective experience or feeling, QOL may or may not be something that people think about. It is probably only during the highs and lows in life that anyone devotes much thought to QOL. In fact, most people would not use the phrase "quality of life" to describe their feelings about their existence.

Factors external to individuals can and do influence their QOL (O'Brien, 1987). One can assume that the abusive and dehumanizing conditions described and depicted so vividly in Blatt's institutional exposés (Blatt & Kaplan, 1974; Blatt et al., 1980) produced a miserable QOL for the people confined to those institutions. Pattie's story certainly confirms this. Similarly, one can reasonably assume that caring and loving families create a high QOL for their members. Yet factors influencing one's feelings and subjective experience should not be confused with those feelings and subjective experience themselves.

2. QOL May Be Experienced Differently by Different People

As a corollary to the first proposition, people may experience the same circumstances differently. What enhances one person's QOL may detract from another's. While there may be some circumstances that produce a nearly universal response in human beings—for example, the treatment accorded August—QOL cannot be determined *solely* through an examination of the conditions of one's existence.

Considerations of the QOL of another person are likely to be characterized by ethnocentrism or chauvinism. The stereotype of the European explorer appalled at the "savagery" of the American Indian provides the clearest illustration of this tendency. Even within cultures, it is common for one class or race to question the folkways and hence the QOL of another. For example, the upper class denigrates the lifestyle and tastes of the working class. Yet who is to say that theatre, literature, and opera create a higher QOL than television and sports?

This is not to suggest that one should not draw on one's own experiences and feelings to understand another person's. In looking at the QOL of another person, it is useful to ask oneself, "How would I feel if I were in that position?" This question can provide a useful starting point for inquiries into QOL. For example, in reading August's story, we must ask ourselves what it would feel like to be restrained for years and to be subjected to constant sedation. In order to understand another person's subjective experience, one must be able to emphathize with that person without substituting one's own values, beliefs, and interpretations for those of the other.

3. The Study of the QOL for People Labelled "Mentally Retarded" Requires that the Label Be Set Aside

The label of mental retardation imposes a barrier to understanding people on their own terms. When a person is labelled "mentally retarded," others are less inclined to take his or her perspective seriously. Burton Blatt used to tell a story about a resident of one of the institutions he and Fred Kaplan visited for their photographic exposé of institutions (Blatt & Kaplan, 1974). While Kaplan attempted to take pictures secretly with a camera attached to his belt and hidden by his sports jacket, this resident pointed out the camera to the administrator who was escorting Blatt and Kaplan.

The administrator laughed and dismissed the resident, saying, "Boy, these retardates can really have an imagination!" (quoted in Bogdan & Taylor, 1982).

Mental retardation is a social construct and metaphor that exists in the minds of people who use it to describe the intellectual states of other people. As Braginsky and Braginsky (1971) wrote:

> The term mental retardation is simply a metaphor chosen to connote certain assumed qualities of putative, invisible mental processes. More specifically, it is inferred that it appears *as if* retarded mental processes underlie particular behaviors. Or, we infer that behavior appears *as if* it were retarded. (p. 15)

To characterize mental retardation as a social construct is not to deny differences among people according to intellectual ability or at least certain dimensions of what is referred to as intelligence. It is to suggest that the nature and significance of these differences depend on how they are viewed and interpreted. Just as the existence of people who disturbed or upset others in the Middle Ages does not prove the existence of witches (Szasz, 1970), the existence of people who seem intellectually deficient does not prove the existence of mental retardation.

Labels like mental retardation affect how people are viewed by others. When people are defined as mentally retarded, this does not engender a closeness or empathy with them. To the contrary, the label provides a filter through which to interpret what they say and do. It becomes easy to dismiss their perspectives, feelings, and experiences as symptomatic of an underlying pathological state. In August's case, for example, staff interpreted his behavior in terms of profound mental retardation, rather than trying to find out what he was feeling. Whatever utility the label mental retardation may have for administrative or programmatic purposes, it can stand in the way of understanding people on their own terms and studying QOL as they experience it.

If, as suggested above, QOL has to do with people's subjective experience, then anything that interferes with grasping that experience must be put aside. The study of the QOL of people defined as mentally retarded requires that we suspend or bracket assumptions and beliefs about mental retardation.

4. An Inquiry into the QOL of People with Mental Retardation Requires Looking at the World from Their Perspective

Because QOL is something that i2s subjectively experienced by the individual, the individual's perspective or point of view must be the primary focus of any study of QOL. In order to study QOL we must strive for what

Max Weber (1968) called *verstehen*, understanding on a personal level. That is, we must attempt to create in our minds their feelings and experiences.

Citing William James, Bruyn (1966) made the distinction between *knowledge of* people and *knowledge about* people: "Knowledge *of* people is personal and social, whereas knowledge *about* people is intellectual and theoretical" (p. 34). It is important to know *about* people with mental retardation and their situations, where they live, how they spend their time, how others treat them, what opportunities they have. All of these things can impact on their QOL. However, studying these aspects of their lives is not the same as studying their QOL. To study their QOL requires a knowledge *of* them; in other words, knowing how they feel about and view their circumstances.

5. The Study of the QOL and Hence Subjective Experience of Some People May Pose a Methodological Challenge

It is easier to study people's life circumstances than how they feel about them. Knowing what another person means and feels is always problematic (Douglas, 1976). Even seemingly objective words that people use to describe their experiences can have different meanings. Deutscher (1973), in a book on the discrepancy between what people say, especially in attitude surveys, and what they do, wrote:

> When an American truck driver complains to the waitress at the diner about his "warm" beer and "cold" soup, the "warm" liquid may have a temperature of 50, while the "cold" one is 75 . . . The standard for the same objects may well vary from culture to culture, from nation to nation, from region to region and, for that matter, within any given social unit—between classes, age groups, sexes, or what have you; what is "cold" soup for an adult may be too "hot" to give a child. (p. 191)

For people with mental retardation, the study of their perspectives and subjective experience may be especially complex. First of all, it may be difficult to interpret interview data. As indicated by Sigelman, Schoenrock, Winer, Spanhel, Hromas, Martin, Budd, and Bensberg (1981), obtaining valid and reliable data from interviews with people who have developmental disabilities may be a challenging task. They report that acquiescence, saying what they think the interviewer wants to hear, is a significant problem. During our interviews with Ed, we often had to ask him the same question several times in different ways to find out what he really thought. In short, one cannot ask a person with mental retardation, or perhaps anyone for that matter, "How do you view your quality of life?" and expect to receive a meaningful answer.

Second, many people with mental retardation cannot talk or use words to communicate their feelings. August provides an example. Because their inner states or perspectives are not readily accessible, it has often been assumed that they have no inner states, that is, that they do not have subjective experience.

Whether or not people with severe disabilities who cannot speak experience the world as other people do is probably unprovable. However, it is just as reasonable to assume that they have subjective experience as to assume that they do not. Family members and others involved in close relationships with people with severe disabilities often state that they can recognize signs of thinking and feeling in their severely disabled loved ones (Bogdan & Taylor, 1989; Goode, 1980a). They can often talk at length about what severely disabled persons think, like, feel, and so on, based on an interpretation of subtle gestures or signs that may not even be apparent to an outsider.

To understand the subjective experience of people with mental retardation, including those with the most severe disabilities, is a methodological problem and challenge. The issue is not whether people have subjective experience, but how we can learn about that experience.

6. Studying QOL Requires an Indepth Knowledge of People and their Perspectives

People who know each other well know how to interpret each other's words and acts. For example, spouses usually know when "yes" means "no" and "no" means "yes."

Because it may be difficult to learn about the subjective experience of people with mental retardation, the study of their QOL calls for knowing them well enough to make reasonable inferences about what they feel and how they experience their lives. This may entail repeated open-ended interviews over a period of time, as well as other procedures designed to enter into their worlds. We interviewed Ed for a total of approximately 50 hours and Pattie for approximately 25 hours.

August could not tell his own story. Yet to say that August could not talk is not the same as saying that he could not communicate. While inferences about the subjective experience of someone who cannot speak or use language must be viewed as tentative, August's behavior seemed to say a lot about how he felt and, hence, his QOL.

In a study of a deaf-blind young girl with mental retardation, Goode (1980b) described how he used various techniques to understand and relate to her on her own terms. According to Goode, many of the young girl's behaviors that seemed meaningless at first inspection became understandable and rational when viewed from her perspective.

7. Definitions and Conceptions of QOL Must Respect People's Subjective Experience

Because QOL is only meaningful in terms of people's subjective experience, any definition or conception of QOL must be broad enough to encompass the range of people's subjective experience. No single instrument is likely to capture QOL as actually experienced by people. To attempt to define QOL too narrowly may be to distort its meaning.

It is perhaps most meaningful to think of QOL as a *sensitizing concept*. Blumer (1969), a sociologist, made the distinction between *sensitizing concepts* and *definitive concepts*:

> I think that thoughtful study shows conclusively that the concepts of our discipline are fundamentally sensitizing instruments. Hence, I call them "sensitizing concepts" and put them in contrast with definitive concepts . . . A definitive concept refers precisely to what is common in a class of objects, by the aid of a clear definition in terms of attributes or fixed bench marks. This definition, or the bench marks, serve as a means of clearly identifying the individual instance of the class and the make-up of that instance that is covered by the concept. A sensitizing concept lacks the specification of attributes or bench marks and consequently it does not enable the user to move directly to the instance and its relevant content. Instead, it gives the user a general sense of reference and guidance in approaching empirical instances. Whereas definitive concepts provide prescriptions of what to see, sensitizing concepts merely suggest directions along which to look. (pp. 147–148)

Thus, as a concept, QOL sensitizes us to look at how people with mental retardation experience and feel about their lives and situations.

CONCLUSION

By listening closely to people's stories and attempting to understand how they experience the world, we learn what QOL means in human terms. Ed speaks about his struggle "not to give in to that mental retardation image." Pattie recalls childhood memories filled with misery on the back ward of an institution. August seems to tell us about his QOL through his actions, first his aggressiveness, then his self-isolation, and finally, his kind and gentle way. It is seldom, if ever, easy to understand what any person feels and experiences. But without an understanding of how people with mental retardation view and experience their lives, quality of life becomes at best a hollow concept and at worst a justification for treating them in ways that we ourselves would not like to be treated.

REFERENCES

The Association for Persons with Severe Handicaps. (1984). *Legal, economic, psychological, and moral considerations on the practice of withholding medical treatment from infants with congenital defects.* Seattle, WA: Author.

Blatt, B., & Kaplan, F. (1974). *Christmas in purgatory.* Syracuse, NY: Human Policy Press.

Blatt, B., Ozolins, A., & McNally, J. (1980). *The family papers: A return to purgatory.* New York: Longman.

Blumer, H. (1969). *Symbolic interactionism: Perspective and method.* Englewood Cliffs, NJ: Prentice-Hall.

Bogdan, R., & Taylor, S.J. (1982). *Inside out: The social meaning of mental retardation.* Toronto: University of Toronto Press.

Bogdan, R., & Taylor, S.J. (1989). Relationships with severely disabled people: The social construction of humanness. *Social Problems, 36*(2), 135–148.

Braginsky, D., & Braginsky, B. (1971). *Hansels and Gretels.* New York: Holt, Rinehart & Winston.

Bruyn, S.T. (1966). *The human perspective in sociology: The methodology of participant observation.* Englewood Cliffs, NJ: Prentice-Hall.

Deutscher, I. (1973). *What we say/what we do: Sentiments and acts.* Glenview, IL: Scott, Foresman.

Douglas, J.D. (1976). *Investigative social research.* Bevery Hills, CA: Sage.

Goode, D.A. (1980a). Behavior sculpting: Parent-child interactions in families with retarded children. In J. Jacobs (Ed.), *Mental retardation: A phenomenological approach* (pp. 94–118). Springfield, IL: Scott Foresman.

Goode, D.A. (1980b). The world of the congenitally deaf-blind: Toward the grounds for achieving human understanding. In J. Jacobs (Ed.), *Mental retardation: A phenomenological approach* (pp. 187–207). Springfield, IL: Charles C Thomas.

Gross, R.H., Cox, A., Tatyrek, R., Pollay, M., & Barnes, W.A. (1983). Early management and decision making for the treatment of myelomeningocele. *Pediatrics, 72,* (4), 450–58.

Hentoff, N. (1985). The awful privacy of Baby Doe. *The Atlantic Monthly,* January, 54–62.

O'Brien, J. (1987). A guide to life-style planning: Using the *Activities Catalog* to integrate services and natural support systems. In B. Wilcox & G.T. Bellamy (Eds.), *A comprehensive guide to the Activities Catalog: An alternative curriculum for youth and adults with severe disabilities* (pp. 175–89). Baltimore: Paul Brookes.

Sigelman, C.K., Schoenrock, C.J., Winer, J.L., Spanhel, C.L., Hromas, S.G., Martin, P.W., Budd, E.C., & Bensberg, G.J. (1981). Issues in interviewing mentally retarded persons: An empirical study. In R.H. Bruininks, C.E. Meyers, B.B. Sigford, & K.C. Lakin (Eds.), *Deinstitutionalization and community adjustment of mentally retarded people* (pp. 114–129). Washington, DC: American Association on Mental Deficiency.

Szasz, T.S. (1970). *The manufacture of madness.* New York: Dell.

Taylor, S.J. (1984). A man named August. *Institutions, Etc., 7* (10), 20–23.

Taylor, S.J., & Bogdan, R. (1984). *Introduction to qualitative research methods: The search for meanings* (2nd ed.). New York: John Wiley.

Weber, M. (1968). *Economy and society.* New York: Bedminster Press.

6
Thinking About and Discussing
Quality of Life

David A. Goode

College of Staten Island
City University of New York

Quality of life (QOL) is a phrase that has achieved national and international notoriety. In America in the 1980s it is a term whose appeal is general, and it has become part of our common lexicon. Further, this growth of interest in QOL is not unique to the United States; indeed, there is particular interest, both national and international, in QOL for persons with disabilities. Expressions of this concern can be found in both western and eastern societies and are growing. While some reasons why this may be the case will be suggested at the end of this chapter, it is important to bear in mind that the historical and social forces that led to the current concern with quality of life, including the work described below, are very large and powerful forces. As the reader is led through the complexities of a national project attempting to explore and define QOL for persons with disabilities, it is critical to consider broad frames of explanation for the current interest in QOL. Questions to bear in mind while reading this chapter are "why are people thinking about QOL in this way now?" and "how is it that a project such as that described would come to be in America in 1987?"

The chapter has five parts: an overview of the National Quality of Life for Persons with Disabilities Project; a description of the research used in this project's approach; overviews of two sets of procedures used in the project for group discussion of QOL issues; and a consideration of the future of QOL policy development in the field of disabilities.

THE QUALITY OF LIFE FOR PERSONS WITH
DISABILITIES PROJECT

Responding to an increased interest in QOL within the field of disabilities, the Administration on Developmental Disabilities gave a grant to the Mental Retardation Institute to examine the potential of QOL as a social policy concept for persons with disabilities and their families. The purposes of the QOL Project were to develop a framework in which to discuss QOL that was consistent with what was known in the research literature; to assess the potential for such a framework to produce consensus about QOL issues and serve as the groundwork for QOL indicators; to enhance the input of persons with disabilities into all aspects of decisionmaking regarding the development of QOL as a social concept; and to formulate a comprehensive set of recommendations about enhancing the QOL for persons with disabilities and their families.

The project began with a review and synthesis of the QOL literature (Goode, 1988a; Kuehn, Goode, & Powers, 1987) that was shared with 10 persons, including professionals and people with physical and cognitive disabilities. With their input, a discussion framework for QOL issues was designed and field tested. This framework was then utilized by a group of 40 people, including persons with disabilities, relatives of persons with disabilities, professionals in the disabilities field, advocates, and others who met in Leesburg, Virginia, in September, 1987. The purpose of this group was to explore the ability of the framework to define QOL issues across the lifespan. The approach and some results of the Leesburg Group will be described below (see also Goode, 1988b). Based upon the success of the Leesburg meetings in achieving agreement about an approach to QOL, a National Conference on Quality of Life for Persons with Disabilities was conducted. The goal of the National Conference was to get further input from the same constituencies about major QOL issues and recommendations to address them. The procedures and results of the National Conference will also be discussed below (see also Goode, 1988c).

SYNTHESIS OF LITERATURE AND FRAMEWORK OF THE LEESBURG GROUP

The review and synthesis of the research on QOL (see Goode, 1988a) was a major undertaking. This review took as an assumption and orientation that the 50-year history of QOL research would have produced many approaches to the topic, but that we were interested in an approach that was client centered; that is, QOL as seen from the viewpoint of the individual.

A synthesis of the literature entailed many decisions about what variables and relationships to stress. These choices were guided by (a) a desire to remain faithful to empirical findings and to formulate a QOL model that contained as many critical elements as were consistent with these findings; (b) the current state of knowledge of social research and policy in the field of disabilities; (c) current philosophies of providing supports to persons with disabilities and particularly those emphasizing the choices made by persons with disabilities; and (d) our own experiences with persons with disabilities.

The following model (Figure 6.1) was formulated as a result of the review of literature. The model is a nonlinear, process model that is client centered. It is meant to suggest relationships between both subjective and objective variables (circles and squares respectively) rather than a pattern of causation. The circles are the core of the model, representing the individual's perception of his own needs and capabilities and his perception of the resources and demands within the environment.

The subjective core of the model emphasizes the relationships among needs, capabilities, demands, and resources. The model suggests that a misfit in the individual's perception of personal needs and environmental/social resources, and between environmental demands and personal capabilities, will influence the individual's satisfaction in specific life settings and thereby affect the person's overall assessment of QOL. The model also shows that degree of life satisfaction and perceived QOL also have a direct effect upon the individual's behavior, implying a circularity between subjective and behavioral/objective factors.

The objective variables in the model are factors directly observable to an outsider. One set of variables is called *life events*, by which is meant economic, political, educational, cultural, familial, or natural events outsided the direct control of the individual. The *objective individual* refers to biopsychosocial attributes of the individual such as health, mental health, and socioeconomic status. The *objective environment* represents the specific life setting, including physical and social properties and elements of the setting. *Individual outcome behaviors* represent the actual behaviors of individuals with disabilities in settings. These outcome behaviors, when satisfactory both to individuals with a disability and to significant others in the setting, are conducive to experiencing a higher QOL. There are various direct and indirect relationships between objective variables and between objective and subjective variables that, while interesting, cannot be commented upon in this context (see Goode, 1988a).

Environment is taken to mean the immediate macrosystem surrounding the individual as described by Goode (1987) and shown in Figure 6.2. Figure 6.2 shows that in each major life setting there exists a set of relationships between the individual, those who surround him, and available resources that constitute QOL for that person. This conceptual approach to QOL was taken from Powers and Goode (1986), who argued that QOL is specific to the kind of setting being discussed. The "Quality Principle," as formulated by Powers and Goode, asserts that QOL is primarily a product of relationships between people in each life setting, that these relationships compose a Quality-Set (Q-Set), and that they may be expressed axiomatically through statements such as "the quality of life of a person with a disability

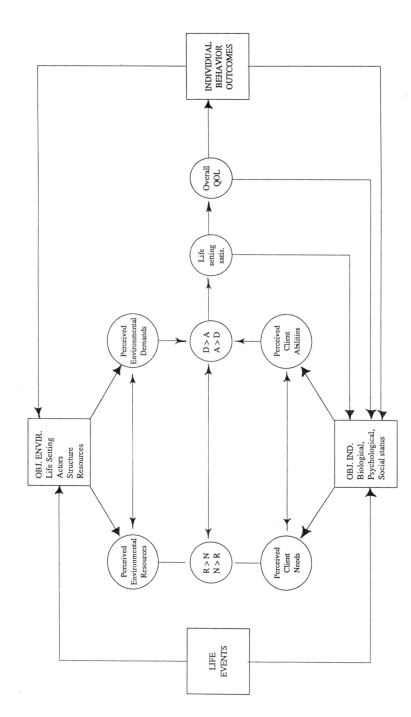

FIGURE 6.1.   A Client-Driven, Ecological, QOL Model

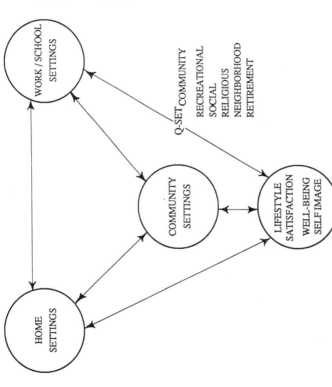

Q-SET WORK
COMPETITIVE EMPLOYMENT
SUPPORTED EMPLOYMENT
WORKSHOP EMPLOYMENT

Q-SET SCHOOL
INTEGRATED
RESIDENTIAL

WORK / SCHOOL
SETTINGS

Q-SET COMMUNITY
RECREATIONAL
SOCIAL
RELIGIOUS
NEIGHBORHOOD
RETIREMENT

COMMUNITY
SETTINGS

LIFESTYLE
SATISFACTION
WELL-BEING
SELF IMAGE

QUALITY OF LIFE

HOME
SETTINGS

Q - SET HOME
NATURAL FAMILY
FOSTER FAMILY
COMMUNITY RESIDENCE

FIGURE 6.2. Interactive Relationships of Major Life Settings that Affect Quality of Life

living at home will vary directly and significantly with the quality of family life experienced by family members."

The essential point made in the approach reflected in Figure 6.2 is that QOL is something experienced in particular settings and is highly responsive to the social relationships the individual with disabilities has in those settings. It was in this way that the factors and relationships named in Figure 6.1 were seen to function from a client-centered perspective. The dimensions and relationships named in Figure 6.1 were specific to settings and critical to the social relationships in those settings. The discussion framework that was employed by the Leesburg group was based upon this understanding.

In summary, the comprehensive model was client centered, social, included many of the variables and relationships known to the QOL literature, and emphasized the "goodness of fit" between client's perceptions of environmental resources and personal needs and between environmental demands and personal capabilities.

PROCESS AND RESULTS OF THE VIRGINIA WORK GROUPS

The discussion framework used in Virginia involved a matrix emphasizing the following five essential QOL factors: the needs of the person with disabilities; the expectations others have for them (phrased in legislative language taken from the Developmental Disabilities Act); the outcome behaviors that satisfy both needs and expectations; the resources needed by the person with the disability to meet demands; and the resources needed by other actors in the setting to enable the person with a disability to meet demands and achieve desired behavioral outcomes. These factors were among those selected from the research model and were judged on a variety of bases to be critical to contemporary discussions of QOL for persons with disabilities. Their relationship is graphically displayed in Figure 6.3. These relationships, as perceived by the person with disabilities, constitute the essential part of the QOL framework employed in discussions. This framework argues that *when an individual, with or without disabilities, is able to meet important needs in major life settings (work, school, home, community) while also satisfying the normative expectations that others hold for him or her in those settings, he or she is more likely to experience a high QOL.* The framework made groups identify major needs in important life settings and expectations associated with those needs. It then asked the group to resolve individual needs with social expectations. To use an example that will appear below, if an adult has a need for friendship at work, what are the expectations that are associated with being a friend at work? Can one

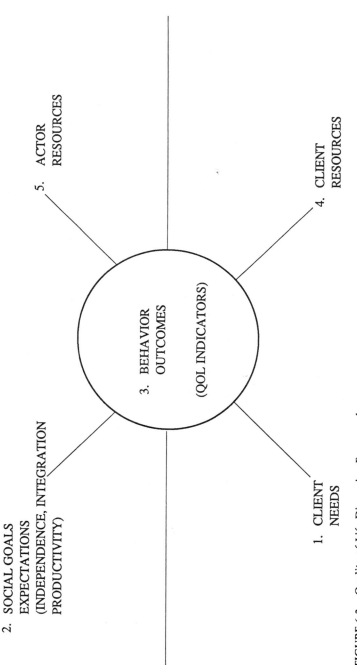

FIGURE 6.3. Quality of Life Discussion Framework

specify what the skills/behaviors are that are required to be successful at workplace friendships? If this were possible to do, one could then ask, what are the resources that a person with disability would need to achieve the desired skills/behaviors, and the related question, what do others around the person with a disability need to know in order to help them achieve the desired behaviors.

The groups were asked to use this way of thinking about QOL in filling out QOL matrices for specific settings. To complete the matrix, the group first defined the discussion in terms of stages in a person's lifecycle. Then a specific setting was identified, as were other significant actors present in the setting with the person with a disability. Thus, the discussions of quality of life were age graded, setting specific, and socially specific. An example, shown in Figure 6.4 and Table 6.1, from a group who replicated procedures with good fidelity, gives a sense of how the framework led group members to think about QOL. The example examines QOL in integrated work settings. The most critical needs were seen as acceptance, personal growth, health, financial security, and stability, while possessions and friendships were of moderate importance. The group filled in the boxes of the matrix (i.e., the behavioral outcomes required to meet need and social expectations) for all needs except those of low salience. Selecting friendship as an example, the group specified that a person with a disability should be able to choose to be friendly with people and relate to them, participate in groups during breaks and lunch, initiate friendships, and have the ability to socialize with others. The group then went on to consider the resources required by the person with disability to achieve these friendship-at-work related outcomes, the resources required by significant others in the setting in order to facilitate the person with a handicap to achieve the outcomes, and the environmental issues posed. These results appear in Table 6.1.

One thing evident in the matrix and table is that even this initial treatment of the issues around quality of life at work for adults with disabilities produced detailed and rich descriptions. One implication that can be drawn from the client resources and actor resources columns in Table 6.1 is that the current training and curricula for persons with disabilities, and for persons who serve them, would have to be radically changed in order to accommodate the information and skills required to support friendship making and maintenance. These columns represent an initial attempt at specifying what skills persons with disabilities and their co-workers must have in order for persons with disabilities to find and keep friends in the work place.

These two examples can only give the reader a flavor of the framework and how groups worked with it. The full report of each group displays much more of an individual character and shows the extensiveness of each group's effort. The process was generally considered to be highly suc-

Table 6.1   Friendship At Work

GROUP: Adult
SETTING: Integrated work
NEED: Friendship

Client Resources	Actor Resources	Environmental Issues

Self-esteem
 	
Discrimination skills
	Skills & social skills
	  training
	Social learning theory
		Not allowing people with DD to
		  access bars, health clubs,
		  leisure centers, dating
		  systems, work settings

Social skills	Role-playing strategies	Accessible settings, e.g., churches
		Negative attitudes of individuals in social areas

Ideas and/or experiences
  to share
	Feedback
	Opportunities in different
	  environments
		Opportunities for social
		  experiences, e.g., in
		  neighborhood

Desire for friends	Teaching Motivation	Inadequate transportation

Be supported in taking a
  chance or risk
	Encouragement and
	  support in risktaking
		Money
		
		Overprotective behaviors

Knowledge of where to
  find friends
	Assistance in accessing
	  places
	Information, instruction,
	  supervision	

Ability to use available
  transportation, meet
  friends
	Developing augmentative
	  communication systems	

Communication skills		
To be able to dress as an adult		

Note: Across all behaviors the following client skills are needed: transportation; communicative/expressive; social; safety.

cessful, having demonstrated consensus around QOL issues in all of the groups.

AGE GROUP: *Adult*   SETTING: *Integrated Work Setting*   OTHER PRIMARY ACTORS: *Supervisor, Co-Workers*

NEED	NEED SALIENCE[a]	SOCIAL GOALS AND EXPECTATIONS		
		Independence (Decision-Making)	Integration (Participation)	Productivity (Responsibility)
LOVE	H_ M_ L×̲			
ACCEPTANCE	H×̲ M_ L_	choose a work environment in which you will be able to relate favorably to others	optional work environments & opportunity to accept or reject	recognize your supervisor's position & authority; accept cultural & behavioral differences among co-workers
SEXUALITY	H_ M_ L×̲			
FRIENDSHIP	H_ M×̲ L_	choose people to be friendly with and relate to	access to informal groups during breaks and lunch	initiate inter-relationships & talk or socialize with other people
PERSONAL GROWTH	H×̲ M_ L_	choose to work in an environment that gives opportunity for advancement	available options to move ahead	finish options for training; seek out & develop knowledge & skills to move up the ladder
HEALTH	H×̲ M_ L_	choose a safe environment to work within	seek out safe working conditions; sit with non-smokers	maintain your own health, safe working conditions; report unsafe working conditions
POSSESSIONS	H_ M×̲ L_	be able to choose your own supplies and equipment; work space	opportunity to provide & receive feedback regarding supplies, equipment & work space	accept the parameters of the organization & maintain equipment & supplies

FIGURE 6.4. Example of Completed Needs/Goals Matrix

		choose a job with wages & benefits you need to do what you want to do	opportunity for jobs with optimum wage scales & benefits & the potential for increases	seek jobs that give wage and benefits
FINANCIAL SECURITY	H×M̲L̲			
STABLE ENVIRONMENT	H×M̲L̲	choose a job with long-term prospects	assess the jobs	be an efficient, productive worker
RECREATION/LEISURE	H̲M̲L×̲			
CULTURE/FAITH	H̲M̲L×̲			
PRIVACY	H̲M̲L×̲			

[a]H = high; M = medium; L = low.

FIGURE 6.4. (Continued)

THE NATIONAL QOL CONFERENCE FOR PERSONS
WITH DISABILITIES

The next stage of the QOL Project was to build upon experience in Virginia and formulate a national agenda for enhancing QOL for persons with disabilities. This involved a larger conference in which a similar constituency to that of the Virginia groups could define critical QOL issues and formulate recommendations. Some 120 persons, one-quarter of whom were persons with disabilities and/or relatives, assembled at the National Conference in Washington in April, 1988. These persons participated in a series of workshops that were designed to identify critical QOL issues and to formulate recommendations about them.

Workshops were divided into the following topic areas: community life, work life, family life, research, program planning, program evaluation, QOL of young children, QOL of school-age children, QOL of adults, and QOL of the aged. In each workshop, a facilitator (often a professional who had been involved in the Virginia meeting) and a reactor (sometimes a person with a disability) presented material related to the workshop topic to participants. Their remarks included a brief, one-page summary of the findings of the Virginia work groups provided to them by the project. In addition, the facilitator and the reactor presented information that assessed the current state of practice in the area under consideration. Participants discussed these remarks before breaking up into smaller groups that were intended to identify related critical QOL issues and formulate recommendations. Critical issues were identified by open discussion and listing of issues, group ranking of issues in order of their importance, selecting the two most important, and then considering recommendations to address the issues. Workshop facilitators and reactors then worked with each other to provide an overall workshop report that included didactic remarks and issues/recommendations (see Goode, 1988c, for detailed reports).

A look at synopses of the content in two group reports—program evaluation and school-age children—provides but a flavor of the work of these groups.

Evaluation Work Group

Several critical issues were identified. The first was the definition and measurement of QOL. The workgroup felt that alternative methods to define QOL had to be examined and that further studies involving persons with disabilities defining QOL factors and outcomes had to occur. The actual process of evaluating QOL was seen as multidimensional. The process should be based upon consumer-defined outcomes and involve consumers in directly assessing services. General QOL indicators and ones more specific to individuals must be incorporated into this process. The use of evaluation data was also a critical issue. Results of QOL evaluation should be used proactively, not punitively. Staff would receive support and training to achieve QOL outcomes. It was recommended that payment for services provide incentives for performance that enhances QOL, to ensure that evaluation will be taken seriously by providers.

School-Age Children

The issue of participation of children and parents in educational, medical, and therapeutic decisions was seen as central. The group noted that active engagement of parents and children in decisionmaking in schools has not been fully realized. They felt that there should be a greater emphasis on policies on the national level that promote full partnership and collaboration in decisionmaking. They also described a lack of definition in decisionmaking roles for children and parents, especially in medical and therapeutic contexts. Policies clarifying child and parent rights in these situations must be formulated so that professionals can form partnerships with parents during decisionmaking. A major QOL issue was the need to reorient the current assessment procedures that are professionally controlled and deficit oriented. Educational self-assessment protocols oriented around QOL outcomes were suggested. A final critical issue was the need to define the place of risktaking in special education. Most educators agree that risktaking is crucial in the educational process. Special education curricula should actively and systematically address independence and integration as goals. Special education must deal with this issue, foster independent decisionmaking, and address the students' present and future concerns about QOL.

The activities of the QOL Project produced so many ideas related to QOL that it is only possible here to describe the kinds of information available and their character. A final indication of the viewpoint developed by the QOL Project can be seen in a set of QOL Principles that were distilled from all of the Project data and activities. These are presented in Table 6.2.

THE FUTURE OF QOL IN THE FIELD OF DEVELOPMENTAL DISABILITIES

This section briefly describes two state-level projects on QOL for persons with disabilities, QOL as an international issue in disabilities, and the future of QOL as a disability issue.

Table 6.2   QOL Principles

1. QOL for persons with disabilities is made up of the same factors and relationships that have been shown to be important to persons without disabilities.

2. QOL is experienced when a person's basic needs are met and when he or she has the opportunity to pursue and achieve goals in major life settings.

3. The meaning of QOL in major life settings can be consensually validated by a wide array of persons representing the viewpoints of persons with disabilities, their families, professionals, service providers, advocates, and others.

4. The QOL of an individual is intrinsically related to the QOL of other persons in her or his environment.

5. QOL of a person reflects the cultural heritage of the person and of those that surround him or her.

6. The development of measurement and assessment procedures that are based upon the concept of QOL is important in the development of resources and supports for persons with disabilities and their families.

7. QOL is a construct best assessed through primary consideration of subjective factors as determined by individuals with disabilities and their families, as well as through a consideration of social factors as determined through social validation.

8. QOL enhancement is made up of activities that emphasize the strengths and capabilities of persons with disabilities and their families.

9. The concept of QOL is important to examine as the basis for social policy in our country generally, as well as for its specific application to social policy for persons with disabilities.

Setting QOL Enhancement Agendas on the State Level

At the time of this writing, two state-wide QOL for persons with disabilities projects are being conducted in New York and California. The general purpose of both projects is to obtain input from persons with disabilities and their families about issues related to their QOL. The California project, funded by the Administration on Developmental Disabilities, is specifically designed to build upon the approach taken by the National QOL Project and to conduct focus groups around the state further exploring and defining issues. The ultimate goal of the California project is to construct a statewide QOL Enhancement Agenda for persons with disabilities and their families that is consistent with federal policy and reflects the input of people with disabilities and their families. The project is being conducted by the World Institute on Disabilities, an organization run by persons with disabilities, and will involve direct input from more than 300 persons with disabilities and relatives.

The purpose of the New York project is similar, with the exception that it is being conducted by the New York State Developmental Disabilities

Planning Council with its own funds. The relationship between this project and the findings and procedures of the National QOL Project is less clear. While the Project Coordinator of the National QOL Project serves as consultant to both state projects, as of this writing the specific direction that New York will take in collection of QOL data has not been determined.

What is important about both projects is that they will amass data about QOL issues on a large scale—perhaps as many as 600–700 people with disabilities will have had the opportunity to participate in a group process that will make their opinions and concerns known. This activity will have multiple results including increased networking in the disability community around QOL issues; increased awareness of QOL as a social policy concept by persons with disabilities and their families; a document that describes a QOL Enhancement Agenda for each state; a statement of critical issues and recommendations to address them based upon the input of people with disabilities; a more concise definition of QOL issues in major life settings; and the development of self-advocacy skills for participants in the groups. The activities in these two projects may well serve as models for future products in other states.

International Research Policy in QOL

At the most recent meeting of the International Association for the Scientific Study of Mental Deficiency, held in Dublin, Ireland, in August, 1988, there were no less than four sessions devoted exclusively to QOL research and policy. In Europe and elsewhere, there has been active QOL research for many years in disabilities and other fields. The degree of activity internationally however is somewhat shocking, even to a person with some familiarity in the area. QOL for persons with disabilities is of interest to cultures all over the world.

Perhaps even more surprising was the content of the discussion about QOL policy and research findings. Most of the speakers were not aware of one another's work and yet the agreement about matters of definition and about research findings was uncanny! It was clear that multiple, independent discoveries of the same phenomena were occurring, and that to some degree these phenomena did not seem to vary in their general features between cultures. For a researcher with a background in anthropology and a healthy skepticism about cultural universals, many of the presentations were unsettling in their similarities. A more comprehensive analysis of international QOL studies must be undertaken to examine the degree to which this impression is empirically true. Should these parallels prove valid and continue to develop, there will follow immense implications for disability policy and research. It may be possible to think about an International Disability Policy that would be linked to policy-generating activities such as described above. International research databases founded upon the same assumptions and procedures may also begin to make sense.

On the Future of QOL for Persons with Disabilities

When beginning the examination of QOL as a basis for disability policy, there was some trepidation. Some felt that the project was too risky and the concept too subjective to be a social policy term of value. Over the past several years, this frame of reference has changed considerably. The question "can QOL serve as the basis for disability policy in America?" is now "how can we construct disability policy based upon QOL?" People involved in the project noted that the logic of QOL is not disability specific and even asked why QOL should not serve as the basis for social policy in the United States generally. This thinking is far from the exploratory and tentative beginnings of the National QOL Project.

QOL as a policy concept may become a permanent fixture in the field of disabilities and certainly will become more influential on policy, training, research, and evaluation. Judging from the National Project, it will likely be a concept embraced by people with all kinds of degrees of disabilities, their relatives, advocates, professionals, providers, and regulators. One of the strengths of the concept is its ability to collect issues from varying perspectives. This is at least true in the experience of persons involved in the QOL Project.

Since becoming involved in QOL research and policy several years ago, the author has had numerous occasions to consider the timeliness of this concept. Why QOL now? The answer may be that QOL constitutes a generic frame of reference for understanding human activities; it is essentially, and potently, egalitarian and democratic. QOL discussions produced powerful reactions in workshop participants during the National QOL Project, requiring persons without disabilities to think about people with disabilities in the same way they thought about themselves. QOL represents the growth of ideology, language, and helping forms that recognize the rights and abilities of persons with disabilities. It has grown out of other historical developments that were similarly motivated and is linked to and partially a result of them. Examples of these include normalization, deinstitutionalization, community integration, and education in the least restrictive setting.

Thus the current concern for QOL in the disability field is anchored in the efforts of societies to think about and include people with disabilities as ordinary citizens with the same rights and responsibilities as other citizens. These efforts historically grow from international activities and exist at this time in many countries around the world. In this sense QOL may be the international disability issue *par excellence* and part of the macro-historical processes of change that have been affecting persons with disabilities around the world. Existing as we do in what will be increasingly a "global village," it would not be surprising to see our international relatedness around shared concern for QOL increase in the future. There is no current social policy vehicle that captures and fits neatly together so many parts of the citizenship puzzle.

REFERENCES

Goode, D.A. (1987). *The interim report of the work group on QOL for persons with disabilities.* Valhalla, NY: The Mental Retardation Institute.

Goode D.A. (1988a). *Quality of life: A review and synthesis of the literature.* Valhalla, NY: The Mental Retardation Institute.

Goode D.A. (1988b). *Discussing quality of life: Framework and findings of the work group on quality of life for persons with disabilities.* Valhalla, NY: The Mental Retardation Institute.

Goode, D.A. (1988c). *The proceedings of the National Conference on Quality of Life for Persons with Disabilities.*Valhalla, NY: The Mental Retardation Institute.

Kuehn, M., Goode, D.A., & Powers, J. (1987). *A framework to facilitate discussion about quality of life among consumers, service providers and researchers.* Unpublished paper.

Powers, J., & Goode, D.A. (1986). *Partnerships for people.* Unpublished paper.

Part II
Quality of Life: Service Delivery Issues

An improved quality of life for persons with mental retardation and closely related disabilities will undoubtedly require a values-based change in our current service delivery system. Authors in this section discuss those changes as they relate to:

- being in and of the community
- transitioning into environments that are more independent, productive, and community integrated
- focusing on outcomes from service delivery programs that reflect a person's enhanced QOL

The section begins at the point where the experiences of families with a child with disabilities usually begin: with the physician. In his chapter, David Coulter stresses the need to empower families to promote the quality of life of young children and to receive the assistance and support to maintain home placement. In the next chapter, Jack Stark and Tammi Goldsbury continue this focus by discussing a quality of life model that includes the domains of health, living environment, family, social and emotional relationships, education, work, and leisure. Their final sentence containing the quotation from Martin Luther King, "injustice anywhere is a threat to justice everywhere," is a thought well worth remembering.

The next four chapters in this section relate to significant QOL issues for persons in transition (Orv Karan, Gary Lambour, and Stephen Greenspan), those being integrated into the community (Ken Keith), those entering the world of work (Bill Kiernan and Kari Knutson), and those who are growing old (Matt Janicki). Each of these chapters reflects the challenges, opportunities, frustrations, and successes that we have all experienced during the last decade of policy and programmatic changes.

One of the most significant of those changes has been the increased quality of life emphasis in programmatic outcomes, addressed by Tom Bellamy, Steve Newton, Nancy LeBaron, and Rob Horner in chapter 13. This chapter is essential reading for anyone who is either involved in or concerned about current service delivery patterns and practices. It also provides the basis for the third section on assessment and measurement issues.

7

Home is the Place: Quality of Life for Young Children with Developmental Disabilities

David L. Coulter
Boston University

Quality of life is such an intensely personal concept that one who writes about it owes the reader a description of his own assumptions about what it means. Others writing in this volume have provided the reader with their understanding of the concept. In this chapter, *quality of life* means a sense of personal satisfaction with life that is more than just pleasure or happiness and yet something less than "meaning" or fulfillment. An individual with mental retardation need not have the cognitive capacity to appreciate "meaning" in order to have a life of satisfying quality. This sense of satisfaction is understood best from the individual's point of view. In other words, one must put oneself into the other person's viewpoint and try to see the world as that person would in order to get an idea of his or her quality of life.

With that conception of quality of life, the reader may wonder how a physician could possibly understand what it might be like to live with a developmental disability such as mental retardation. Indeed, I claim no personal or family experience that could provide such knowledge. What I do rely upon is a clinical style or method in which I try to put myself into the other person's viewpoint, a method which was shown to me by a professor at the University of Notre Dame (Dunne, 1978). Dunne describes a process of "passing over" from oneself to another person's viewpoint, and then returning with a deeper understanding of how that person thinks and feels about life. As a clinician involved in the lives of patients with developmental disabilities and with their families, this method provides some (albeit limited and imperfect) idea of what it is like to live with a neurological disorder. The strongest impressions that this experience provides are of the remarkable strength of individuals and families, of the marked variability of coping styles that characterize satisfying lives, and of my own humility as I try to protect and enhance their quality of life.

This chapter cannot be a review of the medical literature on quality of

61

life. Such a review would be very brief, because physicians have not written much on the subject. Yet physicians talk about it all the time and presume to make quality of life part of their clinical assessment and judgment about medical treatment. Understandably then, we do not do a very good job of measuring quality of life. We rely too often on inaccurate knowledge about the real prognosis for adaptive performance of people with mental retardation (Wolraich, Siperstein, & O'Keefe, 1987), assuming too low a level of performance and thereby too limited a quality of life. In some instances, we rely on simplistic and highly debatable formulas such as QOL = NE(H + S), or quality of life equals the product of one's natural endowment and the sum of the contributions of home and society (Gross, Cox, Tatyrek, Pollay, & Barnes, 1983). Even if this formula were conceptually sound, there is no evidence that we have methodologically valid means for measuring its components.

In this chapter about the quality of life for infants and toddlers with developmental disabilities, I will address two issues that seem to be most important, despite our limited ability to measure their contribution to quality of life. One issue is the tremendous amount of uncertainty we have about predicting the young child's subsequent degree of disability or level of neurological function, despite the fact that physicians often use quality of life judgments, however imperfect, in making these predictions. The second issue is the paramount importance of the family and environment in determining the child's physical, mental, emotional, and psychosocial growth and development. The following case, which describes a patient I have cared for, illustrates these issues.

CASE SUMMARY

This 3-month-old girl was happy and healthy and developing normally and was a source of joy and pride to her parents and grandparents. Both parents had grown up in homes that were financially limited but rich in love, support, and pride in their African-American heritage. The parents, both of whom are special education teachers who work with children with developmental disabilities, were married and had planned for this first child. On Sunday the child was full of life; on Monday she was in the Intensive Care Unit with Group B streptococcal meningitis. By Thursday, she was in a deep coma, unresponsive except to the strongest stimulation, unable to breathe on her own, and with evidence of only minimal brainstem function. A computed tomographic (CT) scan showed what seemed to be extensive brain damage. The family was understandably distraught and asked whether the child would be "a vegetable" if she survived. They wondered if it would be better to withdraw medical support to prevent such a tragic outcome.

The family was advised that in this acute situation, we could not predict the outcome with any degree of certainty. The best course would be to reassess on a daily basis and see in what direction things would go. By the next day, Friday, the child was somewhat more responsive but still in coma and still with minimal brainstem function. Nonetheless, this change seemed sufficient to rule out the possibility that the child would deteriorate further and suffer brain death. The family was now advised that if the child survived, possible outcomes included a persistent vegetative state or some degree of neurological disability, but a normal outcome seemed very unlikely. The family chose to wait until the following Monday to see what a repeat CT scan showed before making any decisions about limiting treatment.

The weekend was very difficult for the family as they struggled with what was best for their child. They expressed to a nurse that they felt the doctors were telling them the child was brain dead, but they saw evidence of continuing improvement. They shared their grief and prayed to God with their family and community, seeking guidance for themselves and healing for their child. When Monday came, the child's improvement was obvious. She had begun to open her eyes and was starting to breathe on her own. The CT scan was improved and showed less evidence of brain damage from the meningitis than might have been expected. The family was now advised that survival in a persistent vegetative state was unlikely, and the child could be expected to survive with some degree of disability.

The family's response was immediate and positive. This was an outcome they could accept. Indeed, with their unique personal, family, community, and professional resources, there was reason to believe that their child might grow up with a satisfying quality of life. The family and medical staff now joined in a shared commitment to provide whatever level of care was needed.

UNCERTAINTY

This case illustrates vividly how difficult it is to predict what will happen and the importance of obtaining new data (such as the CT scan) and waiting to observe possible signs of recovery. Resolving neurological uncertainty is often much more difficult, however (Coulter, 1987). One way to approach this general problem is to examine its components.

Uncertainty may exist because of insufficient knowledge about the actual diagnosis. In the case above, the diagnosis was fairly clear (meningitis). For most children with mental retardation, however, the diagnosis is much less obvious. Biomedical causes account for no more than a third of all cases of mental retardation, but in many such instances the biomedical cause is some imprecise label such as "cerebral maldevelopment." The mechanism of mental retardation attributable to sociocultural causes is even less clear. Indeed, in many cases even the diagnosis of mental retardation is uncertain in young children, and clinicians use the term "developmental delay" instead. Yet many children with developmental delay will not prove to have mental retardation once adequate testing becomes possible.

Uncertainty may also exist because of insufficient knowledge about the effects of treatment. In the case above, effective antibiotic treatment could be expected to clear the infection. Other types of treatment are less predictable. In this regard, the controversy over the effect of early intervention continues, although a recent meta-analysis showed evidence for the effectiveness of early intervention programs that involve the family (Shonkoff & Hauser-Cram, 1987). Although studies of physical therapy programs for young children (Palmer et al., 1988) have failed to show much benefit, these studies cannot be generalized to all physical therapy programs and it is possible that other programs would be beneficial. Medical treatment such as anticonvulsant drugs (which ultimately prove ineffective in as many as 10% to 20% of patients with refractory seizures) may also have unpredictable outcomes and therefore contribute to uncertainty about the outcome.

The most difficult aspect of uncertainty, however, may be lack of knowledge about the exact prognosis. Every experienced clinician can tell a story about a "miraculous" case of completely unexpected recovery in a child with severe neurological illness. Children with virtually identical illnesses may have completely different outcomes for reasons that no one can explain. Many cases of apparent cerebral palsy resolve spontaneously by school age (Nelson & Ellenberg, 1982); yet others may not be diagnosed until several years have passed and the deficit becomes increasingly apparent. At least some of the explanation for this variability in prognosis may reflect the plasticity of the child's brain, which continues to grow and develop throughout the first few years of life. There may well be some as yet unknown "host factor" that determines the extent to which the brain will reorganize itself to recover lost function during childhood.

The net result of this diagnostic, therapeutic, and prognostic uncertainty in early childhood is that one often cannot tell the family exactly what to expect. Clinicians learn to live with this uncertainty and to take every day for what it brings, adjusting to new problems and achievements as they occur. Families who have no such clinical training and whose only experience with disability is their own have much more difficulty adopting such a coping strategy. Yet coming to terms with uncertainty is an essential task for families and how well they accomplish this may influence the quality of their lives and the life of their child.

COPING: THE REST OF THE STORY

To examine the impact of family coping on the quality of life of a young child, we can resume the story of the child described above. After several weeks in the hospital, the acute medical condition of meningitis had passed and she was medically stable. She had recovered to the point that she would wake up and respond to visual, auditory, and tactile stimulation. Her responses were very limited, however, and she fatigued easily. She had difficulty sucking and had to be fed by a nasogastric tube for a while. Her muscle tone was very abnormal, with poor head and trunk control and increased tone or spasticity in her extremities.

A treatment plan for post-hospital care was developed with the family. This included referral to an early intervention program that would assist the family with providing physical therapy and developmentally appropriate stimulation. However, it was clear that the family would have to participate actively in this therapy for it to be successful. Rather than delegate this responsibility to a relative or babysitter, the mother decided to take an extended leave of absence from her job so that she could be home with the child.

As time passed, it became apparent that the child had significant neurological disabilities. A diagnosis of cerebral palsy (spastic quadriparesis) was made. The feeding problems continued and the family found that it took a long time to feed her even minimally adequate calories by mouth. As her growth leveled off and she was failing to thrive, the family rejected a gastrostomy tube in favor of high calorie feeding and oral motor therapy to enhance her swallowing reflexes. She became more social and enjoyed simple games and activities with her family. Her speech was limited to simple sounds, although she seemed to understand what was said to her and responded appropriately.

The child's disability proved to be highly stressful to the family. After several heated arguments between the parents over how the mother was neglecting the father's needs, they agreed to get family counseling. During counseling, it became apparent that an older sibling was also feeling ignored as the parents spent all their time with their disabled child. The decreased family income from the mother's absence from work, as well as the increased financial demands for medical and rehabilitative care for their infant, resulted in a severe financial crisis. With the assistance of a social worker, they were able to qualify for health insurance that covered most of the medical expenses, but many other expenses were not covered. The family was unable to take an extended vacation because they could not trust inexperienced respite care workers to provide adequately for their child.

Service Delivery

QUALITY OF LIFE

The quality of life in this case can be considered in terms of independence (decisionmaking), integration (participation), and productivity (responsibility). However, it is necessary to adapt these terms in a way that makes sense for a young child.

Independence has a very different meaning for a young child, who remains highly dependent on parents or other caregivers for physical and emotional sustenance. Yet anyone who has encountered a typical 2-year-old boy knows how much that child is trying to assert himself and control his world. Young children with disabilities need to work through the same developmental tasks as other children (basic trust, autonomy, and initiative), and the quality of their lives will reflect the opportunities they have to achieve these tasks. Parents and caregivers must recognize and respect that the child with a disability has to make decisions when appropriate and is able to choose within limits. There is an understandable desire to "do for" the child, out of either sympathy, pity, or frustration because it takes the child such a long time and the parent is in a hurry. Many children are only too happy to let their parents do things for them, which often leads to a crisis years later over the parent's frustration with the child's presumed (actually taught or reinforced) helplessness. My point is that this crisis can be prevented by intervening early to encourage and allow the young child to make appropriate choices, take some risks and do as much as he can for himself (Coulter, Murray, & Cerreto, 1988).

Integration into the family and the family's community is important for young children with disabilities. The family is the primary focus of integration and acceptance. Success achieved here will promote integration and acceptance elsewhere. The ability of the family to integrate a young child with severe disabilities, however, should not be presumed. Conflict between parents and conflict with siblings are probably more the rule than the exception. Anticipating these conflicts and helping the family resolve them will promote integration at this most basic level. The family is then empowered to fight for the child's integration in the larger community. This includes such basic activities as bringing the child with severe disabilities to church with the family, or including the child in shopping trips to the grocery or the toy store, or bringing the child to the company picnic. A family that has integrated their child will not permit that child's exclusion from the family's activities in the community.

A separate issue arises when the family brings the child with a severe disability to be enrolled in the educational process. The family then all too often encounters the educational bias toward segregated programs and feels powerless to oppose this bias. To my knowledge, early intervention programs that exclude them do not help them. On the contrary, it makes sense that young children with and without disabilities can learn important lessons about acceptance from each other. A few early intervention programs that have tried this approach (in some instances by including staff children as a form of daycare) have found it to be successful. These lessons about integration and acceptance may be more important educational achievements than traditional "therapy" provided in the classroom setting.

Productivity is tied to the other aspects of the young child's quality of life and follows from them. A child who has the opportunity to make appropriate choices and to interact with others in the family and in the community will develop desired behaviors. These include trust in other people, feasible competence in self-help skills, exploration of the environment, and social interactions outside the family. It is important to reward these desired behaviors when they occur to prevent frustration and to encourage further development. Success at this early age will set the stage for greater productivity as the child matures.

ACHIEVEMENT: THE CHILD MOVES ON

It is appropriate to end this chapter by continuing the story of the child as she grew up and moved on to the next stage of her life. Because of her severe cerebral palsy, she did not sit up independently until she was three years old and was learning to stand with support by age five. Her cognitive abilities were difficult to measure accurately, but testing when she was five years of age showed her language skills to be at about an eighteen-month level. Her teachers felt she was making slow but steady progress and arranged for a smooth transition into the local elementary school when she was five. The school was going to try an experimental program that would include her in many regular kindergarten activities with the other children.

Her feeding behavior improved greatly when her parents discovered that there were some foods she really liked and others she did not like. The nutritionist worked with them to develop a complete, balanced dietary program that included foods she liked. Her swallowing improved and she gained weight on this diet. Mealtimes became a pleasant family affair. The family learned to understand her other wishes as well. They also learned that there were many things she could do for herself if they took the time and encouraged her to try. They stopped picking her up all the time and let her get around by herself as much as possible. This allowed her to "get into trouble" by exploring her environment, but they learned to enjoy her curiosity while protecting her (and the household) from danger.

The family was surprised at how readily their church welcomed their daughter into the community. Their minister told them that God did not see her disability but did see a child whose soul was perfect and, somehow, she seemed to sense her acceptance and enjoyed being in church. This acceptance encouraged the family to take her with them wherever they went, and they learned to cope with the reactions of other people. She also seemed to behave better as she was able to be around other people more. Going to the doctor was a problem until they found a pediatrician who was comfortable with children with disabilities and formed a warm, caring relationship with their daughter.

Gradually, the family came to live normally from day to day without making a "big deal" out of their daughter's disabilities. They came to know other parents of children with disabilities and were able to share their frustrations and accomplishments. Their ability to help other parents also gave them a sense of satisfaction. Acting together, the parents were able to get decent respite care services so that they could finally get away for a little while at least. As their daughter prepared to go to the elementary school, her mother planned to resume her career by teaching special education at the same school so she could still watch out for her daughter.

All in all, it wasn't the way they had planned it when their daughter was born, but somehow it had turned out okay. The love they had started with was still there, changed as their daugher had changed but grown stronger through adversity and through overcoming the challenges of these early years. Their daughter was loved, happy, satisfied, developing new skills, and enjoying her achievements at home and at school. How could they ask for more?

CONCLUSIONS

It should be apparent that the quality of life for a young child with severe disabilities, such as the child described in the case report above, is highly dependent on the child's family. Interventions to promote the child's quality of life must thus be focused on helping the family to cope with the child's ordinary and special needs. As a general statement, it is probably more true than not that the medical care, educational, and social systems are not prepared to accomplish this. A reasonable sense of justice would argue that appropriate resources should be provided to allow the child an opportunity to achieve success (Veatch, 1986). These resources include assistance with health care costs, family and social support services (such as peer groups, counseling, daycare, home health care, and respite care), and high quality public educational and habilitative services from birth or from the time of diagnosis.

Case management has to become a reality that works for families and not just the present agency buzzword that all too often covers up business as usual. Indeed, the best case manager is an informed, assertive, and empowered parent, whose success as a case manager will maximize the young child's quality of life. If we are seriously interested in promoting the quality of life of young children with severe disabilities, we must get serious about accomplishing this agenda for the present and for the future.

REFERENCES

Coulter, D.L. (1987). Neurologic uncertainty in newborn intensive care. *New England Journal of Medicine, 316*, 840–844.

Coulter, D.L., Murray, T.H., & Cerreto, M.C. (1988). Practical ethics in pediatrics. *Current Problems in Pediatrics, 18*, 137–195.

Dunne, J.S. (1978). *The reasons of the heart.* New York: MacMillan.

Gross, R.H., Cox, A., Tatyrek, R., Pollay, M., & Barnes, W.A. (1983). Early management and decision making for the treatment of myelomeningocele. *Pediatrics, 72*, 450–458.

Nelson, K.B., & Ellenberg, J.H. (1982). Children who "outgrew" cerebral palsy. *Pediatrics, 69*, 529–536.

Palmer, F.B., Shapiro, B.K., Wachtel, R.C., Allen, M.C., Hiller, J.E., Harryman, S.E., Mosher, B.S., Meinert, C.L., & Capute, A.J. (1988). The effects of physical therapy on cerebral palsy: A controlled trial in infants with spastic diplegia. *New England Journal of Medicine, 318*, 803–808.

Shonkoff, J.P., & Hauser-Cram, P. (1987). Early intervention for disabled infants and their families. A quantitative analysis. *Pediatrics, 80*, 650–658.

Veatch, R.M. (1986). *The foundations of justice: Why the retarded and the rest of us have claims to equality.* New York: Oxford University Press.

Wolraich, M.L., Siperstein, G.N., & O'Keefe, P. (1987). Pediatricians' perceptions of mentally retarded individuals. *Pediatrics, 80*, 643–649.

8
Quality of Life from Childhood to Adulthood

Jack A. Stark and Tammi Goldsbury
National Center for Persons with Mental Retardation/Mental Illness
Omaha, Nebraska

"Quality" is the *in* word of the 1990s. We seem to be witnessing the beginning of a national shift away from quantitatively evaluating our life-styles to focusing on how we can choose to live our lives in a more meaningful, qualitative way. The emphasis on evaluating and desiring quality is found throughout our society and ranges from the products we produce to the services we demand and receive. This emphasis is particularly needed in our delivery of human services, where hard decisions must be made with limited resources. Despite the billions of dollars that have been allocated in implementing policies such as deinstitutionalization, mainstreaming, early intervention, and community integration, we have not yet answered the critical question: "Has it really made a difference in improving the *quality* of life for persons with mental retardation?" The purpose of this chapter is to construct a *process* by which we can begin to answer this question of quality of life as it pertains to those individuals with mental retardation during the developmental period of 6 to 21 years of age.

CURRENT EDUCATIONAL PRACTICES

Persons with mental retardation served via Chapter 1 funds represent a total of 665,000 individuals, or 15% of the total 4.4 million disabled individuals receiving special educational services in the public education system. Mental retardation ranked third behind learning disabilities and speech or language impaired individuals, respectively, but ahead of a fourth group, the emotionally disturbed (some 400,000 individuals). During the 1985–86 school year, the majority of students with disabilities received special education related services in settings with non-handicapped peers. More than 26% received special education in regular classes, while 41% were served in primary resource rooms. Another 24% were served in separate classes in regular education buildings. Students with learning disabilities or speech impairments were served primarily in regular classes or resource rooms. Yet, on a national basis, approximately 56% of persons with mental retardation were placed in separate classes (U.S. Department of Education, 1988). Regretfully, we still have too many individuals with mental retardation who are out of the mainstream of education, particularly those with more severe multiple disabilities.

LIFESPAN RESEARCH

Research into the concept of quality of life for persons with mental retardation has generally lagged behind and has been influenced by other disciplines. The professional fields of social psychology, lifespan psychology, gerontology, and medicine have primarily helped shape this relatively new and increasingly popular interest in quality of life research with persons who are developmentally disabled. Of particular interest in this chapter is the research from lifespan psychology. Lifespan psychologists have contributed to our overall understanding and development of quality of life measures. The lifespan developmental paradigm was originally proposed by Baltes and his colleagues at the Center for Psychology and Development in West Germany (Baltes, Cornelius, & Nesselroade, 1978). An important point made by Baltes and his colleagues is that their lifespan developmental paradigm is not considered so much a theory as it is a heuristic scheme upon which to generate new ideas and to provide a framework for future theory development (i.e., quality of life measures). They noted that their definition of lifespan allows for additional adaptations and these adaptations will vary among researchers, particularly as the concept is approached from different disciplines. Other lifespan psychologists, such as Dannefer (1984), Featherman (1983), and Gergen (1980), offered additional insight into this complex concept through the utilization of lifespan development, which provides a reference basis and body of research data from which we can now begin a one- to two-decade process of investigation and identification of life measures, instruments, and field tested studies to establish a national impetus to foster meaningful lifestyles that we all want for persons with or without mental retardation.

QUALITY OF LIFE: A DECISIONMAKING MODEL

The chapters in Parts I and IV of this book address the complexities of agreeing upon an operational definition of quality of life as well as *who* determines *what* is quality and *how* these standards can be best applied.

As Bradley (1988; see also Chapter 20) pointed out, "persons with mental retardation are more concerned with the range of personal freedom and choices made available to them . . . whereas service professionals are usually more interested in the technology and theory of service delivery, while public officials tend to focus on accountability issues" (p. 277). In essence, all the authors of this book seem to be unequivocal in their emphasis on having available an array of choices that individuals may select from as to what constitutes these quality of life parameters based upon each individual's unique needs.

It seems to the authors of this chapter, however, that there does not exist a theoretical construct or model of the basic process by which decisions can be made in regard to those critical components upon which to establish standards that measure a person's quality of life. Therefore, we offer Figure 8.1, which represents a six-component decisionmaking model that can be refined as we gain more knowledge in actually conducting quality of life studies with this population across the life span.

Component 1: Definitional Issue

We define quality of life as representing a "general well-being," which is used synonomously with overall life satisfaction, happiness, contentment, or success. This state of general well-being (as expressed in the formula QOL = f(IC + "O" QOL + "S" QOL) is defined as: a function (f) of one's individual characteristics (IC) (i.e., age, sex, social/cultural background, level of cognitive/adaptive functioning, educational status, health conditions) and environmental supports (i.e., parent[s], sibling[s], friends[s], etc.). These individual characteristics are impacted by objective quality of life (QOL) dimensions, which consist of the seven life domains: health, living environment, family, social/emotional relationships, education, work, and leisure. The objective QOL indicators can be analyzed through observation and measurements of satisfaction in each of these domains. The parameters of these seven life domains are discussed in detail in a later section of this chapter.

Added to the individual characteristics and objective quality of life domains are the subjective QOL domains, which are the same as the objective domains but vary in the sense of how these domains are perceived by the person with mental retardation and their immediate support system of family, direct caregivers, etc. It should be noted that although this definition of the concept of QOL is presented as an adapted (Lehman, 1983) operational framework, it can and should also be utilized in the construction of specific measures that make up measurement instruments.

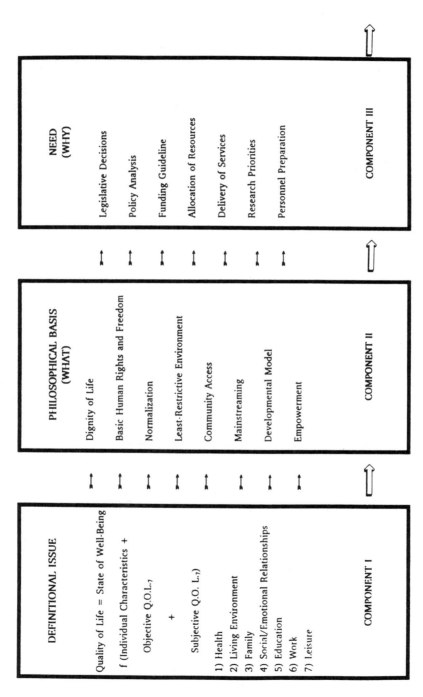

FIGURE 8.1 Proposed decision-making model for establishing QOL measurement standards.

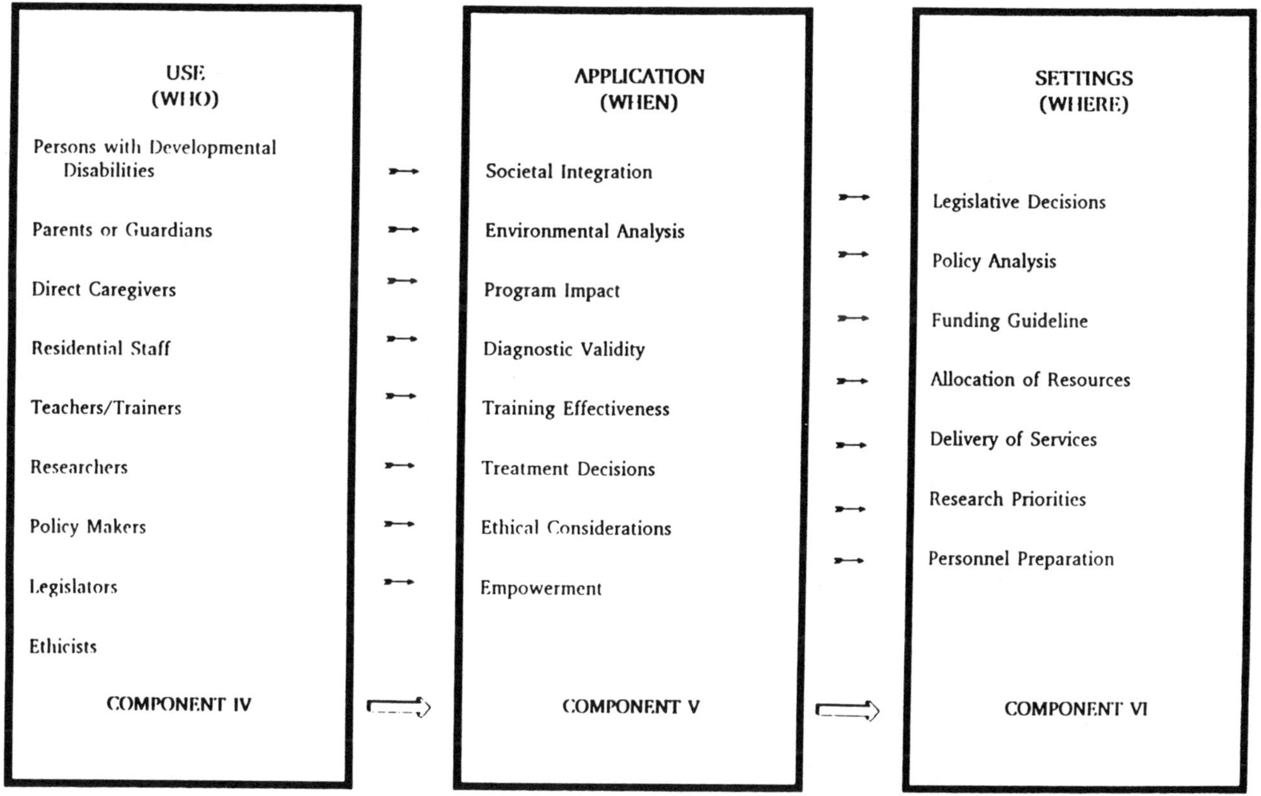

USE:
(WHO)

Persons with Developmental
   Disabilities

Parents or Guardians

Direct Caregivers

Residential Staff

Teachers/Trainers

Researchers

Policy Makers

Legislators

Ethicists

COMPONENT IV

APPLICATION
(WHEN)

Societal Integration

Environmental Analysis

Program Impact

Diagnostic Validity

Training Effectiveness

Treatment Decisions

Ethical Considerations

Empowerment

COMPONENT V

SETTINGS
(WHERE)

Legislative Decisions

Policy Analysis

Funding Guideline

Allocation of Resources

Delivery of Services

Research Priorities

Personnel Preparation

COMPONENT VI

FIGURE 8.1 (Continued)

Component 2: Philosophical Basis

Decisions about a person's QOL have to be grounded and based upon philosophical tenets. Although additional concepts could be added, certainly the dignity of life, basic human rights, and freedom are fundamental and *a priori* philosophical tenets from which QOL measures must be constructed (Luckasson, 1985). It would seem also that most would agree that the concepts of normalization, least restrictive alternative community access, participation in the mainstream of education, and the developmental (model) assumption that all individuals are capable of learning and should have access to age-appropriate educational programs are additional essential philosophical tenets. *Normalization* is used here in the traditional sense of assisting persons with mental retardation to be as normal as possible in the way they appear, behave, and live as well as the provision of opportunities for empowerment—choosing and independent decisionmaking.

Component 3: Need

Quality of life decisions should be derived from the needs of persons with mental retardation, which can range from decisions about research, training, and service to legislative policy funding decisions.

Component 4: Use

The QOL model will change based upon who will be using or making the decisions, ranging from persons who are developmentally disabled, to direct caregivers, policy makers, ethicists, etc. Obviously, caregivers and professionals may have different agendas than legislators or even parents or guardians of persons with mental retardation.

Component 5: Application

The QOL model will also vary depending upon its application and use; that is, whether it is used for societal integration or for developing diagnostic and treatment criteria.

Component 6: Settings

Finally, the decisions that must be made in identifying the quality of life depend upon the context in which persons with mental retardation are being served. These settings range from intensive care units, home and work environments, and the larger community.

Discussion

In essence, this decisionmaking model dictates both vertical and horizontal processes selecting from within and between components depending upon need, the basic philosophical tenets, why it is being used, who is using it, when the model is applied, and in what setting. This model allows for a specific decisionmaking process via the vertical selection of any one of the numerous criteria within each of these components. For example, decisions may be made utilizing this model (I), as it relates to dignity of life (II), in deciding to allocate resources (III), for persons who are severely medically impaired (IV), which health care personnel can utilize in looking at ethical considerations (V) in deciding upon the quality of care for each individual in a health care facility (VI).

QUALITY OF LIFE: DEVELOPMENTAL ASPECTS

In constructing QOL measures, particularly for individuals 6 to 21 years of age, researchers should find the above described model essential as a process framework in constructing and measuring a person's life satisfaction. However, the content of quality of life domains during the developmental period is difficult to identify because we lack an all-inclusive theory of normal development. This process becomes even more complicated when it is applied to persons who are mentally retarded. For example, if we take causality alone, there are some 250 to 350 causes (Menolascino & Stark, 1988) of mental retardation. This variation, along with the individual differences and personal characteristics, mandates a fluidity and a variability in identifying the content of quality of life during the development period of 6 to 21 years for persons with mental retardation.

It would seem, however, that before we can discuss the content of the seven life domains during this age span, we must first address the issue of what is normal development among persons with mental retardation during their developmental years. In other words, we need a reference point upon which to develop measurement criteria, keeping in mind the need for individual variation. It would seem appropriate, as we have traditionally done, to base these criteria on normal development. This complex issue was first addressed by Zigler (1969), who advocated the developmental theory of mental retardation. It was Zigler's contention that cognitive development, particularly among persons who are identified as mentally retarded, is characterized by a slower progression through the same sequence of cognitive stages as persons without mental retardation. Additionally, he hypothesized that the upper stage of cognitive development is more limited than is characteristic of those of average intellectual ability. There has been a considerable amount of debate in the field as to whether cognitive development, for example, should be viewed in this manner (that is, as delayed normal development) or whether it is different from the normal developmental sequence (Zigler, Balla, & Hodapp, 1984). In addition, Weisz and Zigler (1979) concluded that, with a few exceptions, people with identifiable developmental disabilities go through the same sequences of development as those without disability.

While much of this research supports the model of disability as a developmental delay, there also is considerable evidence that it would be overly simplistic to characterize entirely the development of those with disabilities as "like normal children only progressing slowly" (Clements, 1988). Individuals in this age span with disabilities may be much more likely to show progression/regression in their development by alternating back and forth between stages of development. That is, they may show far greater discrepancies between levels of function in different areas of development even though they may progress through the same sequences in each area. In short, there seem to be qualitative differences, oftentimes based upon cognitive factors of the developmental disability.

QUALITY OF LIFE DOMAINS

Health

Frequency, types, and severity of illness; one's access to the health care system; need and use for surgery or medication; and capability of preventive health care service.

Over the last decade, the number of students with medical problems has significantly increased, thereby requiring further clarification of the role of the family and school in the provision of such service. Seven to fifteen percent of adolescents in special education classes and some 40% to 60% of mentally retarded individuals in residential facilities are on medication (Gadow & Kalachink, 1981). In one particular study, Shore, Smalky, and Neff (1981) analyzed medical care for a group of children ages 6 to 17 years in a community-based residential facility. Two-thirds of this sample were between the ages of 13 and 17. It was noted that this sample of children had five times as many medical encounters as an age-matched general population. Approximately half of this sample growth was attributed to children in the severe/profound mental retardation range. Chronic problems were much more frequent than in the general population, with convulsive disorders present in 31% of the sample.

Certainly in constructing criteria for this domain, one must consider the tremendous economic cost and the changes that require new models of health care; availability of medical specialists serving the 6 to 21 year age group; and an expressed interest in working with this growing population in the community (Buehler, Menolascino, & Stark, 1986).

Living Environment

The availability and accessibility of privacy, security, autonomy, and normalized living.

In Sweden, for example, the most important QOL indicator of progress towards full integration of developmentally disabled individuals is the percentage of handicapped disabled young adults who are living in their own independent homes with whatever degree of supervision they need (rather than continuing to live in their parental homes). A person's living environment may be considered by many as perhaps the most important domain in that it is, to a great extent, the major influence on social and emotional development of young adolescents with mental retardation (Rutter, 1985). Most developmentally disabled individuals today remain in the family home until young adulthood. Those who are more severely disabled or medically fragile/complex at times need specialized types of residential settings in the community after "graduation" from the school system. For example, Meyers, Borthwick, and Eyman (1985) examined different types of residential settings in a survey of some 60,000 developmentally disabled persons in California. Meyers and his colleagues found that of all people surveyed (birth to 65 years of age), 53% continued to live at home, 29% lived in community settings, 13% lived in state institutions, and 5% were in health facilities. The majority of younger individuals lived at home, and as they entered the 25 to 30 years of age range, over 50% moved outside the parents' homes.

Family

Frequency and intensity of contact; emotional support; level of intimacy; the structure, interaction, and function of the family.

These characteristics will perhaps have the most significant impact on the development of a young person with mental retardation, particularly during this age span. The family lifecycle theory as advocated by Turnbull, Summers, and Brotherson (1986) provides a framework that considers the uniqueness of each family and a model by which to anticipate and plan for both the immediate and long-term needs of developmentally disabled individuals vis-à-vis their families (Turnbull, Turnbull, Bronicki, Summers, & Gordon, 1988).

Social and Emotional Relationships

The number of social and emotional activities engaged in; the quality and quantity of these experiences; and satisfaction of these social and emotional activities.

Quality of life among mentally retarded persons, particularly at the adolescent stage, is significantly impacted by the bonding and caring of parents, caregivers, peers, and the social/emotional context in which they spend their days (that is, school and residential settings). The school system, which in most cases serves as the primary social agent, must also plan for transition to other social service networks. There also must be an emphasis placed on shifting social relationships toward peer groups and adjustment skills that will result in independent living. Indices that tap these main criteria will be essential in arriving at meaningful measures of this important domain.

Education

Curriculum; the mainstreaming process; peer involvement; and transitional success.

The traditional focus of special education for our handicapped youth is in need of change. The function of the school system has been to identify and place disabled children; to test and classify them educationally; to provide the least restrictive educational setting; to recruit, train, hire staff; to designate curriculum methods of instruction; and to assess all of the cognitive, affective, and behavioral changes of the students, regardless of the degree of disability. The end product of education has been to prepare children with a skills repertoire that will enable them to participate if they so choose in the mainstream of society (Gottlieb, Alter, & Gottlieb, 1983).

Identification of criteria for this important domain has been enhanced by the development of new curriculum models that emphasize critical skills necessary for social transition and development for enhanced quality of life (Wilcox & Bellamy, 1987). In addition, the development of principles that have been introduced in special education during the last 10 years must be broadened. These principles, as advocated by Turnbull and Turnbull (1986), consist of zero reject; nondiscriminatory evaluation; appropriate individualized education; leisure, educational, and vocational placement; procedural process; and parental participation.

Work

Number of hours of real pay; derived benefits; improved self-concept and self-esteem; opportunities to engage in activities that fulfill one's contribution to society.

One of the most gratifying observations in the 1980s has been the rapid improvement in the emphasis on transitional services leading towards full employment with such concepts as supported employment and transitional services (Kiernan & Stark, 1986). A staggering number of persons with mental retardation have graduated from special education with real occupational alternatives. The President's Committee on Employment of the Handicapped has, however, estimated that only 21% of the approximately 650,000 students with disabilities who leave school annually will become fully employed. A total of 26% will be on welfare. Of those working, 40% will be underemployed or paid at poverty wage levels (Patten, 1985). Construction of individual items for this domain offers a rich body of new research from which to draw, especially when including the more difficult to serve and the medically complex individual (Wehman, Wood, Everson, Goodwyn, & Conley, 1985).

Leisure

Recreational aspects; hobbies; free time; and cultural activities.

Leisure, hobbies, recreation, and how we spend our free time, perhaps more than any other major aspect of day-to-day life, often serves as a criterion against which to measure one's quality of life in today's complex society. Enjoyment, happiness, and satisfaction are often enhanced by this critical domain, particularly for this age group, because so much effort goes into their education in preparation for transitioning from school to work. Early childhood provides a critical medium for learning, which later takes on a more complex social phenomenon, particularly in later stages of childhood and adolescence. Hobbies, crafts, and organized sports help to explore one's interests and test out career alternatives. In designing this domain, criteria must be based upon activities that increase the fullness, richness, and complexity of developmentally disabled individuals' lives; lead to acquisition of skills and active participation; can involve development and expression of social concerns through the contribution of well-being and enjoyment of others; and give enjoyment and satisfaction to individuals who engage in them (Schoultz & Jessing, 1986).

CONCLUSION

Clearly, the concept of quality of life is emerging in the field of mental retardation as a critical philosophical and theoretical movement that will most likely provide the driving force for the provision of services and the evaluation of programs in the 1990s, just as deinstitutionalization, mainstreaming, and normalization have done in recent years past. As Borthwick-Duffy (1986) pointed out, quality of life has been identified as a construct in need of a measureable, conceptual model. Hopefully, this chapter will go a long way toward constructing an overall quality of life model, that must now be field tested with measurable indices. This field testing process can result in reliable and valid instruments from which judgments can be made on the provision of the quality of care in service programs and accreditation standards can be developed.

In this chapter we have attempted to identify the cost, nature, and scope of services for individuals between the ages of 6 and 21. Although the research into the quality of life for persons with mental retardation is relatively new, such fields as social psychology, lifespan psychology, gerontology, and medical care have provided an extensive, heuristic, and diverse research base upon which to draw in constructing our own instruments—instruments that must be inherently flexible in order to measure the quality of life for persons with mental retardation with all of these individual characteristics. In addition, the decisionmaking model presented in this chapter will hopefully provide a philosophical reference and guide *vis-à-vis* the construction of both the content and process of quality of life measures.

Unfortunately, far too many persons with developmental disabilities are still excluded from full participation in the mainstream of society only because they have characteristics about which there continue to be inaccurate stereotyping and misinformation (Dart, 1986). We continue to see too many citizens with mental retardation denied their basic rights and forced to exist in situations that foster dependency and thereby lower their quality of life. Hopefully, in some small way this chapter will promote Martin Luther King's statement when he said, "Injustice anywhere is a threat to justice everywhere."

REFERENCES

Baltes, P. B., Cornelius, S. W., & Nesselroade, J. R. (1978). Cohort effects in behavioral development: Theoretical and methodological perspectives. In W. A. Collins (Ed.), *Minnesota Symposium on Child Psychology* (pp. 1–63). Hillsdale, NJ: Erlbaum.

Borthwick-Duffy, S. (1986). Quality of life of mentally retarded people: Development of a model. *Dissertation Abstracts, 34* (3), 245–247. Riverside, CA: University of California.

Bradley, V. (1988). Ensuring the quality of services to persons with mental retardation. In B. Ludlow, A. Turnbull, & R. Luckasson (Eds.), *Transitions to adult life for people with mental retardation: Principles and practices.* (pp. 270–280). Baltimore: Paul H. Brookes.

Buehler, B., Menolascino, F., & Stark, J. (1986). Medical care of individuals with developmental disabilities: Future implications. In W. E. Kiernan & J. A. Stark (Eds.), *Pathways to employment for adults with developmental disabilities.* Baltimore: Paul H. Brookes.

Clements, J. (1988). Early childhood. In J. Matson & A. Marchetta (Eds.), *Developmental disabilities: Lifespan perspective.* New York: Grune & Stratton.

Dannefer, D. (1984). Adult development and social theory: A paradigmatic reappraisal. *American Sociological Review, 49,* 100–116.

Dart, J. W. (1986). Quality of life for Americans with disabilities. In J.W. Dart (Ed.), *Maximizing the quality of life for individuals with mental retardation and other developmental disabilities.* President's Committee on Mental Retardation, 20th Annual Symposium. Washington, DC: U.S. Government Printing Office.

Featherman, D. L. (1983). The life-span perspective in social research. In P. B. Baltes & O. G. Brim, Jr. (Eds.), *Lifespan development and behavior,* Vol. 5 (pp. 1–59). New York: Academic Press.

Gadow, K. D., & Kalachink, J. (1981). Prevalence and pattern of drug treatment for behavior deviance disorders for TMR students. *American Journal of Mental Deficiency, 85,* 588–595.

Gergen, K. J. (1980). The emerging crisis in life-span developmental theory. In P. B. Baltes & O. G. Brim, Jr., (Eds.), *Life-span development and behavior,* Vol. 3 (pp. 32–63). New York: Academic Press.

Gottlieb, J., Alter, M., & Gottlieb, B. (1983). Mainstreaming mentally retarded children. In J. Matson & J. Mulick (Eds.), *Handbook of mental retardation.* New York: Pergamon.

Kiernan, W. E., & Stark, J. A. (1986). *Pathways to employment for adults with development disabilities.* Baltimore: Paul H. Brookes.

Lehman, A. F. (1983). The well-being of chronic mental patients. *Archives of General Psychiatry, 40,* 369–373.

Luckasson, R. (1985). In law and policy. *Mental Retardation, 23*(3), 148–154.

Menolascino, F. J., & Stark, J. A. (1988). *Preventive and curative intervention in mental retardation.* Baltimore: Paul H. Brookes.

Meyers, C. E., Borthwick, S. A., & Eyman, R. K. (1985). Place of residence by age, ethnicity, and level of retardation in mentally retarded/developmentally disabled population in California. *American Journal of Mental Deficiency, 90,* 266–270.

Patten, M. (1985). Introduction. *Journal of Job Placement, 1*(2), 4–6.

Rutter, M. (1985). Family and school influences on cognitive development. *Journal of Child Psychology and Psychiatry, 26*(5), 683–704.

Schoultz, B., & Jessing, B. (1986). Participation in cultural leisure and recreational activities. In J. Summers (Ed.), *The right to grow up.* Baltimore: Paul H. Brookes.

Shore, E. L., Smalky, K. A., & Neff, J. (1981). The primary care of previously institutionalized retarded children. *Pediatrics, 67,* 536–540.

Turnbull, A., Summers, J., & Brotherson, M. J. (1986). Theoretical and empirical implications and future directions for families with mentally retarded members. In J. J. Gallagher & P. M. Vietze (Eds.), *Families of handicapped persons: Research programs and policy issues.* Baltimore: Paul H. Brookes.

Turnbull, A. P., & Turnbull, H. R. (1986). *Families, professionals, and exceptionality: Special partnerships.* Columbus, OH: Charles E. Merrill.

Turnbull, H. R., Turnbull, A. P., Bronicki, G., Summers, J., & Gordon, C. R. (1988). *Disability in the family: A guide to decisions for adulthood.* Baltimore: Paul H. Brookes.

U.S. Department of Education. (1988). *To assure the free appropriate public education of all handicapped children.* Washington, DC: Author.

Wehman, P., Wood, W., Everson, J., Goodwyn, R., & Conley, S. (1985). *Vocational education for a multihandicapped youth with cerebral palsy.* Baltimore: Paul H. Brookes.

Weisz, J., & Zigler, E. (1979). Cognitive development in retarded and non-retarded persons: Piagetian test of a similar sequence hypothesis. *Psychological Bulletin, 86,* 831–851.

Wilcox, B., & Bellamy, G. T. (1987). *The activities catalog: An alternative curriculum for youth and adults with severe disabilities.* Baltimore: Paul H. Brookes.

Zigler, E. (1969). Developmental versus difference theories of mental retardation and the problem of motivation. *American Journal of Mental Deficiency, 73,* 536–556.

Zigler, E., Balla, D., & Hodapp, R. (1984). On the definition and classification of mental retardation. *American Journal of Mental Deficiency, 89,* 215–230.

9
Persons in Transition

Orv C. Karan, Gary Lambour, and Stephen Greenspan
Connecticut's University Affiliated Program, University of Connecticut

We believe the essence of a high quality of life is being able to adopt a lifestyle that satisfies one's unique wants and needs. In this respect, transition poses a real challenge to all persons because it involves a change in one's lifestyle. The uncertainty caused by these changes and the loss of familiar routines, relationships, and control is often stressful. Yet choice, the exercise of free will, and movement into environments that are more productive and fulfilling are central to one's quality of life.

Within this chapter we reflect on our observations drawn from the transition literature and offer suggestions for better facilitating transitional processes for persons with disabilities through planning, coordination, and support. Inherent in these suggestions is the groundwork for contributing to a better quality of life for persons in transition.

OBSERVATIONS ON TRANSITION

In its broader sense, transition involves the passage of individuals from one status or position in society to another at various stages throughout the life span (Patton & Browder, 1988). Examples of such stages include the beginning of school, the development of an adult identity, movement into the world of work, family development, and movement out of the social and work mainstream of life beginning with retirement (Ludlow, Turnbull, & Luckasson, 1988).

These multiple transitions have no definite beginning or ending points other than birth and death. In order to facilitate sensible decisionmaking regarding an individual, it is essential that one's total life span be taken into account while remembering that each transition will in some fashion impact upon future transitions (Chadsey-Rusch, 1984). Whether the transition represents the passage of individuals from one environment to another or from one status or position in society to another, all are forms of change, and individuals react to change. Transition theory suggests that changes alter a person's familiar routines and therefore produce variations in the person's life space (Stark & Karan, 1987).

85

Although transitions can result in a higher quality of life, there is also evidence to suggest that this does not always occur and, even if it does, there still may be extended periods of transitional stress or shock (Coffman & Harris, 1980).

No matter how attractive a particular community setting may be or how well it meets some philosophic ideal, there are no guarantees that an individual in transition will in fact participate in that setting in a personally satisfying, socially productive, and socially accountable manner. Because such behavior may represent a person's adaptation to a social environment she/he does not understand, attempting to modify such behavior without first attending to the person's emotional needs resulting from the transition may actually exacerbate a problem.

A person's adaptability is an important factor in the examination of how successful an individual is in handling transitions (Browder, 1987). However, one's adjustment is not some static entity. Because each environment is an interactive one (Pearce & Shaw, 1987), different environments and/ or differences within the same environment can significantly affect the behavior of persons in those environments (Schalock & Stark, 1988). One's behavior may fluctuate markedly representing the individual's way of revealing that environmental demands and available resources for meeting these are not synchronized. Careful transitional planning, however, provides "a powerful tactic for facilitating the successful interaction between the individual and his or her environment" (Sobsey & McDonald, 1988, p. 40).

TRANSITION PLANNING

Transition planning must incorporate several considerations. This section discusses three considerations that are considered critical to successful transitions.

Individual/Environmental Perspective

There should be an effort to adapt one's program to the needs of the person rather than forcing the person to adapt to a particular program (Weisenstein & Elrod, 1987). In too many cases when there is a mismatch between an individual and his or her environment, the focus of attention is on trying to "fix" the individual's behavior. By focusing on the individual alone, the person's social definition is lost (Lovett, 1985). Fortunately, there is growth in appreciation and empirical support for maximizing the fit between individuals and their environments (Keyes & Dean, 1988).

Flexibility

Second, transition plans must be flexible enough not only to respond to changes in values, goals, and experiences of the participants, but also to incorporate known events as well as spontaneous ones (Patton & Bowder, 1988). Obviously, one's life is not simply an unfolding sequence of planned events. Spontaneous events, circumstances, and opportunities can profoundly influence one's momentary quality of life and can even have permanent effects. The extent to which the person and his/her significant others are emotionally supported during these unplanned transitions can make a difference in how well the person copes with both the frustrations and the joys of life in the community.

Coordination

Another essential consideration in transition plans is coordination. When cooperative program planning efforts are attempted, the following four basic actions are recommended:

1. Assessment, or the determination of what services and resources a person will need for support during the transition period.
2. A plan that identifies roles, responsibilities, and timelines for who will do what for whom and when.
3. Implementation of the plan and subsequent delivery of the services.
4. Evaluation of the transition program and its outcomes to provide measures of an individual's quality of life.

A critical topic related to service delivery in transitional programs involves the adequacy and responsiveness of the person's social and interpersonal networks (Carney & Orelove, 1988; Edgerton & Bercovici, 1976; Halpern, 1985). The availability of support resources valued by the individual has been shown to contribute to successful transitions (Karan, Leahy, & Schwebke, 1985). The next section will therefore elaborate on the role of social support as a necessary ingredient for facilitating the transition process and anticipated enhanced quality of life.

SOCIAL SUPPORT

Social support is a critical mediator of a wide variety of life's stresses. *Social support* refers to the presence of meaningful supportive relationships with others that serve to buffer the negative impact of stressful events (Stoneman & Crapps, 1988). A social life and interactions with others are important. Individuals with social ties have been found to be less vulnerable to stress and to be socially better adjusted (Edgerton, Bollinger, & Herr, 1984).

Many individuals, including professionals, parents, peers, paraprofessionals, and friends, play important roles in providing support. Because communication is the essence of relationships, and because relationships are the primary ingredients of supportive environments, there is a need to assess social interaction processes and to use such information for mobilizing more adequate social supports. This implies that efforts for those who are more socially limited should focus both on teaching them acceptable methods for expressing their needs and on teaching the significant others in their lives how better to assess the communicative intent of their behaviors (Karan & Berger-Knight, 1986).

Family Support

The family is obviously an important part of the individual's social support network, and the role family members play in their successful transitions is receiving increasing attention. Parents and other family members play a variety of roles as advocates, service providers, role models, case managers, evaluators, risk takers, financial planners, and fund raisers (Turnbull & Turnbull, 1986). Within the family structure, parents have been identified as the most salient persons contributing to the success of their child's adjustment to community-based programs (Carney & Orelove, 1988; Conroy & Bradley, 1985; Intagliata, Willer, & Wicks, 1981; Wehman, Everson, Walker, Wood, & Marchant, 1987).

During times of transition, every family experiences changes in routines, patterns, and familiar environments. While such stresses occur for families of nonhandicapped children experiencing expected developmental transitions, changes occurring outside the expected sequence of human development and family life cause the most intense stress (Anderson, 1987). Fear and uncertainty about the future and concern for the welfare of their offspring cause considerable stress for the family (Zetlin & Turner, 1985). Because of uncertainty, families will sometimes delay transition decisions or never complete them at all (Knowlton, Turnbull, Backus, & Turnbull, 1988). One result is that instead of providing an opportunity to prepare in an orderly way, transitions sometimes are forced upon families under emergency situations, such as when a parent dies or when an aging parent can no longer care for a middle-aged offspring.

Peer Relationships

Peer relationships play an important role in one's successful community adjustment, especially as older adults may be placed in community settings among people with whom they have very little in common. (Greenspan, 1979; Greenspan & Shoultz, 1981). At such times, the availability of a placement takes on more importance to those doing the placement than whether the placement discounts or maintains friendships established over years. Krauss and Erickson (1988) found that peers play a critical role in the informal support networks of persons with disabilities and so they advise program planners to prioritize maintenance of these friendships as much as possible.

Support for Support Providers

It has been estimated that 80% of the care provided to individuals with disabilities comes from informal sources. For the younger person, these sources are usually family members, relatives, and friends; whereas for adults, care is provided mostly by paraprofessionals (Gartner, 1979). Regardless of the source of the support, however, no program is complete if it does not pay attention to the needs of those providing the service at least as efficiently as it does to the needs of the person receiving the service (Lovett, 1985).

At some point, it is almost certain that those providing support will need to call upon family members, friends, trusted colleagues, and others to assist them in making careful decisions. The transition from one program or situation to the next will be more successful when careful consideration is given by significant others to the implications of those providing the support (Anderson, 1987; see also Chapter 6, this volume). Meeting the support needs of those providing support can influence the quality of care provided to consumers as well as assist in the retention of qualified providers.

CONSUMER INPUT AND CHOICES

A fundamental aspect of transition planning involves the increasing exercise of direct consent by the individual in making decisions about his/ her life (Knowlton et al., 1988). Transition planning must therefore include many opportunities for choices with a wide range of both career and learning options. One's perception of personal control is necessary for the development of a sense of competence. Those who are given the opportunity for choice acquire a sense of personal control and competency and therefore will most likely experience a higher quality of life.

Service providers, support staff, parents, and friends should allow individuals to choose for themselves. Whether on major or minor issues, decisionmaking opportunities help individuals with disabilities cope more effectively in a variety of community environments and situations (Carney & Orelove, 1988). However, care should be taken not to impose presumed quality of life standards on others, for whom existing or alternate standards may be more appropriate. Because most conceptualizations of quality of life have been framed from professional viewpoints rather than from the perceptions of consumers whose life quality is being affected (Karan, 1986), we must be careful not to put too much confidence in our current assessment of quality of life.

For example, Kregel, Wehman, Seyfarth, and Marshall (1986) conducted interviews on 300 young people who had exited schools from 1978 to 1983. They found at the time of the interviews that 86% of the individuals still lived at home with their natural families and a majority of the social activities and interpersonal relationships in which they participated focused on passively oriented activities conducted within their own homes. Although these young people were not well integrated into the community, an important indicator in current quality of life conceptualizations, over 75% were reported as being very satisfied or somewhat satisfied with their lives. Findings from studies such as this, as well as growing recognition of the importance of consumer input (Karan & Mettel, 1989), present new challenges to program planners and those pursuing quality of life measurement.

Clearly, perceptions of quality of life vary considerably. However, now that consumer input is being incorporated into program decisions, such input can be expected to vary from conventional professional wisdom; yet, it must be heard and it must be respected. The challenges become even greater when the consumers are nonverbal, functionally noncommunicative, or say what they think they should feel rather than what they actually do feel (Lovett, 1985). Those who cannot speak for themselves, however, can still make choices and exercise their will. They, like everyone else, need to have a chance to make decisions, and their decisionmaking should be respected (Boggs, 1985).

SUMMARY AND CONCLUSIONS

This chapter has explored issues relevant to the impact of transitions on quality of life. It has looked at transition as a lifelong concept rather than as applying to one specific point in time. Transition is both a systems issue as well as a highly personal one, and it involves both planned and anticipated events as well as spontaneous alterations in one's expectations. Therefore, transition can be as conspicuous as movement from one environment to another, or as subtle as the movement of one's favorite chair within the same room.

When planning transitional services, programs and opportunities should be built around the needs (including emotional needs) of the individual rather than forcing individuals to fit programs. Transition planning should also include exposing persons to opportunities that will adequately prepare them for skills needed to live, work, and play in the community. Certainly, enabling people to have more control over their lives is an important first step in reducing transition stress while simultaneously contributing to lifestyles that satisfy their unique wants and needs and hopefully improve their real and perceived quality of life.

REFERENCES

Anderson, W. (1987). Transition: A parent advocate perspective. In R. N. Ianacone & R. A. Stodden (Eds.), *Transition issues and directions* (pp. 142–148). Reston, VA: Council for Exceptional Children.
Boggs, E. (1985). *Are we ready to listen?* Video produced by the research and training center. University of Wisconsin-Madison.
Browder, P. M. (1987). Transition services for early adult age individuals with mental retardation. In R. N. Ianacone & R. A. Stodden (Eds.), *Transition issues and directions.* (pp. 77–90). Reston, VA: Council for Exceptional Children.
Carney, I. H., & Orelove, F. (1988). Implementing transition programs. In B. L. Ludlow, A. P. Turnbull, & R. Luckasson (Eds.), *Transition to adult life for people with mental retardation: Principles and practices* (pp. 137–157). Baltimore: Paul H. Brookes.
Chadsey-Rusch, J. (Ed.) (1984). *Conference proceedings document one: Enhancing transition from school to the work place for handicapped youth.* Champaign, IL: National Network for Professional Development and Vocational Special Education, Office of Career Development for Special Populations, University of Illinois.
Coffman, T. L., & Harris, N. C. (1980). Transition shock and adjustment of mentally retarded persons. *Mental Retardation, 18,* 3–7.
Conroy, J., & Bradley, V. (1985). *Pennhurst longitudinal study: A report of 5 years of research and analysis.* Boston: Human Services Research Institute.
Edgerton, R., & Bercovici, S. (1976). The cloak of competence: Years later. *American Journal of Mental Deficiency, 80,* 485–497.
Edgerton, R. B., Bollinger, M., & Herr, B. (1984). The cloak of competence: After two decades. *American Journal of Mental Deficiency, 88,* 345–351.
Gartner, A. (1979). *Career ladders and a training model for the (re)training of direct service workers in community-based programs for the developmentally disabled.* New York: New Career Training Laboratory, Center for Advanced Study and Education, City University of New York.
Greenspan, S. (1979). Social intelligence in the retarded. In N. R. Ellis (Ed.), *Handbook of mental deficiency: Psychological theory and research* (2nd ed.) Hillside, NJ: Lawrence Erlbaum.
Greenspan, S., & Shoultz, B. (1981). Why mentally retarded adults lose their jobs: Social competence as a factor in work adjustment. *Applied Research in Mental Retardation, 2,* 23–38.
Halpern, A. S. (1985). Transition: A look at the foundations. *Exceptional Children, 51*(6), 479–485.
Intagliata, J., Willer, B., & Wicks, N. (1981). Factors related to the quality of community adjustment in family care homes. In R. Bruininks, C. Meyers, B. Sigford, & K. Lakin, *Deinstitutionalization and community adjustment of mentally retarded people* (pp. 217–230). Washington, DC: American Association on Mental Deficiency.
Karan, O. C. (1986, May). *Current approaches to quality of life assessment.* Paper presented at the 110th annual meeting of the American Association of Mental Deficiency, Denver, CO.
Karan, O. C., & Berger-Knight, C. (1986). Developing support networks for individuals who

fail to achieve competitive employment. In F. R. Rusch (Ed.), *Competitive employment: Service delivery models, methods and issues* (pp. 241–255). Baltimore: Paul H. Brookes.

Karan, O. C., Leahy, M., & Schwebke, K. (1985). *Project deinstitutionalization*. Mendocino, CA: Lawren Productions.

Karan, O. C., & Mettel, L. (1989). Staff training needs in integrated settings. In W. E. Kiernan & R. L. Schalock (Eds.), *A look ahead: Economics, industry and disability* (pp. 141–152). Baltimore: Paul H. Brookes.

Keyes, J. B., & Dean, S. F. (1988). Stress inoculation training for direct contact staff working with mentally retarded persons. *Behavioral Residential Treatment, 3*(4), 315–324.

Knowlton, H. E., Turnbull, A. P., Backus, L., & Turnbull, H. R. (1988). Letting go. Consent and the "yes but" problem in transition. In B. L. Ludlow, A. Turnbull, & R. Luckasson (Eds.), *Transitions to adult life for people with mental retardation: Principles and practices* (pp. 45–66). Baltimore: Paul H. Brookes.

Krauss, M. W., & Erickson, M. (1988). Informal support networks among aging persons with mental retardation: A pilot study. *Mental Retardation, 26*(4), 197–201.

Kregel, J., Wehman, P., Seyfarth, J., & Marshall, K. (1986). Community integration of young adults with mental retardation: Transition from school to adulthood. *Education and Training of the Mentally Retarded, 21*(1), 35–42.

Lovett, H. (1985). *Cognitive counseling and persons with special needs: Adapting behavioral approaches to social contexts*. New York: Praeger.

Ludlow, B., Turnbull, A., & Luckasson, R. (1988). Transitions to adult life for people with mental retardation: Principles and practices. In G. Blalock (Ed.), *Transitioning across the life span* (pp. 3–20). Baltimore: Paul H. Brookes.

Patton, J. R., & Browder, P. M. (1988). Transitions into the future. In B. L. Ludlow, A. P. Turnbull, & R. Luckasson (Eds.), *Transitions to adult life for people with mental retardation: Principles and practices* (pp. 293–311). Baltimore: Paul H. Brookes.

Pearce, C. K., & Shaw, K. J. (1987). Transition: A vocational rehabilitation perspective. In R. N. Ianacone & R. A. Stodden (Eds.), *Transition issues and directions* (pp. 125–134). Reston, VA: Council for Exceptional Children.

Schalock, R., & Stark, J. (1988). Identifying programming goals. In B. L. Ludlow, A. P. Turnbull, & R. Luckasson (Eds.), *Transition to adult life for people with mental retardation: Principles and practices* (pp. 85–100). Baltimore: Paul H. Brookes.

Sobsey, D., & McDonald, L. (1988). Special education: Coming of age. In B. L. Ludlow, A. P. Turnbull, & R. Luckasson (Eds.), *Transition to adult life for people with mental retardation: Principles and practices* (pp. 21–63). Baltimore: Paul H. Brookes.

Stark, J., & Karan, O. (1987). Transition services for early adult-age individuals with severe mental retardation. In R. N. Ianacone & R. A. Stodden (Eds.), *Transition issues and directions* (pp. 91–110). Reston, VA: Council for Exceptional Children.

Stoneman, Z., & Crapps, J. M. (1988). Correlates of stress, perceived competence, and depression among family care providers. *American Journal of Mental Retardation, 93*(2), 166–173.

Turnbull, A. P., & Turnbull, H. R. (1986). *Families, professionals and exceptionality: A special partnership*. Columbus, OH: Merrill.

Wehman, P., Everson, J., Walker, R., Wood, W., & Marchant, J. (1987). Transition services for adolescent-age individuals with severe mental retardation. In R. Ianacone & R. A. Stodden (Eds.), *Transition issues and directions* (pp. 49–76). Reston, VA: Council for Exceptional Children.

Weisenstein, G. R., & Elrod, G. F. (1987). Transition services for adolescent-age individuals with mild mental retardation. In R. Ianacone & R. Stoddens (Eds.), *Transition issues and directions* (pp. 39–48). Reston, VA: Council for Exceptional Children.

Zetlin, M., & Turner, J. L. (1985). Transitions from adolescence to adulthood: Perspectives of the mentally retarded individuals and their families. *American Journal of Mental Deficiency, 89*(6), 570–579.

10
Quality of Life: Issues in Community Integration

Kenneth D. Keith

Nebraska Wesleyan University

Integration of persons with mental retardation into ordinary community settings, services, and activities has been considered a desirable goal for at least two decades (Dybwad, 1969). It has also been asserted that such integration produces developmental progress superior to that attained in segregated settings (Menolascino, 1977), in part because of the integration of specialized service and normalization (Keith, 1979; Perske & Perske, 1980). Nevertheless, these are notions that have evolved in comparatively recent times, following a longer history of neglect, abuse, and devaluation (Wolfensberger, 1969). Major issues for the last decade of the twentieth century include the question of the strength of our commitment to community integration for all citizens and the quality of life that should be expected as such integration occurs.

It has become apparent in the past few years that the right to live in the community can no longer be made contingent upon developmental or behavioral criteria. Thus, persons with mental retardation should not be required to "earn" a place in the community by virtue of such standards as skill gains. Instead, quality of life, including such dimensions as personal satisfaction and happiness, becomes increasingly important in the evaluation of community programs and placements (Keith, 1986). This viewpoint makes it essential that we develop an understanding of those aspects of personal lifestyle that contribute to quality of life for persons moving toward full community integration.

DIMENSIONS OF QUALITY OF LIFE

The personal stories of persons with mental retardation suggest that they want the same things from life that other persons do (Hoffman, 1980; Williams & Schoultz, 1982). Some of these things have been summarized as objective or social indicators (Campbell, 1976), including various national statistics, health and employment data, availability of

93

education, and other quantifiable variables. While these measures may be *influential* in the experience of life by individuals, they do not provide direct *assessment* of life experience (Campbell, 1976). Other measures, sometimes designated psychological indicators (Schalock, Keith, Hoffman, & Karan, 1989), are useful in assessing subjective, affective perceptions such as happiness and satisfaction of persons (Campbell, 1976) and the extent to which they experience mental well-being (Campbell, 1981).

Flanagan (1978) organized personal interview responses of about 3,000 people from all regions of the United States into six quality of life components. He reported that six areas correlated most highly with overall quality of life: material comforts; health; work; active recreation; learning; and creative expression.

Lehman (1988) studied nine life domains among chronically mentally ill persons: living situation, relations with family, social relations, leisure activities, work, finances, safety, health, and religion. He also included interview questions regarding personal satisfaction in each of the domains.

Keith, Schalock, and Hoffman (1986) examined quality of life in terms of the three broad factors of control of environment, community involvement, and social relations. Each factor encompassed a variety of items on the *Quality of Life Questionnaire* (Keith et al., 1986) and was tested with persons with mental retardation in a number of settings as well as with several other citizen groups.

Campbell (1981) reported the results of several nationwide studies of psychological well-being in terms of 12 domains of life. These domains and their respective levels of correlation with overall life satisfaction were marriage (.42); family life (.45); friendships (.39); standard of living (.48); work (.37); neighborhood (.29); city or town or residence (.29); the nation (.30); housing (.30); education (.26); health (.29); and the self (.55).

Although the works of Flanagan (1978), Lehman (1988), Keith et al., (1986) and Campbell (1981) differ in important ways, there is considerable overlap in their findings. It would be fair to say that Americans (with or without mental retardation) are concerned in rating the quality of their own lives with relationships, work, general material standard of living, opportunities for learning, the neighborhoods/communities/homes in which they live, health and safety, recreational/social activities, and perception of self. In addition, employment, interpersonal relationships, and independent survival in practical life situations may be the most significant determinants of community adjustment of adults with mental retardation (Toomey & O'Callaghan, 1983). Thus, the availability of these life satisfactions to such persons in their communities is a critical issue that must be addressed.

QUALITY OF LIFE AND COMMUNITY INTEGRATION

Generally speaking, quality of life for persons with mental retardation in the community is directly related to the extent to which services approximate normal models. That is, those persons served in residential models closest to independent living and those whose vocational activity is closest to normal competitive work score highest on measures of quality of life (Schalock et al., 1989).

In a study of personal satisfaction of a small sample of adults with mental retardation living with their parents, Flynn and Saleem (1986) found that two-thirds wanted to leave their parental homes for more independent living. An equal number expressed a desire to move from their workshop situations. Unfortunately, none reported having nonhandicapped friends. Similarly, in a study of adults who had left their parental homes for community residences, Catterole, Jahoda, and Markova (1988) found that all felt their autonomy had been limited at home, that their ability to learn self-help skills at home was restricted, and none had had relationships with nonhandicapped friends prior to their move.

Lovett and Harris (1987) interviewed 48 persons with mental retardation in order to determine the skills that these persons believed important to their success in community living. On average, they rated vocational skills most important, followed by social skills and personal skills. Although these ratings were similar to those obtained from staff members, the authors concluded that it is important to involve persons with mental retardation in identifying their own goals and training needs. Dudley (1987) agreed, arguing that people with mental retardation should be participants in efforts to help themselves, and that they should have meaningful associations with a range of people beyond relatives, staff, and other clients.

Dudley (1987) also suggested that individuals with mental retardation may well be aware of their disabilities and of the labels attached to them. Further, he pointed out that most studies show that these persons dislike the label "mental retardation." Mest (1988) found in a series of group interviews that, while her subjects were critical of prejudice against persons labeled "retarded," they did not attribute their own problems to "being retarded." Instead, they talked about problems in the community (jobs, money, safe homes, etc.) as social problems—not as the problems of persons with mental retardation. In other words, they viewed their problems and needs in much the same way that other citizens might.

Wolfensberger (1980a) deplored the need for research to demonstrate that devalued members of our culture possess the same feelings, behavior, and capacity to change as other, nondevalued citizens. He argued that it should be obvious that all persons would benefit from culturally valued environments, convenient services, warm interactions, positive social images, and the like—factors that would be considered desirable by nearly anyone. Heal, Sigelman, and Switzky (1978), however, cautioned that an empirical base may be necessary to prevent a swing of the pendulum of enthusiasm in the direction of pessimism in residential services.

QUALITY OF LIFE AND SOCIAL INTEGRATION

One question that should be asked with regard to the current status of community integration efforts is this: Compared with their neighbors, how do citizens with mental retardation fare with respect to quality of life? This is an area of research that has significant implications for current community service models and for attempts to achieve true community integration. Existence in the community may denote physical integration, but this may be different from social integration, (Wolfensberger, 1980b). Measures of quality of life will be important in the assessment of the latter.

For example, Keith et al. (1986) studied quality of life questionnaire scores of 101 persons living in two small midwestern towns. Specifically, the scores of 44 adults with mental retardation were compared to scores from 57 of their neighbors. The persons with mental retardation lived in homes or apartments in the two towns, and the neighbors resided next door ($n = 28$) or within two blocks but not next door ($n = 29$). The quality of life scores of the neighbors were found, as a group, to be significantly higher than those of the persons with mental retardation. The two groups of neighbors were compared with each other in order to assess the possibility that living next door to individuals with mental retardation might alter neighbors' perceptions of quality of life. There was no significant difference between the two groups of neighbors.

Subsequent analysis (Kixmiller, Keith, & Schalock, in press) of responses to three specific questions ("How do you like this town?" "How do your neighbors treat you?" "How often do you talk with the neighbors, either in the yard or in their home?") revealed some interesting patterns. Neighbors reported significantly higher scores on the items "How do your neighbors treat you?" and "How often do you talk with your neighbors?" However, on the question "How do you like this town?", no significant difference was found between the groups. Although these citizens with mental retardation seemed to like their towns as well as their neighbors, they clearly viewed their interactions with those neighbors differently, and not as favorably. In addition, a separate analysis (Kixmiller et al., in press) indicated that, on all three questions, persons with lower levels of need (see Schalock & Keith, 1986, and Schalock et al., 1989) had significantly higher quality of life scores.

The pattern for these two communities is clear. Neighborhood residents with mental retardation do not enjoy (or at least perceive) equal treatment from, or as frequent interaction with, their neighbors as do other people living in the same towns. Further, individuals with low levels of need experience more frequent and satisfying interactions with their neighbors than do persons with higher need levels. These findings suggest that while these persons are physically integrated in the community, they are not fully integrated socially. In fact, some might question whether loneliness and unhappiness are characteristic of their existence and a reduced quality of life (Schalock, 1988).

There is some apparent tendency for adults with mild mental retardation living in the community to score higher than other persons on self-reports of depression (Prout & Schaefer, 1985) and for such depression to be associated with low levels of social support and poor social skills (Benson, Reiss, Smith, & Laman, 1985; Laman & Reiss, 1987). However, it is not clear whether these relationships are causal in nature, and it seems to be the case that social skill training can be effective in treating symptoms of depression in this population (Laman & Reiss, 1987). It does seem clear that adults with mental retardation can provide self-reports on their emotional states (Kazdin, Matson, & Senatore, 1983) and that emotional anguish may in some cases be the result of stigmatizing treatment by others (Dudley, 1987).

As a part of a larger study of quality of life in the community, Hoffman (1980) measured self-reports of loneliness among individuals with mental retardation. She found that there were few reports of loneliness and that about three out of four of her interviewees considered themselves less lonely than other people. Additional research has suggested that adults with mental retardation, like other persons, seek intimacy and marriage, but often have difficulty in finding mates (Drew, Logan, & Hardman, 1988).

OUTLOOK

Being a "client," Wolfensberger (1988) asserted, ranks high on the list of those things dangerous to persons with mental retardation. It is likely that satisfactory quality of life levels and true community and social integration will await the emergence of legitimate generic roles. Clients will become employees and persons with mental retardation will become simply neighbors. Individuals are sensitive to the impact of labels and as a result suffer the consequence of their fellow citizens' misconceptions and expectancies (Dudley, 1987). We might predict that true integration will bring less artificial visibility to individuals with mental retardation who will be:

> . . .living in ordinary houses and apartments like yours; passing you or standing next to you on the streets; riding with you on buses, trolleys,

and subways; rubbing elbows with you in shopping centers; going to
public school with the other kids on the block; working in the same
building where you work; making money and paying taxes; seen in
restaurants, theaters, and at athletic events; sitting beside you in churches
and synagogues (Perske & Perske, 1980, p. 77).

It will be necessary that we show sensitivity to the *perception* of quality
of life of *individuals* (Landesman, 1986) and that we give attention to the
integration, service needs, and satisfaction of persons across the lifespan
(Schalock & Lilley, 1985). Continued development of improved quality of
life measures can be expected (see Chapter 16, this volume; Lehman, 1988).

Just as social validation has become a significant issue of interest to
behavioral engineers, it will increase in importance to those planning and
delivering community services. To the extent that community services are
seen as socially acceptable, normal, and useful by their consumers and
neighbors, persons with mental retardation are likely to enjoy more satisfying lives. The attempt to measure quality of life is a step toward a useful
social validation and may help us along to the point to which one such
person aspired:

The community has to accept us. We're handicapped, but we have
needs like everyone else. Some of our needs are special, but they have
to be accepted. We're not asking for your blood—we're just asking to
be treated as you'd want to be treated, if you were in our position
(Williams & Schoultz, 1982, p. 82).

Finally, personal satisfaction depends in large measure upon a sense of
control over one's own life. This has been shown for persons with mental
retardation as well as for the population at large. That is, persons with a
strong sense of control feel high satisfaction with their lives. This sense of
empowerment, autonomy, and independence is likely to provide the foundation for an improved quality of life. Our ability to define and measure
it is the new challenge in program evaluation.

REFERENCES

Benson, B. A., Reiss, S., Smith, D. C., & Laman, D. S. (1985). Psychosocial correlates of
depression in mentally retarded adults. II. Poor social skills. *American Journal of Mental
Deficiency, 89*, 657–659.
Campbell, A. (1976). Subjective measures of well-being. *American Psychologist, 31*, 117–124.
Campbell, A. (1981). *The sense of well-being in America.* New York: McGraw-Hill.
Cattermole, M., Jahoda, A., & Markova, I. (1988). Leaving home: The experience of people
with a mental handicap. *Journal of Mental Deficiency Research, 32*, 47–57.
Drew, C. J., Logan, D. R., & Hardman, M. L. (1988). *Mental retardation: A life cycle approach.*
Columbus, Ohio: Merrill.
Dudley, J. R. (1987). Speaking for themselves: People who are labeled as mentally retarded.
Social Work, 32 (1), 80–82.

Dybwad, G. (1969). Action implications, U.S.A. today. In R. B. Kugel & W. Wolfensberger (Eds.), *Changing patterns in residential services for the mentally retarded* (pp. 383–428). Washington, DC: President's Committee on Mental Retardation.

Flanagan, J. C. (1978). A research approach to improving our quality of life. *American Psychologist, 33*, 138–147.

Flynn, M. C., & Saleem, J. K. (1986). Adults who are mentally handicapped and living with their parents: Satisfaction and perceptions regarding their lives and circumstances. *Journal of Mental Deficiency Research, 30*, 379–387.

Heal, L. W., Sigelman, C. K., & Switzky, H. N. (1978). Research on community residential alternatives for the mentally retarded. In N. Ellis (Ed.), *International review of research on mental retardation* (Vol. 9). New York: Academic Press.

Hoffman, K. (1980). *Quality of life as perceived by persons who were classified as mentally retarded.* Unpublished master's thesis, University of Nebraska, Lincoln.

Kazdin, A. E., Matson, J. L., & Senatore, V. (1983). Assessment of depression in mentally retarded adults. *American Journal of Psychiatry, 140*, 1040–1043.

Keith, K. D. (1979). Behavior analysis and the principle of normalization. *AAESPH Review, 4*, 148–151.

Keith, K. D. (1986, May). *Quality of life in the community: Current status of adults with mental retardation.* Paper presented at annual meeting of the American Association on Mental Deficiency, Denver.

Keith, K. D., Schalock, R. L., & Hoffman, K. (1986). *Quality of life: Measurement and programmatic implications.* Lincoln, Nebraska: Region V Mental Retardation Services.

Kixmiller, J. S., Keith, K. D., & Schalock, R. L. (in press). *Views on town and neighborhood: Adults with mental retardation and their neighbors,* Nebraska Journal of Psychology.

Laman, D. S., Reiss, S. (1987). Social skill deficiencies associated with depressed mood of mentally retarded adults. *American Journal of Mental Deficiency, 92*, 224–229.

Landesman, S. (1986). Quality of life and personal life satisfaction: Definition and measurement issues. *Mental Retardation, 24*, 141–143.

Lehman, A. F. (1988). A quality of life interview for the chronically mentally ill. *Evaluation and Program Planning, 11*, 51–62.

Lovett, D. L., & Harris, M. B. (1987). Important skills for adults with mental retardation: The client's point of view. *Mental Retardation, 25*, 351–356.

Menolascino, F. J. (1977). *Challenges in mental retardation: Progressive ideology and services.* New York: Human Sciences Press.

Mest, G. M. (1988). With a little help from their friends: Use of social support systems by persons with retardation. *Journal of Social Issues, 44*, (1), 117–125.

Perske, R., & Perske, M. (1980). *New life in the neighborhood.* Nashville: Abingdon.

Prout, H. T., & Schaefer, B. M. (1985). Self-reports of depression by community-based mildly mentally retarded adults. *American Journal of Mental Deficiency, 90*, 220–222.

Schalock, R. L. (1988, September). *The concept of quality of life in community-based mental retardation programs: A position paper.* Paper presented at the meeting of the Administration on Developmental Disabilities, Washington, DC.

Schalock, R. L., & Keith, K. D. (1986). Resource allocation approach for determining clients' need status. *Mental Retardation, 24*, 27–35.

Schalock, R. L., Keith, K. D., Hoffman, K., & Karan, O. C. (1989). Quality of Life: Its measurement and use. *Mental Retardation, 27*(1), 25–31.

Schalock, R. L., & Lilley, M. A. (1985, May). *What should one expect from programs for elderly citizens with developmental disabilities?* Paper presented at the annual meeting of American Association on Mental Deficiency, Philadelphia.

Toomey, J. F., & O'Callaghan, R. J. (1983). Adult status of mildly retarded past-pupils from special education. Part II: Social adaptation. *International Journal of Rehabilitation Research, 6*, 301–312.

Williams, P., & Schoultz, B. (1982). *We can speak for ourselves.* London: Souvenir Press.

Wolfensberger, W. (1969). The origin and nature of our institutional models. In R. B. Kugel & W. Wolfensberger (Eds.), *Changing patterns in residential services for the mentally retarded* (pp. 59–171). Washington, DC: President's Committee on Mental Retardation.

Wolfensberger, W. (1980a). Research, empiricism, and the principle of normalization. In R. J. Flynn & K. E. Nitsch (Eds.), *Normalization, social integration, and community services* (pp. 117–129). Baltimore: University Park Press.
Wolfensberger, W. (1980b). The definition of normalization: Update, problems, disagreements, and misunderstandings. In R. J. Flynn & K. E. Nitsch (Eds.), *Normalization, social integration, and community services* (pp. 71–115). Baltimore: University Park Press.
Wolfensberger, W. (1988). Reply to "All People Have Personal Assets." *Mental Retardation, 26,* 75–76.

11
Quality of Work Life

William E. Kiernan and Kari Knutson
Children's Hospital, Boston

Quality of work life (QWL) is a concept and practical tool that has been discussed, examined, and debated by social scientists, psychologists and the business world for more than 20 years (Beer & Walton, 1987; Faucheux, Amado, & Laurent, 1982; Nadler & Lawler, 1983; Sashkin & Burke, 1987; Seashore, 1975). The definition and application of QWL remain rather vague, despite the attention QWL has received over the years. Essentially, QWL is an attempt to understand, both individually and in an interactive fashion, the individual, organizational, and social dynamics of the workplace (Bowditch & Bouno, 1982; Faunce & Dubin, 1975; Sashkin & Burke, 1987).

Recently, QWL has been applied to the human service and disability fields as a component of its parent construct, quality of life (Edgerton, 1975; Goode, 1989; Heal & Chadsey-Rusch, 1985; Schalock & Heal, 1988). Quality of Life (QOL) is becoming an increasingly popular method of evaluating individual, group, and societal satisfaction in all spheres of life: residential, recreational, and vocational (Bowditch & Bouno, 1982; Nadler & Lawler, 1983; Schalock & Heal, 1988; Taylor, 1987). A basic tenet of this chapter is that the individual's QWL cannot be discussed in isolation from the QOL in any other life sphere.

The working environment as a focus for identifying and examining quality issues is just emerging, joining residential, social, and personal spheres as an area of interest (Charland, 1986; Goode, 1989; Kolodny & van Beinum, 1983). There are numerous reasons for this new vision of work, including many historical precedents and contemporary attitudes and events. It is important to emphasize at the onset that work is becoming increasingly important not only because of the amount of time that people spend on the job, but also because work is assuming a larger, more meaningful role in most people's lives (Taylor, 1987).

Work is often a vehicle through which we establish our identity and place in society, our peer groups, and the level of economic independence we realize (Holland, 1983; Super, Starishevsky, Matlin, & Jordaan, 1963). This fact alone supports the need for organizations to take a closer look at how well they provide individuals with opportunities for satisfaction and success on and off the job. Work is clearly playing a more significant role in people's lives; in response, organizations are beginning to recognize that they have a primary responsibility to their employees (Bowditch & Bouno, 1982).

The remaining sections of this chapter examine QWL from three perspectives, including that of industry, as a definitional and operational perspective, and finally a disability-based perspective. When something is so malleable as QWL, it is essential to have one central theme to which one can always return. This theme is presented in the following definition of QWL adopted by the authors:

> . . . QWL is an individual's interpretation of his/her role in the workplace and the interaction of that role with the expectations of others. The quality of one's work life is individually determined, designed, and evaluated. A quality work life means something different to each and every individual, and is likely to vary according to the individual's age, career stage, and/or position in the industry.

INDUSTRY PERSPECTIVE

Historical Precedents

Over the past 20 years, QWL has evolved through various definitional stages, each having contributed to the current conceptualization of the term (Bowditch & Bouno, 1982; Davis & Cherns, 1975; Sashkin & Burke, 1987). Academia and the business world have long been concerned with the psychology of the workplace, particularly focusing on the attitudes and behaviors of workers as they affect individual productivity and, correspondingly, the company's bottom line (Faunce & Dubin, 1975; Goode, 1989). Such issues have been addressed historically under the concept Organizational Development (OD). The more recent focus on quality is an attempt to resolve the conflict between bottom-line and humanistic values in OD (Gadon, 1984; Kanter, Summers, & Stein, 1986; Sashkin & Burke, 1987). In response to this and other changes, QWL has evolved into an expansion of the business world's OD programs.

Origin and Development of QWL

The term QWL was first used in the late 1960s, originating with General Motors and the United Auto Workers to describe workers' levels of job satisfaction. Irving Bluestone coined the term *Quality of Work Life*, which began as a variable expressing the level of worker satisfaction and developed into an approach and series of programs designed ultimately to increase worker productivity (Goode, 1989). Labor-management cooperation guided the development and implementation of these early QWL efforts, resulting in workplaces where employees participated in problem-solving and decisionmaking efforts to improve their work lives. In addition, management attitudes became more concerned with the individual's welfare, stressing positive interpersonal relationships and overall improved working conditions (Bowditch & Bouno, 1982; Goode, 1989).

In the mid 1970s, QWL was considered in light of specific changes and methods that could be instituted in companies not only to enhance bottom line productivity, but also to increase employee identification and a sense of belonging and pride in their work (Davis & Cherns, 1975; Faunce & Dubin, 1975; Sashkin & Burke, 1987). Examples of these approaches include work teams, autonomous groups, job enrichment, and sociotechnical change (Charland, 1986; Gadon, 1984). Such approaches can be very effective, but must not be seen as cure-alls that can be introduced and implemented in a "connect the dots" fashion. These types of programs are frequently what comes to mind when one thinks of QWL.

By far the most complex view of QWL is the social movement or overall commitment not just to the bottom line, the employee, or society, but to the interaction of the three (Kanter et al., 1986; Modic, 1987; Sashkin & Burke, 1987; Taylor, 1987). QWL has come to be seen as more than an array of services; it is a holistic individual, organizational, and societal response to work-related attitudes. It cannot be understood outside the context of the individual's whole life. As reinforced by the scope of the other articles in this book, QOL is a broad phenomenon that must be viewed as the interaction of all life domains. By this discussion of QWL as a separate concept, the reader should not assume that it is a process that can be assured through manipulation of the work environment: it must be considered in light of the whole person if one is to understand and impact the QWL for an individual.

Key Concepts In QWL

To summarize QWL from the perspective of industry, one can use three key concepts that are manifest in QWL attitudes and approaches. These are productivity and job satisfaction, participative management style, and flexibility in meeting individuals' needs (Sashkin & Burke, 1987).

Productivity and Job Satisfaction.

Although the research is inconclusive, there is a prevailing belief within organizations that individuals who are highly satisfied with their jobs are more productive (Bowditch & Bouno, 1982). This is the fundamental reason why management invests the time, money, and energy toward improving the QWL of their employees. Regardless of the bottom line, productivity and job performance are often not presented in QWL aims in order to prevent workers from perceiving that management is merely trying to get more productivity out of them at no cost (Sashkin & Burke, 1987). There has been some evidence showing that QWL efforts result in higher product quality, lower absenteeism, lower employee sabotage, fewer grievances, and good publicity (Goode, 1989).

Participative Management Style.

As noted earlier, a participative management style has become almost universally accepted as a significant QWL concept (Bowditch & Bouno, 1982; Davis & Cherns, 1975; Kolodny & van Beinum, 1983). The core of QWL is the opportunity for employees at all levels in the organization to have an impact upon the working environment by participating in decisionmaking processes regarding the job and thereby enhancing self-esteem and the level of satisfaction realized. Development of decisionmaking mechanisms such as work management problem-solving committees or task forces has been a common strategy to enhance QWL. Essential to the successful improvement of QWL is a meaningful involvement of the worker in all decisionmaking processes (Goode, 1989).

It has become management's responsibility to support the worker's need to be an active participant in the day-to-day decisions that affect his/her job and the company as a whole. The company that is serious about quality, and recognizes those employees who do a good job, produces satisfied and productive employees. The worst thing that management can do is to ask workers for their input, opinions, and concerns, and then not utilize them. The result is disillusioned and frustrated workers who frequently experience such stress-related pathologies as suicide, addiction, and divorce (Yankelovich, 1988).

Flexibility in Meeting Individual's Needs.

This flexibility allows workers to custommake their work spaces while keeping in mind the expectations of the industry. Additionally, flexibility allows employees to balance more effectively the demands of the social and residential aspects of their lives so that they can enhance their entire quality of life (Gadon, 1984; Kanter et al., 1986; Sashkin & Burke, 1987). Again, the theme is that QWL means different things to different people. This attitude increasingly results in more individualized benefits packages to meet the many and varied needs of today's employee. The relationship of this need to be flexible to the changing role of work in our society is addressed further in the next section.

DEFINITIONAL AND OPERATIONAL PERSPECTIVE

As noted above, QWL is currently defined as a social movement. As such, it is interdependent with other aspects of life. QWL is not simply a series of services or programs offered to an employee by an employer or a menu of fringe benefits or perks available. Rather, it is a philosophical commitment to the development of an interactive relationship between the worker and the employer. Each of the three key concepts of QWL discussed in the preceding section—productivity and job satisfaction, participative management, and flexibility—produces a whole set of challenges to individuals, organizations, and society at large. The question is, "What must we do to meet the needs and expectations of all involved, such that people in organizations will have healthy working relationships?"

QWL Is Interactive

In order to better understand the interdependent nature of QWL, we must consider it as part of a larger social system. QWL is not just what the worker needs, but the interaction of the expectations of the work place and the needs of the individual as well. It is when there is a match of the industry expectations with the employee needs that heightened levels of satisfaction are realized (Getzel & Guba, 1957). This social system model notes that the needs of the individual reflect the personality of that individual, while industry's expectations reflect the role that the workers should and must play in that industry. When there is compatibility of the expectations and the needs, the level of satisfaction realized is high. When there is dissonance, where the worker does not meet the expectations of the industry or where the needs of the individual are not met by the industry, the levels of job satisfaction and QWL for industry and the individual are poor. Ultimately, the resolution of this dissonant state is through a change in the individual's needs or a dissolution of the employment relationship.

QWL Is Responsive To The Environment

QWL does not exist in a vacuum. Changes in demand for business services, labor supply, and societal expectations have led to major shifts in the workplace. Concerns about profits persist as industry acknowledges the needs of the marketplace and its valuable asset, the workforce. Some of the factors that have led to this include (Bogue, 1985; Harris, 1987):

- A movement from a manufacturing to a service industry, reflected by a threefold increase in service over manufacturing jobs, with this trend expected to continue and increase to fivefold by 1995;
- Reduction in the number of younger workers entering the labor force, with an estimated 27% reduction in 19-year-olds entering the work force in 1995 (as compared with 1985);
- Continued early retirement patterns, with the average retirement remaining in the upper 50s;
- An increase in the number of persons over the age of 65, thus increasing the demand for services such as shopping, transportation, health care, home services, and so forth; and
- An increase in the number of women entering the work force, with more than one-half of the work force in 1995 expected to be made up of female employees.

Changes in demand with the associated decline in supply has stimulated industry to pay more attention to the needs of the worker as well as the interests of the customer (Bluestone, 1989). The motivation to respond to employee needs has led to an increased interest in the adoption of practices that increase productivity, decrease absenteeism, and improve employee morale and commitment to the company.

Evolution in the Role of Work

The changes noted above have led to a greater awareness of worker needs. As noted by Yankelovich (1988), jobs are critical to identity and general happiness for workers not only on the job but outside the job as well. Work has been a form of self-expression in many ways. The more educated workforce of the baby boom generation is looking to the job not just as a means of economic independence, but also as a mechanism for social and interpersonal support (Bogue, 1985; Harris, 1987). The emphasis upon work and the concepts of work is now coming from the worker, who receives not only pay but also social and emotional support, an outlet for self-expression, and an arena for interpersonal interaction. Work establishes an identity for the worker, creates opportunities for social and peer group development, creates a means of economic independence, and establishes a sense of self-worth (Kiernan, Schalock, & Knutson, 1989).

The role of work is not a constant role, but rather an evolving one. People's needs change over time, with work taking on more or less significance depending on one's age and other factors such as family demands, personal goals, and income expectations. This again reinforces the inter-

Table 11.1   Sociological Classification of Work Stages [a]

Preparatory work period	Development of an orientation to the world of work through home, neighborhood, and school activities
Initial work period	First part-time or summer work experience at about the age of 14 (a marginal worker)
Trial work period	Entry into the regular labor market some time between 16 and 25 years of age and continuing until a stable work position is located (usually after considerable changing of jobs until the type of work is found in which the individual can hold own) at about age 35
Stable work period	At about age 35 and continues until about age 60
Retirement period	Begins at age 60 or 65

[a] Adapted from Holland (1983) and Super et al. (1963).

active character of QWL. When considering an individual's QWL, it is important to pay attention to where the person is in terms of job or career development. The work stages presented in Table 11.1 provide a conceptual frame from which to view QWL. In the preparatory and initial work periods, what the individual views as critical may differ from what is viewed as critical during the trial work period, the stable work period, or the retirement work period. For example, in the early work stages, such as the initial and trial work periods, many people are more concerned about experience than money, whereas in later periods, issues of salary, success, and security seem stronger. The factors that the employee values vary depending upon what the work stage is. Thus, in assessing the QWL, consideration of what work stage the employee is at is important.

QWL as a Series of Services and Programs

In an effort to expand QWL for employees, a number of activities have been attempted, including personal and professional development, work redesign, team building, work scheduling and total organizational change (Gadon, 1984). The specific activities are designed to create opportunities for involvement of employees in the day-to-day work assignments and in the creation and maintenance of their personal work space. The more important of these activities are summarized in Table 11.2. The thrust of these activities is to increase the involvement and the commitment of the employee to the company. The intent of industry in initiating such activities is twofold; increased profitability through decreased turnover and increased productivity and a more invested and satisfied work force. Because

Table 11.2   Activities To Enhance Quality of Work Life

Personal and Professional Development

    Management by objective
    Peer counseling
    Employee assistance support service
    Physical health improvement

Work Redesign

    Job enrichment
    Work flow reorganization
    Work redesign

Team-Building

    Quality circles
    Participation teams
    Task workers
    Project groups
    Joint labor-management productivity committees

Work Scheduling

    Flex time
    Staggered work hours
    Compressed work week
    Job sharing
    Part-time work

Organizational Changes

    Profit-sharing programs
    Joint ventures
    Combined ownership programs

the competitive edge in many areas is quality, management is paying increased attention to what employees need and say (Charland, 1986; Modic, 1987; Taylor, 1987).

The Variables that Constitute QWL

Along with those implementing QWL programs in the private sector, social scientists are also busy attempting to operationalize QWL. A number of reports have identified key variables that enhance QWL (Davis & Cherns, 1975; Gadon, 1984; Seashore, 1975; Taylor, 1987; Walton, 1975). For example, Walton (1975) identified eight key variables that must be present if a high level of QWL is to be experienced. These are summarized in Table

Table 11.3 Quality of Work Life Variables

Adequate and Fair Compensation

Safe and Healthy Working Conditions

- Reasonable hours
- Minimize risk of injury or illness

Immediate Opportunity to Use and Develop Human Capacities

- Autonomy or self-control in job
- Range of skills and abilities used or learned
- Knowledge of results of actions on job
- Knowledge of entire task and meaningfulness of tasks
- Opportunity to get involved in planning

Opportunity for Continued Growth and Security

- Development of one's capabilities
- Possibility of using skills in the future
- Advancement opportunities
- Job or income level security

Social Integration in the Work Organization

- Freedom from prejudice
- Equal opportunities
- Percentage of job mobility
- Supportive primary work group
- Sense of community beyond work group
- Interpersonal openness

Constitutionalism in the Work Organization

- Privacy
- Free speech
- Equity
- Due process

Work and the Total Life Space

- Balanced role of work

Social Relevance of Work Life

- Social responsibility of the work organization

11.3. It is clear from this listing that QWL pertains not just to earnings and work space, but also to a number of factors that impact work directly and indirectly, including working conditions, growth opportunities, social integration, constitutionalism, and the social relevance of work life. QWL, like quality of life, is a complex set of factors that contribute to the workers' sense that their contributions and involvement will make a difference in the production of the materials or delivery of services, and that those services and materials are valued by society.

DISABILITY-BASED PERSPECTIVE

As the reader has no doubt noted, no reference to persons with disabilities has yet been made by the authors. This is intentional and reflects the authors' strong conviction that the variables constituting QWL are consistent, regardless of the presence or absence of a disabling condition. Thus, we have examined what constitutes QWL in general. This is, however, not to say that the authors feel that persons with disabilities have or will have the same or similar employment opportunities as persons without disabilities. The lack of employment opportunities is certainly a critical issue for those of us interested in integrated employment for persons with disabilities (Kiernan & Schalock, 1989). If there is no opportunity to work, then there can be no QWL for the individual. It is up to each of us to advocate, encourage, and create employment opportunities for persons with disabilities so that the QOL variables presented thus far in the chapter will help to maximize the independence, productivity, and integration for all adults.

Implications for Persons with Disabilities

Many people are concerned about how to enhance the QWL for individuals with disabilities. Some initial efforts to define QWL implications for such individuals have been done. At a national conference on QOL for persons with developmental disabilities (see Goode, Chapter 6), it was the consensus of those professionals, consumers, advocates, parents, and providers participating that in defining QWL there is no need to differentiate the factors that constitute QWL between persons with and without disabilities (Schalock, 1987). At that same meeting, the following three resolves were made:

1. QWL is the same for people with and without disabilities.
2. QWL is a matter of consumer rather than professional definition.
3. QWL is a social phenomenon and a product primarily of interactions with others.

There is a need for the disability field to make a conceptual commitment to the philosophy of QWL. Professionals and policy makers must begin to adopt the precepts of the participative management style by confronting the issues that perpetuate low QWL for both consumers (individual employees who have disabilities) and human service providers. More specifically, if the concepts of QWL are felt to be important, then the role of the person with disabilities in the decisionmaking process must be clearly supported by parents, professionals, employers, and society. To assure QWL, we must assure opportunities, choice, and experience for persons with disabilities.

Policy and Research Implications

The concept of QWL does not reflect the presence or absence of a disabling condition, but rather the acknowledgement that workers must be involved in the decisionmaking process and feel ownership in all aspects of the job if they are to feel that their QWL is sufficient. For persons with disabilities, the evaluation of QWL begins not with an assessment of the individual's perception of the key characteristics that constitute QWL, but with an examination of the job selection process. Frequently for persons with disabilities, development of employment opportunities is done by an external source seeking out job openings, placing the individual in employment, and assuming the person with a disability should be satisfied with the position for many years to come. Overall, the QWL for individuals with disabilities is considerably compromised in many instances because persons with disabilities are not incorporated into the decisionmaking process for identifying, obtaining, and maintaining employment. It is critical that persons with disabilities participate in the decisionmaking process and that they have full involvement in the selection of their jobs. The right to choose is an important right for all persons. We need to teach persons with disabilities how to recognize their options and how to make choices. They must be given sufficient experience and opportunity to do so.

Given the involvement of the individual with disabilities in the job selection process, it is appropriate to examine the more traditional concepts of QWL. Because work is a dynamic experience, one must frequently make choices based on changing expectations (that is, new job demands, different co-workers/supervisors, etc.). Thus, any QWL evaluation must be flexible and able to reflect the changing needs of the individual and the evolving expectations of the job. The key variables summarized in Table 11.3 can serve as a basis for such an evaluation.

Additionally, any assessment of QWL must consider the issues of presence, opportunity, access, and interpretation. The work environment must provide the basic characteristics constituting QWL. When some or all of the key variables are not present, as in those instances where the work space is hazardous, the wages are inadequate, and/or the options for growth are limited, the chances of achieving a high QWL are poor. In other instances, when such key variables are present yet the individual is not given the opportunity to participate, again the level of QWL will be reduced. In these two instances, the issue is a reflection of a deficiency in the workplace. There are occasions when the presence and opportunity are available yet the worker will not access these. The reasons for lack of access can be many and might include lack of skills, unwillingness or lack of intent, or absence of interest. All three situations—presence, opportunity, and/or access—can adversely impact the QWL achieved by the employee. However, even if the key variables are present, the opportunity to participate is available, and the worker accesses that opportunity, the perception of QWL for the individual may be low because of incompatibility of need and expectation for the worker and the job.

The measurement of QWL is a complex process that reflects numerous variables and the interaction of the individual worker with these variables in a specific environment. What is quality for one individual in one situation may not be perceived as quality to someone else. Additionally, QWL may change with changes in job expectations or changes in the needs of the individual. It is essential that any assessment of QWL take into consideration a set of key variables that may fluctuate over time and in importance for the individual. Furthermore, the perception of the individual regarding his or her specific environment at a point in time is what will ultimately constitute the individual's sense of QWL. Therefore, a thoughtful assessment procedure for documenting QWL must include:

- Identification of key variables constituting QWL;
- Clear strategies to assess these variables upon the following domains, including the presence of these on the job, the opportunity for the individual to interact with these variables, the level of access that the individual exercise, and the level of satisfaction expressed by the worker with each variable at a specific point in time;
- A procedure to evaluate (quantitatively and qualitatively) the match of the needs of the individual to the expectations of the job (the "goodness of fit" measure of the persons to the position using the key variables constituting QWL).

Thus, measurement of QWL, just as measurements of success in employment, is not solely through dollars earned, but involves a combination of factors including the perception of individuals and their roles in the decisionmaking process, actual and perceived level of control of the workspace, options for growth, level of perceived significance of the contribution made by the worker to the goods or service provided, the impact of work on other life areas, and the feel of economic independence realized through work.

Additionally, there are a number of policy implications that emerge. For persons with disabilities, frequently the opportunity to decide what types of work to enter is compromised. Thus, the QWL for persons with disabilities may include some measure of independence, decisionmaking, and opportunity for selection of types of jobs sought. Also, as for all employees, it is important to ascertain the level of satisfaction regarding tasks performed, level of integration, level of autonomy, level of opportunity for independent decisionmaking, and, ultimately, the acceptance and satisfaction derived through employment.

In conclusion, it is clear from the above discussion that QWL is a complicated phenomenon. It reflects a philosophical commitment by employers and employees to work constructively to establish an interactive communication system that allows each to have an opportunity to influence the levels of independence, autonomy, and self-esteem realized through employment. QWL changes over time and must reflect the differences for individuals in their early, stable, and retirement years. In examining QWL, it is clear that the variables that are important for persons without disabilities are the same variables that are important for those individuals with disabilities. Thus, the authors have not made a distinction between persons with and without disabilities in looking at the variables that contribute to QWL. However, to achieve an increased QWL for persons with disabilities, additional efforts are necessary to incorporate these individuals into the decisionmaking processes, not only in the workspace but also in the selection of the types of work involved. This level of involvement by employees will lead to an increased sense of QWL. This increased sense will have the secondary benefits of increased productivity and reduced costs to industry. Thus, by attending to those areas that enhance QWL, employees, industry, and society all win.

REFERENCES

Beer, N., & Walton, A. E. (1987). Organizational development. In M. R. Rosenzweig & R. W. Porter (Eds.), *Annual Review of Psychology* (pp. 339–367). Palo Alto: Annual Reviews.

Bluestone, B. (1989). Employment prospects for persons with disabilities. In W. E. Kiernan & R. L. Schalock (Eds.), *Economics, industry and disability: A look ahead* (pp. 17–26). Baltimore: Paul H. Brookes.

Bogue, D. J. (1985). *The population of the United States: Historical trends and future projections.* New York: Free Press.

Bowditch, J. R., & Bouno, A. F. (1982). *Quality of work life assessment: A survey-based approach.* Boston: Auburn House.

Charland, W. A. (1986). *Life work: Meaningful employment in an age of limits.* New York: The Continuum Publishing Company.

Davis, L. E., & Cherns, A. B. (Eds.) (1975). *Quality of working life.* Volume 2. New York: Free Press.

Edgerton, R. B. (1975). Issues relating to quality of life in mentally retarded individuals. In M. J. Begab & S. A. Richardson (Eds.), *Mental retardation in society: A social service perspective* (pp. 127–140). Baltimore: University Park Press.

Faucheux, C., Amado, G., & Laurent, A. (1982). Organizational development. In M. R.

Rosenzweig & L. W. Porter (Eds.), *Annual Review of Psychology* (pp. 343–370). Palo Alto: Annual Reviews.

Faunce, W. A., & Dubin, R. (1975). Individual investment in working and living. In L. E. Davis & A. B. Cherns (Eds.), *Quality of working life*. Volume 1. (pp. 313–314). New York: Free Press.

Gadon, H. (1984). Making sense of quality of working life programs. *Business Horizons, 27,* 42–46.

Getzel, J. W., & Guba, E. G.. (1957). Social behavior in the administrative process. *School Review, 65,* 423–441.

Goode, D. A. (1989). Quality of life, quality of work life. In W. E. Kiernan & R. L. Schalock (Eds.), *Economics, industry and disability: A look ahead* (pp. 337–349). Baltimore: Paul H. Brookes.

Harris, L. (1987). *Inside America*. New York: Heritage Books.

Heal, L. W., & Chadsey-Rusch, J. (1985). The lifestyle satisfaction scale (LSS): Assessing individuals' satisfaction with residence, community setting, and associated services. *Applied Research in Mental Retardation, 6,* 475–490.

Holland, J. R. (1983). Vocational preference. In M. Dunnette (Ed.), *Handbook of industrial and organizational psychology* (pp. 521–571). New York: John Wiley & Sons.

Kanter, R. M., Summers, D. V., & Stein, B. (1986). The future workplace alternatives. *Management Review, 75,* 30–34.

Kiernan, W. E., Schalock, R. L., & Knutson, K. (1989). Economic and demographic trends influencing employment opportunities for adults with disabilities. In W. E. Kiernan & R. L. Schalock (Eds.), *Economics, industry and disability: A look ahead* (pp. 3–16). Baltimore: Paul H. Brookes.

Kiernan, W. E., & Schalock, R. L., (Eds.) (1989). *Economics, industry and disability: A look ahead.* Baltimore: Paul H. Brookes.

Kolodny, H., & van Beinum, H. (1983). *Quality of work life in the 1980's.* New York: Praeger Publications.

Modic, S. J. (1987, June 15). Higher quality of work (editorial in *Industrial Week*).

Nadler, D. A., & Lawler, E. E., III (1983). Quality of work life: Perceptions and direction. *Organizational Dynamics, 11*(3), 20–30.

Sashkin, M., & Burke, W. W. (1987). Quality of work life. *Journal of Management, 13*(2), 393–418.

Schalock, R. L. (1987). The concept of quality of life in community based mental retardation programs: A position paper. Hastings, NE: Hastings College, Department of Psychology.

Schalock, R. L., & Heal, L. W. (1988). Research in quality of life: Current status and policy recommendations. Unpublished manuscript. Hastings, NE: Hastings College, Department of Psychology.

Seashore, S. E. (1975). Defining and measuring the quality of work life. In L. E. David & A. B. Cherns (Eds.), *Quality of working life*. Volume 1. (pp. 93–110). New York: Free Press.

Super, D. E., Starishevsky, R., Matlin, V., & Jordaan, J. T. (1963). *Career development: Concept theory.* New York: College Examination Board.

Taylor, H. (1987). Evaluating our quality of life. *Industrial Development, 156,* 1–4.

Walton, R. D. (1975). Quality of work life: What is it? *Sloan Management Review, 15*(1), 11–21.

Yankelovich, D. (1988). Our turn. *American Health, 7*(7), 56–60.

12
Growing Old with Dignity: On Quality of Life for Older Persons with a Lifelong Disability

Matthew P. Janicki

*New York State Office of Mental Retardation and
Developmental Disabilities*

The difficulties inherent in defining the factors associated with the notion of quality of life (QOL) for persons who are elderly and who are mentally retarded are analogous to those associated with those for others who are just elderly or who are living their lives with a disability. The key difference between daily life for a person in the general population with at least minimal capacity for self-determination and independence and one who has special needs because of dependency is that the individual who is independent can potentially define what his or her day will be like. Dependency often denies an individual that freedom of choice and brings with it the onus of responsibility for others to provide. The interaction of the definition of freedom by two individuals with conflicting needs is what tests quality of life—for the provider must give care and the recipient of the care must be provided for. Who defines what is to be done? Freedom to make choices is the root of this concept.

In our culture, we highly value the ability to define our lives and make independent decisions about what we do, where we live, how we spend our time, what we eat, with whom we socialize, and so on. Of course, realism tempers these freedoms. Our income level defines our options for where we live, our experiences and opportunities define what we can do, and our networks define with whom we socialize. Persons with lifelong disabilities who are elderly may have limited options to exercise these decisions.

Gerontologists have long debated the qualitative points of old age (Achenbaum, 1986; Neugarten & Neugarten, 1986). However, there is general recognition that with social and financial supports, old age for contemporary Americans is easier than it was for age peers several generations ago. In many instances this is also the case for adults with mental retardation. However, generational differences in lifestyle and service availability do exist. The question can be posed: Is life better now for older Americans with a lifelong disability?

FACTORS THAT CONTRIBUTE TO QOL

What factors contribute to what we consider quality of life? Lawton (1983) characterized "the good life" for older persons as composed of four sectors: behavioral competence, psychological well-being, perceived quality of life, and objective environment. Within the sector of behavioral competence, he included a hierarchy that includes health, functional health, cognition, time use, and social behavior. He posited an interrelation among these sectors that influences the self, which in turn reenergizes the factors.

Blunden (1988) offered several dimensions that he considered integral to quality of life for all persons, including those with mental retardation: (a) physical well-being, (b) material well-being, (c) social well-being, and (d) cognitive well-being. Each is described briefly below.

Physical Well-Being

Certainly, health or physical well-being is fundamental to other aspects of quality of life. Freedom from the debilitating effects of illness or disability is an important consideration for persons with mental retardation who are aging or elderly. The limitations of old age or lifelong physical disability can confound the individual's ability to continue to be independent and this can lead to profound impediments to lifestyle.

Material Well-being

Material well-being is the ability to gain and use at one's discretion disposable income, to live in quarters of acceptable physical quality, and to have material possessions of a desirable quantity and quality. Such objective environmental factors have a relationship to perceived quality of life (Lawton, 1983). The implication is that where one lives and under what conditions have a significant effect upon one's perceived level of satisfaction.

Social Well-being

Blunden (1988) noted that the dimension of social well-being offers a vital element to most people's lives. Being part of the greater community, having relationships, being able to make choices, exercising competence (in communication, mobility, self-help, and social and leisure skills), and being the object of respect are all important ingredients of social well-being. Indeed, class differences can affect social involvement and consequently subjective well-being (Kearney, Plax, & Lentz, 1985). Although choice is a factor in life satisfaction, being able to exercise choice means having the social and economic status that permit the exercise of choice among options. Further, being able to express one's being as a member of society with the same entitlements and rights as others have is an important facet of social well-being (Cotten & Spirrison, 1986).

Cognitive Well-being

This dimension is particularly important when one examines the gerontological literature, because it involves one's own perception of QOL and life satisfaction. Most research has shown that well-being is strongly related to socioeconomic factors, degree of social interaction, and aspects of living situations (Larson, 1978). Again, the notion of being in a position to exercise choice apparently is tied to greater cognitive well-being and life satisfaction. Further, societal referents are important contributors to self-perception. Clark (1988) made the point that advertent or inadvertent perjorative labelling of older persons can lead to diminished self-esteem. He noted that such labelling can restrict autonomy, life chances, and opportunities.

What is evident from this brief overview is that these notions are not particularly different from those noted in other chapters in this book or by writers in the gerontological literature. However, what makes these notions special is the confluence of age and disability and their relation to a number of contextual variables. The balance of this chapter will address three of these contextual variables. To set the tone for the ensuing discussion, I would like to pose several assumptions:

- We are becoming an aging society.
- Societal attitudes will affect the quality of life for older adults with mental retardation.
- The degree and extent of quality of life factors for older adults with mental retardation will be qualitatively similar to those for other older adults.
- Transitional occurrences will present challenges that affect the lifestyle of older adults with mental retardation.

THE NATURE OF THE OLDER POPULATION

Societal attitudes are often framed by what a majority of the population thinks about minorities within that population. Minorities are characterized as groups of people who, because of age, racial, physical, cultural, or other characteristics, are singled out from others in the society in which they live for differential and unequal treatment and who therefore regard themselves as objects of collective discrimination (Wirth, 1945).

Elderly persons in our nation have been viewed as a minority group; as a consequence, they have been stereotyped and discriminated against because of their age. Such discrimination occurs when the minority is ascribed a devalued status. Minority populations can also have valued status. Valued status can come from numbers, power, or wealth. Although the population of the United States will never be totally elderly, the character of the population is changing dramatically, and what many have viewed as a passive minority may not remain such for long. Indeed, economists are already predicting that our nation's senior citizens will control a significant share of the available disposable income in the nation. This will continue to increase well into the twenty-first century. Such economic wealth should translate into considerable economic power, enhanced valued status, and a changed perception of what it means to be elderly.

In fact, current demographic trends portend that older persons will become a sizable segment of our nation's population. In 1960, there were approximately 16.7 million persons in the United States age 65 and older, comprising slightly more than 9% of the population. In contrast, the same age population numbered 25.5 million persons in 1980, representing slightly more than 11% of the nation's total population—a 53% increase in just 20 years. Expectations are that by 2040, this same age group will have grown to represent 20% of the population. Further, there has been a dramatic growth among older generational groups. In the 20-year period 1960–1980, the number of individuals aged 75 to 84 rose 65%, and the number of those age 85 and older increased by 174%. Indeed, the age group 85+ is the second fastest growing segment of the nation's population. Currently, over 60% of all older persons are between the ages of 65 and 74, 30% are between the ages of 75 and 84, and about 9% are aged 85 and older. Because women tend to outlive men, the majority of the nation's older population are women; this disparity in longevity increases with advancing age.

Many of these same trends hold true for older individuals with mental retardation and hold significant implications for service providers. Expectations are that the nation's population of older mentally retarded persons will also double over the next 30 years. (National Institute on Aging, 1987).

What of the current older population of adults with mental retardation? Some estimates put this population at between 200,000 and 500,000—depending upon which prevalence estimation factors are used (Janicki, Seltzer, & Krauss, 1987). A conservative estimate is that for every 1,000 older persons, 4 are expected to be persons with mental retardation. Studies have also shown that up to one-fifth of the populations of state registries of mentally retarded individuals are composed of seniors. Of this older group, about 50% comprise the "young-old" (60–74) group, about 32% comprise the "middle-old" (75–84) group, and about 18% comprise the "old-new" (85 +) group. Age trends also show that women generally outnumber men among mentally retarded persons over the age of 50 and, while the life expectancy of men is increasing, the predominance of older women will continue. Anecdotal information also indicates that many older mentally retarded persons live with their families and continue to work well beyond the typical retirement age of the mid-60s.

These demographics show us that we must consider old age as an important aspect of the lifespan. An increasing older population will constantly force us to contend with what and how services are to be provided. These changes will also bear upon lifestyle and QOL factors. What other factors can influence lifestyle? One is the manner in which society views the elderly in general and older adults with mental retardation specifically. Another is the challenges associated with the points of transition that particularly affect older adults with mental retardation and how these are resolved.

SOCIETAL FACTORS THAT DEFINE VALUED STATUS

One of the underlying facets of the definition of quality of life for older adults is how society defines this population and what status it ascribes to it. What is important to consider is that older and elderly mentally retarded persons do have to contend with the dual problems of how society views both being old and being disabled. Indeed, our society has had a built-in negative bias toward old age. Further, our society still exhibits negative bias toward being disabled.

Consequently, one factor to consider is how cultural factors shape our attitudes toward older and elderly persons with mental retardation. We recognize that societal attitudes toward aging and societal perceptions of aging persons with mental retardation interact to affect the nature of the integration of older adults with mental retardation into the fabric of society.

Our society ascribes positive value to youth and a negative value to age. Butler (1975), who coined the term *ageism*, noted that ageism is manifested in a wide range of phenomena in the form of stereotypes and myths, outright disdain and dislike, or simply subtle avoidance of contact; discriminatory practices in housing, employment, and services of all kinds; as well as epithets, cartoons, and jokes. Ageism represents a negative societal attitude. It is a blatant prejudice against people who are old and is demonstrated by an emphasis on youth and wellness—the antithesis of our stereotypic perception of the elderly.

There are some gerontologists, however, who believe that the notion that older people are not valued is a social myth that has been perpetuated without cause. Old age is a social problem in that aged persons have been seen and see themselves as a minority group. As with the self-advocacy movement in the mental retardation field, many older activists have moved toward greater collective self-interest in order to overcome their subordinate position in society.

A parallel negative attitude exists in terms of how some members of our society manifest attitudes toward persons with handicapping conditions. The term *handicapism* has been coined to characterize this attitude. Handicapism is also culture and generation bound; while many younger persons are constantly exposed to mentally retarded and physically handicapped persons, many older persons have not been so for the better part of their lives. Many negative attitudes toward handicap among elderly persons stem from a fear that they themselves can or will become infirm or disabled. Further, different facets of American society show different levels of acceptance of differentness. People also tend to view disabilities along a basic value continuum in relation to their ability to conform to majority standards.

Because of the polycultural nature of American society, each subculture and class within it brings with it its own attitudes and perceptions toward disablement and age. Some cultural groups are family and kin oriented and perceive disabled members no differently than other members. Others see disability as a stigma and the disabled individual becomes an outcast. Between these two extremes are many variations (Janicki, 1987).

Research has shown that, in the greater scheme of society, persons with a disability such as mental retardation are socially devalued. The implications of devaluation mean that it is difficult for that individual to be accepted and to move freely within society. Further, how a person is perceived affects how that person will be treated. If one of the tenets of community integration is using generic or mainstream services—thus expanding options and choices—then what are the implications of how disabled people are perceived by other users of mainstream services? With regard to older adults with mental retardation, the issue is how other users of senior services react to seniors with disabilities who want to use those services.

Many older adults in the United States have stereotypes and attitudes toward disabled peers. I have been told by a number of senior program administrators that the individuals using their programs have very set ideas about the center and what it is used for. These set ideas include how they react to "outsiders," irrespective of whether they are disabled or not. Consequently, one major consideration with regard to quality of life is how community attitudes of generational groups as well as cultural groups impinge on the choices that older adults with mental retardation can make. Certainly, attempting to exercise one's options will be affected by how a select group of elderly persons accommodate newcomers within their midst and, in particular, newcomers who have had a lifelong disability.

Our society is changing; it is growing progressively older and as such it should become more accepting of old age. However, we are not yet free from ageism in all of its forms. Our society has also made more accommodations for its citizens with handicapping conditions, but has yet to become fully accessible. We have a growing population of older and elderly persons with lifelong disabilities such as mental retardation. We have mixed notions of how best to provide services for this growing population. We are torn between doing it ourselves and using generic elder care system. We understand that it does not make sense to continue offering only segregated programs; yet we are fearful that what others have to offer will not measure up to our standards. What we do, in light of these attitudes, wil be a measure of the QOL experiences in the future by seniors with mental retardation.

FACTORS INTRINSIC TO OUR PROVIDER EFFORTS: THE CHALLENGES

Among the factors that contributed to the historical lack of awareness or concern about the aging of older adults with mental retardation, two stand out: in the past, persons with severe mental retardation had a relatively short lifespan; and many adults with mental retardation spent much of their lives in public institutions. However, both more readily available medical services and improved overall health status have contributed to increased longevity. Further, with the nation's deinstitutionalization efforts over the past 20 years and an increased emphasis on the availability of community living and support programs, many more older adults with mental retardation are visible and present in the community. Consequently, the combination of greater longevity with the increase in the number of known individuals with mental retardation residing among the general population has contributed to the greater awareness of aging among this population.

Qualitative factors affecting the ability of older adults with a disability to define their own lifestyle interact with what can best characterized as *problems of transition*. These problems of transition pose a number of challenges to maintaining lifestyle and addressing quality of life concerns.

The Challenge of Setting Up Senior Services

In many states, increased longevity has created a demand for services and programs that public authorities are unprepared to address. Over the years, states have developed child-oriented developmental and remedial educational services as well as adult-oriented vocational and social developmental services. The transition to senior-oriented retardation services (and the divergence from child to work-age adult program practices that these demand) has been slow in coming.

Probably more importantly, there is still disagreement among mental retardation policymakers and administrators as to the auspices and nature of these senior services. Whether to create parallel senior programs within the mental retardation service system or to collaborate with the aging network in the use of existing or augmented senior services within that network has not been resolved. This lack of consistency in policy has significant implications for how services are defined and developed and the manner in which the age-defined needs of seniors can be met. If service providers build off younger adult work or habilitative models for programs and extend these models to senior services, they will create different challenges than if they adapt models of senior services from the aging network. Further, senior service models must recognize a different set of personal development goals. These goals, in turn, will significantly affect quality of life in the latter years.

The Challenge of Aging Families

Another challenge is related to the increasing number of adults with mental retardation remaining at home throughout the lifespan. Living with one's family may be very facilitative and certainly offers opportunities for an enriched lifestyle. In some instances, however, living with one's parents can also be very restrictive and adversely affect lifestyle and QOL factors.

In the general population, it is primarily the family that provides most services for an elderly person. Unlike other elderly persons, older adults with mental retardation generally do not have children or a spouse on whom they can depend for aid and support in old age. In some instances, they live with very old parents who still provide for their day-to-day support; thus, the notion of the "two-generation elderly family." In other instances, siblings or the children of siblings provide care. However, because of advancing age, a deteriorating situation can lead to serious concerns about well-being, particularly when an elderly parent (or parents) retains the responsibility for the care of an aging adult son or daughter with mental retardation.

The Challenge of Growing Old in One's Home

Gerontologists refer to the phenomenon of *aging in place*, which means growing older while remaining in the same residential setting. The aging in place of older mentally retarded adults currently living in a variety of community residential situations also poses a challenge to maintenance or enhancement of lifestyle. Generally, this notion refers to the problem of the growing frailty of older individuals already living in a community setting and the changing demands that growing frailty makes upon the staff and the environment. Many older adults with mental retardation living in group homes and other similar settings began to reside in the settings as young or middle-aged adults. With the passage of time, they have aged, and their abilities and needs have changed. Some experience the medical complications or increased frailty that accompany the normal aging process (such as difficulties in ambulation, sensitivity to temperature changes, diminished vision and hearing, and impairments in fine motor dexterity). Changes in quality of life may result from situations where ease of movement and participation in loved activities become restricted and labored because of the physical changes associated with aging. In such situations, agencies face certain problems, including finding the right residential and day program mix and attempting to keep intact friendship networks that the individual has developed and upon which he or she relies.

The Challenge of Retirement

Of all the transition issues related to aging, the most challenging is retirement. Retirement is a particularly vexing issue because of its impact on all facets of life. Minimally, it presents an immediate change in lifestyle; maximally, it may threaten one's living situation, health, social and financial supports, and friendship network. This is why retirement should be seen as "retirement to" and not "retirement from." Among nondisabled persons, the material benefit associated with work—a salary—is usually substituted by Social Security benefits and/or a pension. Further, most pensioners, when considering what to do upon leaving the workforce, also think in terms of what will replace work and the social and psychological benefits associated with the workplace, such as friendships, a place to go, and the personal intensity that is defined by one's job. This is not always the case with older adults with mental retardation.

The challenge to lifestyle in these situations is closely associated with the lack of appropriate alternatives defined as senior services. For example, available alternatives may not compensate for the loss of the social and financial benefits associated with continued involvement in vocational services. Further, social and personal changes that are associated with retirement can be traumatic when bridging does not occur as part of the transition process. The loss or change of friends when moving to new daily activities (or lack of them) can pose significant difficulties to the overall well-being of the individual.

Certainly, one of the challenges of enhancing lifestyle is to blend services available within the mental retardation system with those available to other seniors in the local community. For example, for older adults who are relatively independent and capable, such senior services can include joining in activities in a local senior center, attending a congregate meal site, or enrolling in social model adult daycare. For older adults who are severely mentally impaired, specialty senior programs may be the preferred option. Whichever are used, the transition to retirement activities and participation in a new range of experiences will affect lifestyle. Further, the ease of social integration experienced when attempting to make use of mainstream senior services will pose its own challenges.

All of these transitions pose certain challenges; some are easily overcome, others much more complex in nature. The notions explored earlier, as posed by Lawton (1983) and Blunden (1988), bear heavily on the dignity of older adults with mental retardation. A key question is how these challenges can be used constructively to improve lifestyle and minimize the restrictions posed by growing old.

CONCLUSIONS

In summary, QOL factors related to elderly persons with mental retardation are not necessarily different from those affecting other older adults. There are the same needs for acceptable living environment, freedom to choose activities and friends, social and psychological well-being, and physical independence through good health. It was proposed that external influences may impinge upon these factors. Such factors include cultural and societal perceptions and attitudes toward the elderly and persons with disabilities; they may also include familial and institutional factors related to living and care arrangements. In addition, it was noted that points of transition in the lives of older persons with mental retardation will offer challenges that may enhance or diminish factors contributing to quality of life. These transitions include growing older within an overall system of care that has not previously accommodated older persons, living within a two-generation elderly family, aging in place in one's residential setting, facing the transition to retirement, and gaining acceptance into mainstream aging network programs.

Each successive generation of persons with mental retardation will hold a collective set of experiences that will be its own. Contemporary adults with mental retardation are living longer, in better health, enjoying a broader range of experiences, and growing older with greater dignity than did previous generations. This will be doubly true for future generations of seniors; no two generations will be the same. Our current expectations of the potential limits of a valued lifestyle will be redefined over the years to come. This is healthy: it shows that life is a valued commodity and that we are constantly stretching the limit on what we, as a society, can offer to persons with special needs.

REFERENCES

Achenbaum, W. A. (1986). American as an aging society: Myths and images. *Daedalus, 115*(1), 13–30.

Blunden, R. (1988). Programmatic feature of quality settings. In M. P. Janicki, M. W. Krauss, & M. M. Seltzer (Eds.), *Community residences for persons with developmental disabilities: Here to stay* (pp. 117–122). Baltimore: Paul H. Brookes.

Butler, R. (1975). *Why survive? Being old in America.* New York: Harper & Row.

Clark, P. G. (1988). Autonomy, personal empowerment, and quality of life in long term care. *Journal of Applied Gerontology, 7,* 279–297.

Cotten, P. D., & Spirrison, C. L. (1986). The elderly mentally retarded (developmentally disabled) population: A challenge for the service delivery system. In S. J. Brody & G. E. Ruff (Eds.), *Aging and rehabilitation: Advances in the state of the art* (pp. 112–114). New York: Springer.

Janicki, M. P. (1987, May). Cultural attitude perspectives toward elderly persons with mental retardation. Paper presented at symposium, *Cultural Factors in Mental Retardation.* Los Angeles: Annual Meeting of the American Association on Mental Retardation.

Janicki, M. P., Seltzer, M. M., & Krauss, M. W. (1987). *Contemporary issues in the aging of persons with mental retardation and other developmental disabilities.* A Rehabilitation Research Review prepared for the National Rehabilitation Information Center, Washington, DC.

Kearney, P., Plax, T. G., & Lentz, P. S. (1985). Participation in community organizations and socioeconomic status as determinants of seniors' life satisfaction. *Activities, Adaptation & Aging, 6*(4), 31–37.

Larson, R. (1978). Thirty years of research on the subjective well-being of older Americans. *Journal of Gerontology, 33,* 109–125.

Lawton, M. P. (1983). Environment and other determinants of well-being in older people. *The Gerontologist, 23,* 349–357.

National Institute on Aging. (1987). *Personnel for health needs of the elderly.* Washington: U.S. Department of Health and Human Services.

Neugarten, B. L., & Neugarten, D. A. (1986). Age in the aging society. *Daedalus, 115* (1), 31–49.

Wirth, L. (1945). The problem of minority groups. In R. Linton (Ed.), *The science of man in the world crisis.* New York: Columbia University Press.

13
Quality of Life and Lifestyle Outcomes: A Challenge for Residential Programs

G. Thomas Bellamy
U.S. Department of Education

J. Stephen Newton
University of Oregon

Nancy M. LeBaron
Oregon Technical Assistance Corporation

Robert H. Horner
University of Oregon

An important strength of residential services for nearly 20 years has been the widely shared ideology (ideas and values) collectively referred to as *normalization* that includes a concern for independence and enhanced adaptive functioning, a normal routine and rhythm of life, normal economic and environmental standards, integration with individuals with and without handicaps, the dignity of risk, the right to live in the least restrictive appropriate environment, and the opportunity to experience an enhanced quality of life. Together, these values have structured professional discussion, legal opinion, legislation, and research on residential services (Wolfensberger, 1972).

Despite this widely shared value base, however, opinions continue to vary about how local residential services should be designed and operated to actualize the normalization and quality of life ideals. These differences

Acknowledgments. This chapter was supported in part by the Office of Special Education and Rehabilitative Services, U.S. Department of Education as part of Grant #G008430096. The opinions expressed here are those of the authors and do not necessarily reflect the position and policy of the Office of Special Education, U.S. Department of Education. The authors extend appreciation to Dr. Philip Ferguson for his comments on early drafts of this chapter. This paper was written while Dr. Bellamy was director of the Specialized Training Program of the University of Oregon, Eugene. The paper was written by Dr. Bellamy in a private capacity. No official support or endorsement by the Department of Education is intended or should be inferred.

are readily apparent in the program evaluation instruments that have emerged in response to the continuing demands for accountability in service programs. In general, measures of quality or effectiveness in residential services have evolved along three broad paths, termed here measures of *capacity, progress,* and *lifestyle.* While such broad classifications necessarily miss finer distinctions among evaluation instruments, comparison at this level provides an excellent vantage point from which to analyze important differences in the practical application of normalization, including quality of life.

CAPACITY MEASURES

Capacity measures index the quality of a residential service by analyzing program procedures and environmental features that seem to promote quality. Essentially, these measures deduce important inputs and processes for the service delivery enterprise. For example, the value of social integration might be reflected in capacity measures as a requirement for small program size and presence of persons without disabilities in the immediate vicinity.

Reviews by Rotegard, Hill, and Bruininks (1983) and Rotegard, Bruininks, Holman, and Lakin (1985) documented the extensive use of capacity-focused evaluation instruments in residential services. Perhaps the best known of these are conducted in conjunction with Accreditation Council for Facilities for the Mentally Retarded and Developmentally Disabled and Commission on Accreditation of Rehabilitation Facilities accreditation, ICF/MR certification of programs, and the Program Analysis of Service Systems (Wolfensberger & Glen, 1975).

The primary benefits of capacity measures are administrative: they are easy to administer and offer protection against flagrant abuses in service programs. They also serve as important measures of some values not reflected in direct measures of service results. For example, it is important that people are treated with dignity and respect, regardless of the outcomes they receive from services.

Despite these advantages, at least three major drawbacks of capacity measures have led to a growing focus on alternative outcome measures. First, capacity measures provide at best a very indirect index of whether normalization and quality of life (QOL) values are achieved in a program. Capacity-focused instruments may well be necessary, but there is little or no evidence that they are sufficient to produce the desired impact on the lives of persons with mental retardation. Second, capacity measures treat all service consumers the same. Implicit to the capacity approach is the questionable assumption that the same program inputs and processes will affect different people in similar ways. Finally, capacity measures reflect a program-centered, rather than a person-centered, approach to services. When capacity measures reveal discrepancies between the program and the standards, the expected response is to change the physical environment, the program's resources, and/or the process of service delivery. These changes may or may not affect the lives of persons served by the program.

PROGRESS MEASURES

Progress measures assess the quality of a residential service in terms of its success in increasing an individual's skills, adaptive behavior, or community adjustment. In this developmental model context, *progress* refers to individual behavior changes achieved in pursuit of the long-range goal of independence. In effect, the progress approach has used the values of normalization to deduce the mission of services as helping persons with mental retardation to achieve independent living, competitive employment, or other adaptations to normal living. It then defines service goals in terms of the gradual development of the skills and behaviors needed to achieve that mission. The argument is that as an individual's skills or adaptive behavior improves, he or she is likely to experience a normal, high quality lifestyle that requires less costly services. A program with a progress orientation might measure its success with regard to the value of social integration by examining the number of social skills acquired by service consumers.

The literature references this emphasis on progress as a measure of the quality of residential services in two ways. The first is with a direct focus on skill development as an outcome of services (see Halpern, Lehmann, Irvin, and Heiry (1982) and Mayeda, Pelzer, & Van Zuylen (1978)). The second way in which program measures are used to index service quality is through movement from one program to another, with each succeeding program being presumably one step closer to an independent, high quality lifestyle (Schalock & Harper, 1982).

By focusing on an actual outcome received by service consumers (that is, skill development), the progress approach to defining quality has several advantages over capacity measures. Attention to outcomes allows programs to innovate, to be creative in ways that are difficult or impossible when capacity measures alone are used to define quality. Outcome measures challenge service providers to find program approaches that work, whatever their departure from traditional service methods. Outcome measures also help to individualize services. Evidence that outcomes are not being achieved provides a foundation for systematic adjustment of the training strategies used with each individual. The progress orientation is also useful in judging program quality because of the widespread consensus that increased independence is one of the outcomes expected for service consumers.

The primary drawback of a progress orientation as the sole means of defining program quality lies in the fact that increased independence should be but one of the goals of most adult services. As Taylor and Bogdan (1981) suggested, limiting attention to independence, or any other single outcome for that matter, "reduces a complex process into a one-sided variable . . . . Adaptive behavior may or may not signify adjustment to community living and normal rhythms and routines of life" (p. 75). In fact, progress in skill development may at times have little impact on the overall quality of daily living. Many skills targeted in popular skill sequences are unnecessary for community life and work, because alternative performance strategies or support services can be devised to eliminate the need for those particular skills. Other skills have little impact because practical application requires progress through an entire curriculum sequence before the individual skills can be combined into functional behaviors.

By focusing attention on movement to less restrictive programs as a measure of quality, progress measures also do a disservice to persons with more severe disabilities. Frequently individuals with severe disabilities are denied access to many normative activities in the community because they are presumed to lack the readiness to move to programs where those activities are made available (Wilcox & Bellamy, 1982). When movement does occur, the independent living skills learned by people with severe disabilities in one home or apartment may not transfer to another program setting even if the historical patterns of uncoordinated funding, lack of an adequate variety of services, and provider incentives for movement could be resolved (Bronston, 1980).

Perhaps the most extreme expression of frustration with overreliance on a progress orientation to define program quality appeared in testimony in the Wyatt case, where a number of professionals argued that a daily regimen of training activities, as required by the court's right to habilitation decision, might be punitive to individuals whose progress in training gave little hope that functional independence would develop to the extent that individual quality of life would be improved (Ellis et al., 1981).

LIFESTYLE MEASURES

In his classic review of predictive research in rehabilitation, Cobb (1972) highlighted the need for lifestyle or quality of life measures, noting that "in the last analysis, the application of prediction research to the practical business of rehabilitation requires that the counselor determine what kind of success in what sorts of social situations he is interested in" (p. 11). The emerging focus on lifestyle and quality of life as indices of residential program quality reflect this challenge (Landesman, 1986), requiring answers to two questions: What kind of life is desirable for persons with mental retardation? and How can one tell if an individual is leading such a life? The lifestyle approach begins with an assumption that program quality can best be determined by examining the lives of persons served by a residential program. This approach involves using the values of normalization not merely to deduce program processes or long-range goals for service consumers, but also to define features of current individual lifestyles that would reflect the normalization ideals.

To continue an earlier example, the value of social integration in the lifestyle approach might lead to empirical measures of the adequacy of one's social network, the number of activities one performs each week or month with others, or the number of social contacts one has with family and friends. This contrasts sharply with both capacity measures, which might index social integration in terms of program size and location, and progress measures, which might focus on behavioral development in a social skills training program.

Although lifestyle data are less widely reported, the literature affords several examples of lifestyle measures that index the quality of residential services. One approach involves participant observation, in which an investigator lives and shares residential experiences with persons having mental retardation and reports the results of conversations, semi-structured interviews, and observations (for example, Edgerton, 1984). A second measurement strategy relies on consumer and/or staff interviews to gain information about the kinds of activities in which individuals with disabilities engage (Birenbaum & Re, 1979; Scheerenberger & Felsenthal, 1977); the nature of their community interactions and relationships (Bell, Schoenrock, & Bensberg, 1981); and their vocational, economic, social, and personal adjustment (McDevitt, Smith, Schmidt, & Rosen,1978). A third approach comes from the tradition of social ecology and involves naturalistic observation conducted by trained observers using behavior coding systems (for example, Butler & Bjannes, 1978; Landesman-Dwyer & Sackett, 1980). Direct observation measures assess discrete units of behavior that are summarized to provide an indication of how behavior is distributed across broader response categories.

The primary strength of the lifestyle approach to defining quality in residential services is its close relationship with the values upon which services are based. Additionally, it shares with the progress strategies those advantages that result from focusing on outcomes rather than service inputs and processes: program flexibility and creativity increase, and services can be more easily individualized in response to data on performance. In addition to these benefits, the lifestyle approach removes the need to postpone realization of valued aspects of the lives of people with mental retardation while they acquire greater adaptive behavior. Consequently, like some capacity measures, lifestyle measures serve as a protection from the perpetual readiness programming in which many persons with mental retardation now find themselves.

The primary drawback of the lifestyle approach relates to implementation. The developing support for using lifestyle information to make summative judgments about the quality of residential services is not yet matched by procedural guidelines for the internal operation of residential services to achieve these results. The remainder of the chapter addresses these critical implementation issues.

PROGRAM IMPLICATIONS OF LIFESTYLE ACCOUNTABILITY

While the emerging emphasis on lifestyle accountability addresses many of the conceptual problems associated with the program capacity and individual progress, it also raises several important issues for day-to-day operation and management of residential services. This section addresses how lifestyle accountability can be expected to affect program operations, with particular attention to (a) internal data systems that can guide program decisionmaking; (b) service delivery procedures that enhance lifestyle; and (c) administrative practices that support a lifestyle focus in services.

New Internal Measurement Systems

Well-managed organizations of all kinds use information about the success of various program components to guide ongoing operations. In residential services, internal information systems are particularly important in making programmatic decisions about individual treatment and management decisions about allocation of staff time and other resources. Naturally, a program's efficiency increases when the measures that guide these internal decisons are compatible with those used for external, summative judgments about quality.

One measurement system that addresses this need for internal program data on lifestyle was developed by the Neighborhood Living Project (NLP) at the University of Oregon. While detailed descriptions of this system are available elsewhere (Newton, Romer, Bellamy, Horner, & Boles, 1983), a brief description here will illustrate the issues in developing lifestyle measures for internal program use. The NLP internal measurement system was

Table 13.1 Lifestyle Values and Measures

Lifestyle Values	*Operational Measures*
1. Physical integration	The number of activities performed outside the property boundary of the home (or the communal areas of an apartment complex)
2. Social integration	The number of activities performed with individuals who are not housemates or providers
3. Variety	The number of different categories of activities performed within a given time period
4. Independence	The number of activities performed without staff assistance
5. Security	The number of months of continuous support without forced movement to another setting

designed for use in small residential community programs providing 24-hour support to adults with moderate, severe, or profound mental retardation. The objectives of the system are to provide a simple procedure that program staff can use to collect regular information about the lifestyle of people receiving support and to use that information to make effective service decisions. Such a system must combine objective measurement procedures with the personal lifestyle values of individual consumers. To achieve these criteria, the NLP system measures the activities that people perform, organizes the resulting activity pattern data around a critical set of lifestyle values, and evaluates the adequacy of residential support by determining the conformity between the observed activity patterns and those defined as desirable (that is, valued) by the consumer and his/her advocates during construction of the individualized plan.

Use of data from the internal measurement system is tied to values in two ways. The first is through summarization of the results by major lifestyle values. Each week, staff members are presented with activity pattern information summarized in a manner that allows easy assessment of a person's physical integration, social integration, variety of activities, independence, and security. This constellation of lifestyle values has been selected as defining critical variables in normalized life, though by no means forming a comprehensive description of everything valued in a person's lifestyle. Operational measures of the five lifestyle values emphasized in the NLP system are provided in Table 13.1.

A second method in which the measurement system is tied to personal lifestyle values is through the individualized planning process. During the development of individualized plans, the consumer and his/her advocates describe not just new skills to learn and behaviors to be changed, but the type and amount of support needed to ensure certain desired activity patterns as well.

A Broader Service Technology

By defining the purpose of residential services as improving the current quality of lives with persons with mental retardation, the lifestyle focus creates a new basis for developing and evaluating service delivery procedures. If lifestyle results are to be consistently achieved, a service technology is needed to develop, support, and maintain performance of valued activities. The need for such a technology is immediately apparent when individual program plans specify activity patterns as the primary focus of service efforts.

No doubt the developing technology for enhancing lifestyle will include many of the procedures used in conventional skills development efforts, because teaching new skills is one way to improve activity performance. The needed technology should incorporate additional components, however, because developing independent performance of all parts of an activity is only one of many ways to support performance (O'Brien, 1987). One increasingly common strategy for increasing the performance of valued activities involves devising alternative performance strategies and prostheses that allow individuals to perform activities without knowing all the component skills. For example, an individual buying a cup of coffee at a local restaurant could use a cue card with a picture of the coffee for ordering, or always use a one dollar bill for payment in order to avoid money counting skill requirements.

Another procedural option is to structure staff time for sharing selected activities with individuals with disabilities. This reflects the importance of performance of activities and removes skill requirements that would exist with independent performance. For example, a staff member might accompany an individual with severe mental retardation on a shopping trip or sailing outing that would be beyond the person's ability to do independently. A third strategy for increasing performance of valued activities is for the program to foster a network of friends for each individual receiving services. If such a social support network exists, the number and variety of activities that can be performed by an individual will be limited by neither his or her skills alone nor the staff time available to support activities. However, it should be kept in mind that the first step in building a coherent procedural technology from these various strategies is to develop a data system that systematically evaluates their effects.

Program Administration

The shift to a lifestyle focus in residential services has implications for both the mechanics and the underlying rationale for administration of residential services. At a practical level, the major effect of this shift is to focus program evaluation and monitoring efforts on the lifestyle benefits that service recipients receive. Thus, regardless of the type or location of the residential service, the nature or severity of disabilities of persons served, or the level of public funding received, a common standard exists for evaluating the quality of services. In effect, that standard is reflected in the question, "To what extent is the individual enjoying a lifestyle that reflects his or her values and those of the funding agency and the advocates who participate in the planning meeting?"

The focus on lifestyle outcomes also shifts the logic underlying service administration from one of preparation for normal adult living to one of support in normal adult living. The role of publicly funded services is to provide the support necessary for each individual to enjoy a quality lifestyle. This focus on support instead of preparation leads to reconsideration of several current features of service administration. Because valued lifestyle outcomes are not necessarily different for persons with different levels of disability, the differentiation of program goals for persons with various disability levels seems no longer applicable. This, in turn, raises the possibility that the conventional structure of services around homogeneous groups of service recipients is unnecessarily restrictive. Program placement decisions might be made instead on such variables as personal preference for living situation, proximity to family, presence of friends in the neighborhood, and commuting demands for employment. Further, if the primary function of the public agency is to support individuals with disabilities in achieving desired lifestyles, financing of services would have to take into account not only the level of disability of the individual served but also the values that the funding agency uses to define acceptable lifestyle outcomes.

SUMMARY

The increasing emphasis on the lifestyles experienced by persons with mental retardation as a method of evaluating residential services offers an important perspective on the nature and purpose of those services. To date, however, the lifestyle perspective has largely been limited to external evaluations of services, creating a discrepancy between those evaluations and the measures and procedures used within community residential services. Extending this concern for lifestyle accountability to internal program operations requires the development of program level measurement systems that reflect the lifestyles of individuals served. Such a system allows the staff within a program to use the same information in their decisions about individual interventions and resource allocation that external evaluators use to judge the overall quality of the service. By bringing the shift toward lifestyle outcomes to the level of service delivery and management, a measurement system such as the one described could also provide the foundation for a broader and more integrated technology of supporting persons with mental retardation in residential services. Doing so might well build a synthesis among currently competing but not incompatible service strategies, all of which are focusing on improved life quality for persons with mental retardation.

REFERENCES

Bell, N. J., Schoenrock, C., & Bensberg, G. (1981). Change over time in the community: Findings of a longitudinal study. In R. H. Bruininks, C. E. Meyers, B. B. Sigford, & K. C. Lakin (Eds.), *Deinstitutionalization and community adjustment of mentally retarded people.* (Monograph No. 4). Washington, DC: American Association on Mental Deficiency.

Birenbaum, A., & Re, M. A. (1979). Resettling mentally retarded adults in the community: Almost four years later. *American Journal of Mental Deficiency, 83*, 323–329.

Bronston, A. (1980). Matters of design. In T. Apolloni, J. Cappuccilli, & T. Cooke (Eds.), *Achievements in residential services for persons with disabilities* (pp. 1–7). Baltimore: University Park Press.

Butler, E. W., & Bjannes, A. T. (1978). Activities and the use of time by retarded persons in community care facilities. In G. P. Sackett (Ed.), *Observing behavior, Volume I: Theory and applications in mental retardation.* Baltimore: University Park Press.

Cobb, H. V. (1972). *The forecast of fulfillment: A review of research on predictive assessment of the adult retarded for social and vocational adjustment.* New York: Teacher's College Press.

Edgerton, R. B. (1984). The participant-observer approach to research in mental retardation. *American Journal of Mental Deficiency, 88*, 498–505.

Ellis, N., Balla, D., Estes, O., Warren, S., Meyers, L., Hollis, J., Isaacson, R., Palk, B., & Siegel, P. (1981). Common sense in the habituation of mentally retarded persons: A reply to Menolascino and McGee. *Mental Retardation, 19*, 221–225.

Halpern, A. S., Lehmann, J. P., Irvin, L. K., & Heiry, T. J. (1982). *Contemporary assessment for mentally retarded adolescents and adults.* Baltimore: University Park Press.

Landesman, S. (1986). Quality of life and personal life satisfaction: Definition and measurement issues. *Mental Retardation, 24*(3), 141–143.

Landesman-Dwyer, S., & Sackett, G. P. (1980). Relationship of size to resident and staff behavior in small community residences. *American Journal of Mental Deficiency, 85*, 6–17.

Mayeda, T., Pelzer, I., & Van Zuylen, J. E. (1978). *Performance measures of skill and adaptive competencies in the developmentally disabled: Individualized data base.* Pomona, CA: University of California, Los Angeles. Neuropsychiatric Institute Research Group at Pacific State Hospital.

McDevitt, S. C., Smith, P. M., Schmidt, D. W., & Rosen, M. (1978). The deinstitutionalized citizen: Adjustment and quality of life. *Mental Retardation, 16*(1), 22–24.

Newton, S., Romer, M., Bellamy, G. T., Horner, R. H., & Boles, S. M. (1983). *Neighborhood living project tenant support operations manual.* Eugene, OR: University of Oregon, Center on Human Development.

O'Brien, J. (1987). A guide to lifestyle planning: Using the activities catalog to integrate services and natural support systems. In B. Wilcox & G. T. Bellamy (Eds.), *The activities catalog: An implementation guide.* Baltimore: Paul H. Brookes.

Rotegard, L. L., Bruininks, R. H., Holman, J. G., & Lakin, K. C. (1985). Environmental aspects of deinstitutionalization. In R. H. Bruininks & K. C. Lakin (Eds), *Living and learning in the least restrictive environment*. Baltimore: Paul H. Brookes.

Rotegard, L. L., Hill, B. K., & Bruininks, R. H. (1983). Environmental characteristics of residential facilities for mentally retarded persons in the United States. *American Journal of Mental Deficiency, 88,* 49–56.

Schalock, R. L., & Harper, R. S. (1982). Skill acquisition and client movement indices: Implementing cost-effective analysis in rehabilitation programs. *Evaluation and Program Planning, 5,* 223–231.

Scheerenberger, R. C., & Felsenthal, D. (1977). Community settings for mentally retarded persons: Satisfaction and activities. *Mental Retardation, 15*(4), 3–7.

Taylor, S. J., & Bogdan, R. (1981). A qualitative approach to the study of community adjustment. In R. H. Bruininks, C. E. Meyers, B. B. Sigford, & K. C. Lakin (Eds.), *Deinstitutionalization and community adjustment of mentally retarded people* (pp. 70–82). Washington, DC: American Association on Mental Deficiency.

Wilcox, B., & Bellamy, G. T. (1982). *Design of high school programs for severely handicapped students*. Baltimore: Paul H. Brookes.

Wolfensberger, W. (1972). *The principle of normalization in human services*. Toronto: National Institute on Mental Retardation.

Wolfensberger, W., & Glenn, L. (1975). *PASS 3: A method of the quantitative evaluation of human services*. Toronto: National Institute on Mental Retardation.

PART III
Quality of Life: Assessment and Measurement Issues

Of all the issues discussed here, none has generated more heated discussion than how best to assess or measure a person's quality of life. This issue will become even more critical in the future as the field begins to consider the implication and use of quality of life data. This section should provide a good foundation for that discussion.

The section begins with a chapter by Bob Schalock, who gives a brief overview of the various attempts to conceptualize and measure quality of life, especially from the social sciences and disabilities perspectives. Bob Edgerton expands on these attempts by summarizing his 30 years of longitudinal research efforts that suggest strongly that, by its very nature, quality of life and its measurement must be subjective and based on an indepth understanding of the person. Laird Heal and Carol Sigelman begin their chapter by summarizing four major ways in which methodologies for assessing QOL can differ, including objective or subjective, absolute or relative, reported directly or by someone else, and either authored or generated by the investigator or by the subjects of the investigation. The authors then go on to discuss a number of factors that affect responses in survey research, and the implications of these factors on interviewing persons with mental retardation in an effort to assess their quality of life. Chapter 17 by Sharon Borthwick-Duffy stresses two important points: first, we must continue to improve our ability to perceive the needs of persons who are severely or profoundly handicapped and to evaluate their overall happiness and life conditions; and second, the evaluation and measurement of life quality must follow a clear delineation of the important dimensions of quality of life, keeping in mind that, regardless of intelligence level, individuals will differ in their preferences and their own perceptions of what makes a good quality of life.

Throughout these chapters the reader will find both a cautionary note and a critical point to remember: we are just beginning to understand the concept of quality of life and are probably not doing a very good job at this time in measuring it. Thus, as persons attempt to assess a person's quality of life, it is important to restate a cautionary note made by Heal and Sigelman:

> . . . it is a disservice to individuals with mental retardation to 'slap together' a measure and simply hope for the best. Developing any

reliable and valid quality of life measure requires considerable effort, effort that promises to result in a fuller understanding of the lives of developmentally disabled citizens. (p. 174)

14
Attempts to Conceptualize and Measure Quality of Life

Robert L. Schalock

Hastings College and Mid-Nebraska Mental Retardation Services, Inc.

Our attempts at conceptualizing and measuring a person's quality of life do not have a long history, even though since antiquity people have attempted to determine how to identify and implement the conditions of a life of quality. In reference to persons with mental retardation and closely related disabilities, the history is even shorter (Schalock, Keith, Hoffman, & Karan, 1989). The primary purpose of this chapter is to summarize briefly these attempts to conceptualize and measure quality of life (QOL).

Despite their short history, efforts to conceptualize and measure QOL are multiplying rapidly because of three types of interests in life quality research that are much more evident now than a decade ago (Andrews, 1986):

- Increased attention devoted to describing the life quality of particular national subgroups and comparing them with more general national populations such as those described by Andrews and Whithey (1976) and Campbell, Converse, and Rodgers (1976).
- Increased interest in how time-related phenomena link to life quality, and specifically the use of time and the effects of age, period, and cohort.
- Increased concern for the social and psychological dynamics of perceived well-being, including factors related to social support, social integration, interpersonal trust, internal control, antonomy/independence, self-confidence, aspirations/expectations, and values having to do with family, job, and life in general.

THE SOCIAL SCIENCE PERSPECTIVE

Social scientists have attempted to conceptualize and evaluate both objective and subjective indicators of a person's QOL. There is little doubt but that the central issue confronting any examination of a person's perceived quality of life involves the relationship between subjective and objective well-being (Campbell et al., 1976). This historical focus on both the subjective and objective is well summarized by Dalkey (1972), who stated:

> Quality of Life is related not just to the environment and to the external circumstances of an individual's life (pollution, quality of housing, aesthetic surroundings, crime, etc.), but whether [these factors] constitute a major share of an individual's well being, or whether they are dominated by factors such as sense of achievement, love and affection, perceived freedom and so on. (p. 9)

The social scientists' attempts to conceptualize and measure QOL fall into the following three perspectives: social indicators, psychological indicators, and goodness-of-fit/social policy. Each is summarized briefly below.

Social Indicators

Social indicators generally refer to external, environmentally based conditions such as health, social welfare, friendships, standard of living, education, public safety, housing, neighborhood, and leisure. These indicators may be defined as a statistic of direct normative interest that facilitates concise, comprehensive, and balanced judgments about the conditions of major aspects of society (Andrews & Whithey, 1976). Such indicators are good for measuring the collective quality of community life; however, they are probably insufficient to measure either an individual's perceived quality of life or outcomes from (re)habilitation programs. Campbell et al. (1976), for example, argued that social indicators only reflect an outsider's judgment of quality as suggested by external, environmentally based conditions. Thus,

> . . . because we are accustomed to evaluating people's lives in terms of their material possessions, we tend to forget that satisfaction is a psychological experience and that the quality of this experience may not correspond very closely to these external conditions (Campbell et al., 1976, p. 3).

This concern about one's personal satisfaction and well-being has led to the second, or psychological indicators, perspective on conceptualizing and assessing quality of life.

Psychological Indicators

Psychological indicators focus on a person's subjective reactions to life experiences. Recently, there have been attempts to measure these subjective evaluations from one of two perspectives: psychological well-being

Table 14.1   Psychological Indicators of Quality of Life

Psychological Well-Being[a]	*Personal Satisfaction*[b]
Physical and material well-being	Marriage
1. Material comforts and financial security	Family life
2. Health and personal safety	Health
Relations with other people	Neighborhood
3. Relations with spouse	Friendships
4. Having and rearing children	Housework
5. Relations with other relatives	Job
6. Relations with close friends	Life in The United
Social, community, and civic activities	States
7. Helping and encouraging other people	City or country life
8. Participating in local and government affairs	Nonwork
Personal development and fulfillment	Housing
9. Intellectual development	Usefulness of
10. Personal understanding and planning	education
11. Work that is interesting, rewarding, worthwhile	Standard of living
12. Creativity and personal experience	Amount of education
Recreation	Savings
13. Socializing with others	
14. Passive/observational recreational activities	
15. Active/participatory recreational activities	

[a] Adapted from Flanagan (1982, p. 58). [b]Adapted from Campbell et al., (1976, p. 63).

and personal satisfaction/happiness. The first perspective comes primarily from the work of Flanagan (1978; 1982) who attempted to conceptualize and operationalize life domains associated with psychological well-being. On the basis of a review of 6,500 critical incidents collected from nearly 3,000 people of various ages, races, and backgrounds, he identified 15 factors defining quality of life. He then grouped these 15 categories into five general dimensions of quality of life: physical and material well-being; relations with other people; social, community, and civic activities; personal development and fulfillment; and recreation. A summary of these 15 factors is presented in Table 14.1 (left side).

Measures of personal satisfaction and happiness, such as found in the right hand column of Table 14.1, indicate the extent to which persons have positive feelings and attitudes about various aspects of their lives. The underlying assumption of this approach is that the greater one's satisfaction with his/her resources, the greater the feelings of life satisfaction, well-being, personal competence, and control over one's life. One of the best known examples of this approach is that taken by Campbell et al. (1976), who have completed national studies of satisfaction and dissatisfaction in various life domains such as family, work, leisure, income, social relations, and health. These investigators report generally that greater satisfaction in each of the domains is related to a higher perceived quality of life.

Zautra and Goodhart (1979), however, suggested that, although psychological indicators are often considered the best QOL measures because they provide the most direct assessment of people's perceptions and evaluations of their life experiences, they may have at least three validity problems. First, the tendency toward social desirability may tend to inflate the scores, although this concern may be more problematic for research attempting to determine the true level of QOL than for the study that aims to compare levels of well-being between groups. Second, measures that ask for reports of feeling states may be measuring only idiosyncratic ratings of satisfaction and happiness. And finally, psychological indicators might not reflect the realities of external conditions.

Goodness-of-Fit/Social Policy

This perspective proposes that QOL is an important criterion for social policies. A number of analysts, such as Land and Spilerman (1975), Liu (1976), and Milbrath (1979; 1982), have recommended that QOL studies be used to identify unmet needs in different populations and that the information be used to weight differentially the importance of need areas that would then influence resource allocation decisions. For example, the goodness-of-fit model proposed by Murrell and Norris (1983) defined QOL as the criterion for establishing the goodness-of-fit between the person and his/her environment. In this model, it was assumed that the characteristics of a given group interact with the resources and stressors of its environment. A central assumption was that the QOL of a person is a function of the discrepancy between resources and stressors.

The significance of the Murrell-Norris model is that it conceptualizes quality of life as both an outcome from human service programs (application of additional resources should improve a person's QOL) and the criterion for establishing the goodness-of-fit between a population and its environment. Thus, the better the fit, the higher a person's QOL (Schalock et al., 1989).

QOL: THE DISABILITY PERSPECTIVE

The pioneering work by Robert Edgerton (1967; 1975; Chapter 15 of this volume) on issues relating to quality of life among mentally retarded individuals is well known to most readers and represents a significant milestone in the history of QOL research. Since Edgerton's original work,

Table 14.2   Quality of Life Variables from Mental Retardation Literature[a]

References	Independence (Living Environment)	Interpersonal and Community Relationships	Productivity
Bell, Schoenrock, & Bensberg (1981)	Home and family	Relationships/ helpers	Employment
Bruininks (1986)	Normalization-related environment Physical environment Psychosocial environment	Social support Social-interpersonal relationships Activity patterns Involvement in community life	
Halpern, Nave, Close, & Wilson (1986)	Residential environment Neighborhood quality Cleanliness Access to service	Social support Social network Self-satisfaction Leisure-activities Community integration	Income employment
Intagliata, Crosby, & Neider (1981)	Home life Social, affective, habilitative	Social support Interaction Integration in community	Recidivism Movement
Schalock et al. (1989)	Environmental control Residential placement status Pride in residence	Leisure Social interaction Variety of community utilization	Work status Finances
Intagliata, Willer, & Wicks (1981)	Normalized home life	Relationship with caregiver/fellow resident Friends Natural family Use of formal and generic community resources	

[a] Adapted with permission from Borthwick-Duffy (1986).

numerous investigators within the disabilities field have focused on a number of outcome variables that have been associated with successful community adaptation and, in a general sense, quality of life. These variables are summarized in Table 14.2. The table is organized around the three

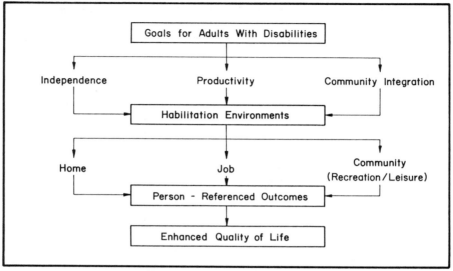

FIGURE 14.1.   Relationships Among Goals, Habilitation Environments, Person-Referenced Outcomes, and Enhanced Quality of Life.

legislative goals for persons with disabilities: to increase a person's independence, productivity, and community integration.

A second direction to conceptualize and measure QOL within the disabilities field has been to develop QOL models that will:

- Help understand better the multidimensionality of a person's quality of life.
- Contribute to a theory of quality of life and facilitate the interpretation and summarization of the research related to the life experiences of persons with mental retardation and closely related developmental disabilities.
- Help establish criteria for assessing outcomes from current habilitation services for persons with mental retardation and closely related developmental disabilities.

A recent model (Schalock & Thornton, 1988) reflecting this focus is shown in Figure 14.1. Other models have been presented in previous chapters. The reader will find that there are a number of commonalities to these models including:

- Community integration and involvement in recreation, clubs, events, and community activities.
- Social and interpersonal relations, including family members, friends, neighbors, and acquaintances.

- Living environment, including some degrees of control, developmental services, safety, and normalization of setting.
- Meaningful work with its financial and status byproducts.

In conclusion, how these four commonalities are implemented and evaluated represents the next historical phase in the "Quality of Life Agenda." Many questions remain to be addressed and issues remain to be resolved regarding the concept of QOL, its impact on public policy, its impact on service delivery, its measurement, and the use of QOL data. The issue of QOL and how we will approach it will undoubtedly influence service provision in the future, just as deinstitutionalization and normalization have done in recent decades.

REFERENCES

Andrews, F. M. (Ed.) (1986). *Research on the quality of life*. Ann Arbor: The University of Michigan, Institute for Social Research.

Andrews, F. R., & Whithey, S. B. (1976). *Social indicators of well-being: Americans' perceptions of life quality*. New York: Plenum Press.

Bell, N. J., Schoenrock, C. J., & Bensberg, G. J. (1981). Change over time in the community: Findings of a longitudinal study. In R. H. Bruininks, C. E. Meyers, B. B. Sigford, & K. C. Lakin (Eds.), *Deinstitutionalization and community adjustment of mentally retarded people* (pp. 195–206). Washington, DC: American Association on Mental Deficiency.

Borthwick-Duffy, S. A. (1986). Quality of life of mentally retarded people: Development of a model. Unpublished doctoral dissertation. Riverside, CA: University of California, School of Education.

Bruininks, R. (1986). The implications of deinstitutionalization for community adjustment. Paper presented at the Annual Meeting of the American Association on Mental Deficiency, Denver, CO, May 25–27.

Campbell, A., Converse, P. E., & Rodgers, W. L. (1976). *The quality of American life: Perceptions, evaluations and satisfactions*. New York: Russell Sage Foundation.

Dalkey, N. C. (1972). *Studies in the quality of life: Delphi and decision-making*. Lexington, MA: Lexington Books.

Edgerton, R. B. (1967). *The cloak of competence: Stigma in the lives of the mentally retarded*. Berkeley and Los Angeles: University of California Press.

Edgerton, R. B. (1975). Issues relating to quality of life among mentally retarded individuals. In M. J. Begab & S. A. Richardson (Eds.), *The mentally retarded and society: A social service perspective* (pp. 128–142). Baltimore: University Park Press.

Flanagan, J. C. (1978). A research approach to improving our quality of life. *American Psychologist, 33*, 138–147.

Flanagan, J. C. (1982). Measurement of quality of life: Current state of the art. *Archives of Physical Medicine and Rehabilitation, 63*, 56–59.

Halpern, A. S., Nave, G., Close, D. W., & Wilson, D. (1986). An empirical analysis of the dimensions of community adjustment for adults with mental retardation in semi-independent living programs. *Australia and New Zealand Journal of Developmental Disabilities, 12*(3), 147–157.

Intagliata, J., Crosby, N., & Neider, L. (1981). Foster family care for mentally retarded people: A qualitative review. In R. H. Bruininks, C. E. Meyers, B. B. Sigford, & K. C. Lakin (Eds.), *Deinstitutionalization and community adjustment of mentally retarded people* (pp. 233–259). Washington, DC: American Association on Mental Deficiency.

Intagliata, J., Willer, B., & Wicks, N. (1981). Factors related to the quality of community adjustment in family care homes. In R. H. Bruininks, C. E. Meyers, B. B. Sigford, & K. C.

Lakin (Eds.), *Deinstitutionalization and community adjustment of mentally retarded people.* (pp. 217–230). Washington, DC: American Association on Mental Deficiency.

Land, K., & Spilerman, S. (Eds.) (1975). *Social indicator models.* New York: Russell Sage Foundation.

Liu, B. C. (1976). *Quality of life indicators in U.S. metropolitan areas: A statistical analysis.* New York: Praeger Publishers.

Milbrath, L. W. (1979). Policy relevant quality of life research. *Annals of the American Academy of Political and Social Science, 444,* 33–45.

Milbrath, L. W. (1982). A conceptualization and research strategy for the study of ecological aspects of the quality of life. *Social Indicators Research, 10,* 133–157.

Murrell, S. A., & Norris, F. H. (1983). Quality of life as the criterion for need assessment and community psychology. *Journal of Community Psychology, 11,* 88–97.

Schalock, R. L., Keith, K. D., Hoffman, K., & Karan, O. C. (1989). Quality of life: Its measurement and use in human service programs. *Mental Retardation, 27*(1), 25–31.

Schalock, R. L., & Thornton, C. V. D. (1988). *Program evaluation: A field guide for administrators.* New York: Plenum Publishing Company.

Zautra, A., & Goodhart, D. (1979). Quality of life indicators: A review of the literature. *Community Mental Health Review, 4*(1), 2–10.

15
Quality of Life from a Longitudinal Research Perspective

Robert B. Edgerton

University of California at Los Angeles

It is unlikely that any of us would criticize efforts to improve the life quality of any of our citizens, particularly those who like many persons with mental retardation may be dependent on human services. We also realize that providing improved objective standards of living does not necessarily increase peoples' sense of well-being because, although the quality of life can be measured by objective criteria, it is experienced subjectively (Schneider, 1976). Many well-intended governmental programs such as low-cost housing projects may in fact provide objectively improved residential amenities without increasing the residents' sense of well-being. The purpose of this chapter is to see what a longitudinal perspective may be able to tell us about the relationship between objective criteria of life quality and the subjective experience of well-being.

THE CURRENT EMPHASIS ON QUALITY OF LIFE

To begin, we might do well to reflect on the currently popular enterprise of raising quality of life to the status of a master concept in our human service industry. Quality of life is not a revolutionary idea; one of its recent progenitors is the concept of normalization. But quality of life has caught on as the challenge—or the shibboleth—of the 1990s (Landesman, 1986).

It has long been characteristic of Western societies to specify the rights of their citizens and, both directly and indirectly, the quality of life they were entitled to enjoy. The Greeks did so as they defined the rights of citizens and slaves. So it was in pre-Roman Egypt. Later, the life to which peasants, merchants, and the nobility were entitled was established

Acknowledgments. I gratefully acknowledge support from the National Institute of Child Health and Human Development Grants No. HD-05540-02 to the author; HD 04612 to the Mental Retardation Research Center, UCLA; and NICHD Program Project Grant No. HD 11944-02, The Community Adaptation of Mildly Retarded Persons.

149

throughout Europe, if not always consensually, as many peasant revolts and the French revolution attested. After our own rebellion against the British, we promulgated our Bill of Rights, which defined the qualities of life that Americans should enjoy (except for slaves and Amerindians). As we are also aware, when the Western European nations imposed their hegemony on much of the rest of the world by the force of arms, they exported their standards of life's quality even as they denied all but a privileged few among their subject peoples access to those qualities.

I make reference to the era of colonial ethnocentrism because, unlike most European countries, which are relatively homogeneous in terms of ethnicity and hence subculture, the United States is culturally heterogeneous, and with our new immigrants from Asia, Latin America, and the Middle-East, we are increasingly so. Hence, whatever our policymakers or service providers decide about defining an acceptable quality of life, they must be aware that no single set of standards can possibly gratify all Americans. They should also be wary if, or perhaps I should say when, they are tempted by the American passion for reducing complex qualitative concepts to simple scalar instruments.

Quality of life scales have existed for 50 years (Thorndike, 1939), and they have proliferated so rapidly in recent years that seemingly every city and town in the country (and even entire nations) has had its quality of life compared to that of every other (Zautra & Goodhart, 1979). So, of course, have residential facilities, including small group homes. Like the Program Analysis of Service Systems of years past, such scales of relative quality may help to prevent neglect or abuse, but they may also lead to the belief (as has happened in individual program planning sessions in many parts of the country) that there truly are absolute life quality standards that should be enjoyed by all. If individual choice is replaced by a "Quality of Life Quotient," the result will not only be absurd, it may be tragic as well. To declare that all people should enjoy a quality of life that includes safety, love, friendship, sexual expression, religious belief, personal growth, self-esteem, recreational options, or whatever else is thought to be desirable, may only represent a harmless, if rather vacuous, expression of values; but if taken as a template for action, such statements may create frustratingly unattainable expectations. Hopefully, this volume, with its leavening of advice from clients themselves, will help to retain individual choice as the guiding principle of any action taken on behalf of enhancing the quality of clients' lives.

This seemingly self-evident point must be emphasized because human service system personnel, often encouraged by parents, employees, and others, have been known to impose their notions of appropriate life styles on unwilling clients. As the literature on normalization within the deinstitutionalization process has shown over and over, clients' wishes to lead lives of their own choosing have very often been rejected in favor of a more restrictive and less risky option. Plans for residential or vocational change, marriage, and childbearing are obvious examples of client options that are often seen by concerned parents and agency personnel as unrealistic or dangerous. Arguments about the dignity of risk are by now passé, and have always been fraught with ethical booby traps. But the fact remains that many mentally retarded persons choose to live in ways that others find objectionable.

When I describe the lives of some of the mentally retarded people we have studied for almost 30 years to audiences of nonretarded people, the reaction is often one of horror or revulsion and demands that I as a "responsible scientist" take action to remove these people from their deplorable life circumstances. When I protest that I have no such right and that the people involved are quite satisfied with their lives—and themselves— the reaction is typically one of frank disbelief.

One of these mentally retarded people whose quality of life worries others is a 58-year-old man with an IQ of 54. He lives in a single room occupancy hotel in a rundown and crime-ridden part of downtown Los Angeles. He has a dangerous yet personally rewarding job as the night manager of a laundromat frequented by homeless people, prostitutes, and drug dealers. His sexual partners are drug-using prostitutes, one of whom recently contracted AIDS. There is no doubt that this man works very hard for the money he makes, that he is frequently in physical danger, and that his repeated exposure to AIDS could be life threatening. Yet he lives in a network of friends and acquaintances who value his friendship and help, and who do not know or care that he can neither read nor write. To many people, he is loved and respected. He is as satisfied with the quality of his life as anyone I know.

Another man, aged 67, with an IQ in the mid-50s, recently retired from his union-protected job loading and unloading trucks after 30 years of employment. His small apartment was incredibly filthy, the women in his life ruthlessly relieved him of his monthly Social Security and pension income in return for very little sex and even less affection, and he had gained so much weight that he was obese. Despite an increasingly severe heart condition and high blood pressure that twice forced his hospitalization, he refused to modify his eating habits, which included five or six meals per day, most of them consisting of heavily salted red meat and eggs. Our research workers joined his doctor in urging him to change his diet, but he refused, arguing that he liked to eat that kind of food and denying that it was unhealthy for him to do so. A few weeks ago he died of a heart attack. Perhaps he would have lived longer if he had been institutionalized and forced to eat less food and fewer fats. But if that had happened, it is by no means certain that he would have been more satisfied with his life.

When intervention does take place, the results are not always happy. For example, in the growing enthusiasm for programs of supported work, many clients have been more or less forced to leave sheltered workshops to accept work placements in the competitive economy. Because many of these people have left all of their friends behind at their workshops and have not made friends at their new workplaces, it is commonplace for them to express great unhappiness about their new and improved lives. Some clients who resist their counsellors' pressure to enter supported work programs are openly threatened, all in the service of improving the quality of their lives, but not, it seems, their sense of well-being.

It is clear that we cannot abdicate all responsibility for setting limits to individuals' freedom of choice. We cannot tolerate risks to the public health, nor can we ignore some kinds of self-injurious behavior, and we must obviously draw the line at behaviors that harm others. But few instances are as clear-cut as these. Most, like those just described, involve far more complex calculations of risks and benefits. When do we, like the colonial administrators in Asia or Africa or the administrators of our own Bureau of Indian Affairs, have the right to impose any set of life standards on other people?

We tend to think of middle-class Anglo-American culture as setting a standard of life's quality for all people, and when immigrants rush to the United States from all over the world, we feel confirmed in this belief. But white middle-class values and life styles are not universally favored, even in the United States. Black, Hispanic, and Asian Americans continue to express their preference for alternative ways of living, often to the discomfiture of well-meaning persons who believe that access to white middle-class culture is a glorious gift that must necessarily be cherished by all. We should not perpetuate this misconception.

As a final consideration, we should keep in mind that, even if unlimited resources were available for meeting certain specified life quality standards for all mentally retarded persons known to our human service agencies, a much larger number of mentally retarded persons would be unaffected by this program. It is a fair assumption that the majority of mentally retarded persons in this country—persons who do not receive mental retardation services—live in ways that diverge dramatically from anything that service agencies would like to provide for them. Many live in poverty, that is certain; but it is not at all certain how many of these would choose to change their lifestyles if they could. And that is all the more reason why mentally retarded persons must be encouraged to participate in program planning that involves quality of life issues.

LONGITUDINAL RESEARCH ON THE QUALITY
OF LIFE

As numerous reviews of the literature reporting longitudinal studies have noted, most of this body of research suffers from serious flaws of research design, with sampling and sample attrition being among the most common weaknesses (Bruininks, Meyers, Sigford, & Lakin, 1981; Heal, Sigelman, & Switsky, 1978; McCarver & Craig, 1974). Moreover, with a very few exceptions, this research reported on brief time spans, or if longer periods were considered, there were no more than two or three points of measurement (Cobb, 1972). Relatively continuous measurement over protected periods of time has rarely been attempted. Because measures of quality of life are inherently temporal, this lack is disappointing.

Even more disappointing for present purposes, this body of research tells us relatively little about changes in quality of life or subjective well-being. Few direct measures of either life's quality or well-being are reported. Instead, reports concentrate on such findings as changes in marital, residential, vocational, or recreational patterns that, while certainly relevant to quality of life considerations, are relatively insensitive indicators of subjective well-being. For example, the recent 40-year follow-up of former special education students in San Francisco by Robert Ross and his associates (Ross, Begab, Dondis, Giampiccolo, & Meyers, 1985) painted an encouraging picture of the long-term community adaptation of these men and women. We can see that these people have generally established lives that do not seem to differ greatly from those of their nonretarded relatives or peers. Yet we are told very little about the actual quality of those lives, the life events that have had the greatest impact on these lives, or the feelings of the people themselves about their lives or themselves.

On balance, the longitudinal research available to us suggests that the majority of mentally retarded persons who are given an opportunity to live in community settings manage to achieve a reasonably successful adjustment to community living and that their adaptation tends to stabilize and improve over time. However, it also indicates that a minority—sometimes a sizable one—encounters serious difficulties in adapting to community living and returns to more restricted residential settings. It tells us very little about how these individual men and women search for friends and relationships, maintain their self-esteem, cope with their jobs or their joblessness, enjoy their leisure time, or worry about their futures. In short, we know all too little about the actual quality of their lives and next to nothing about their satisfaction with those lives. The voices of the people themselves have not been heard.

In any effort to look more closely at the satisfaction of some mentally retarded people with their lives, it may be helpful to refer to some longitudinal research in which I have been involved. For the past 30 years, my colleagues and I have carried out longitudinal research with a number of samples of mildly or moderately retarded persons. Our ethnographic procedures require familiarity with as many aspects of a retarded person's life as possible. Our methodological philosophy derives primarily from naturalism, rather than positivistic behavioral science. We attempt to comprehend and interpret the phenomena under study as faithfully as possible; our goal is to be true to the phenomena themselves. We believe that such an interpretation can best be undertaken by following three principles (Edgerton & Langness, 1978):

- that phenomena be seen in their relevant context;
- that these phenomena be seen not only through the observer's eyes, but those of the subject as well;
- that reactive procedures be avoided at the same time that the investigator regards himself as a part of the phenomenon under investigation.

No existing methodology for the study of human behavior adequately satisfies these three principles, and ours is no exception. Nevertheless, our procedures differ markedly from those commonly employed in the study of mentally retarded people (interviews, tests, formal observation, self-reports, or secondhand accounts) and do, we believe, provide a useful perspective on persons' quality of life as well as their sense of well-being.

To carry out ethnographic naturalism, we must have prolonged contact with people. We must become, if only relatively so, a natural part of their lives. In time, we usually gain access to more than the public domain of their lives. We assume that retarded people, like other people, manage one or another aspect of their lives by saying and doing many things in order to present a favorable face to others. Our ethnographic procedures are sensitized to the Janus-faced quality of self-presentation, and by virtue of our prolonged and somewhat unpredictable presence in their world, we hope to be able to see more than the obvious. We often drop by unannounced, we take retarded persons away from their residences to unfamiliar settings, and we talk to others about them. We attend important events in the lives of the people, going to weddings, family gatherings, or weekend outings, and we introduce them to new recreational experiences. Our procedures do not break down all deception (efforts to deceive are, after all, part of the reality we hope to study), nor do they reduce the complexities of human life to a clear and simple truth. However, they do lessen the likelihood that an obvious deception will go unnoticed and that the contradictory complexity of a human life will be construed too simplistically. The method is not intended to provide simple answers; it is intended to provide the empirical grounds for rejecting simple answers in favor of fuller and more accurate understanding.

In time, people usually tell us how they feel about themselves and their lives. These expressions of satisfaction are not always consistent. Like the rest of us, these people have good days and bad ones, and certain events or circumstances may evoke elation, anxiety, or depression. But over time the accumulation of naturally occurring statements combined with reactions to environmental changes usually allow us to make inferences about individuals' satisfaction with the quality of their lives that we believe are both reliable and valid. Words and deeds are not the same and need not be consistent, as we well know (Deutscher, 1966). Moreover, individuals often have positive and negative domains of affect that can express themselves independently of one another (Bradburn, 1969). But despite these complexities and contradictions, we believe that it is possible to reach valid conclusions about how satisfied most of the mentally retarded people we study are with their lives and what they would most like to change about those lives.

The data that will be summarized here derive from longitudinal research with five principal samples: (a) 67 moderately and mildly retarded adults living in community residential facilities (Edgerton, 1975); (b) close to 100 clients of two large sheltered workshops (Zetlin & Turner, 1984); (c) 48 independently living young adults (Edgerton, 1981; Kaufman, 1984; Koegel, 1982); (d) 48 young Afro-Americans sampled to represent a range of independence and employability (Koegel & Edgerton, 1984; Mitchell-Kernan & Tucker, 1984); and (e) a sample of 48 (now reduced to 17) persons released from a large state institution over 30 years ago. With the exception of sample a, we have seldom gone more than a few months without being in contact with these people, and in some samples contact is more frequent than this.

It is neither possible nor appropriate to do more than briefly summarize the masses of data that have accumulated about the lives of these men and women. However, the findings and inferences that will be reported here represent clear and pronounced patterns that have been observed by many of my colleagues and me for a number of years. First, there is one finding that is quite clear: Younger mentally retarded people who are new to life in community settings are given to complaining about the lives they lead and their own self-esteem. They complain most often about the lack of close relationships and the opportunity to see themselves more positively because they are not able to have reciprocal helping relationships with others around them. These complaints are well taken because, in truth, their lives are turbulent and these young adults give every evidence of being unhappy much of the time. Over time, these same people complain less and seem to become happier as their lives tend to stabilize. As these people grow older, they complain less and instead speak often about the rewards that their lives hold for them and strongly express their beliefs that the future will be at least as positive.

This pattern of growing confidence and satisfaction has been reported before (Edgerton, 1975) and may, therefore, be considered less than fully newsworthy. But if we turn from the kinds of group comparison analysis that led to this finding, to single-person-over-time analysis, another pattern emerges. When we track individuals over a period of 10, 15, or 30 years, a striking pattern of stability in their satisfaction with their lives emerges. As George (1979) has pointed out, we should first make a conceptual distinction between terms such as *happiness* (referring to transient affective states), *life satisfaction* (referring to how well life's expectations have been met), and *well-being* (a more global expression of satisfaction with the nature and quality of one's life). The stability that we observe relates primarily to well-being, and secondarily so to life satisfaction. We find that major life events such as illness, loss of a loved one, or job loss can bring about changes in expressed life satisfaction and in expressed affect. But before long, these people rebound and return to whatever state of global well-being they enjoyed before. In like fashion, there are individuals who enjoy sudden good fortune in the form of a new friendship, a better job, or an improvement in physical health, and respond with undisguised elation. However, in due course, they too return to their prior pattern of life satisfaction and well-being (Lazarus & Lannier, 1979).

Many have endured the death of loved ones, abandonment by friends or lovers, victimization such as rape, robbery, or assault, the loss of a job or a place to live, and life-threatening illness or surgery while remaining cheerful, satisfied with their lives, and optimistic about the future. But others, despite finding better jobs or places to live, making new friends, developing romantic attachments, and winning increased respect from friends or relatives, continue to complain about everything, to disparage themselves and their lives, and to express fear that the future will be as bad, if not worse.

The pattern that emerges again and again is that people who were happy and hopeful 10, 20, or even 30 years ago remain so no matter what ill-fortune they suffer; and those who were sad or negative about life do not change even though their environment improves significantly. The data clearly indicate that major life stressors or major gratifications can bring about changes in affect and expressed life satisfaction, but those changes are short lived.

Counterintuitive as this finding may seem to those like myself who believe in the causal power of environmental factors, these data suggest that internal dispositions—call them *temperament* for want of a better term—

are better predictors of peoples' satisfaction with the quality of their lives than are objective environmental variables. If we take this finding seriously, it would have powerful implications for our ability to program an increased sense of well-being. Because it is such a controversial finding, one that tends to devalue environmental affects, we are obliged to ask whether there is any reason (other than my assertion) to believe that well-being may be relatively independent of objective standards of life's quality (Keogh & Pullis, 1980).

There are research reports from other populations that describe similar findings. Twenty years ago, Maddox (1968) reported that 148 noninstitutionalized persons age 60 and over showed substantial persistence in lifestyle patterns and well-being over the course of time, a finding that was replicated by other investigators who worked in the area of gerontology (Stones & Kozma, 1986). And Ormel (1983), examining data from a 6- to 7-year Dutch longitudinal study, concluded that how people respond to well-being measures over a period of years was primarily dependent on attributes of the persons, not on their environment. According to Ormel, neither deterioration nor improvement in life circumstances seemed to have had any significant effects on the amount of distress or satisfaction reported.

To further examine these challenging findings, let us turn to Costa, McCrae, and Zonderman (1987), who compared the responses given by 4,942 American men and women between 1981 and 1984 with responses these same people gave to the same questions a decade earlier. Subjects responded to 10 to 18 items in the General Well-Being Schedule (Dupuy, 1978); changes in life circumstances were inferred from current demographic data involving sex, race, age, income, education, and marital status, and therefore did not rely on subject's memory.

Because of this study's large and carefully selected stratified probability sample, its findings call for careful consideration. The authors reported that their data showed great stability in well-being measures over a 10-year interval. They asserted that they could predict future happiness more accurately from past measures of happiness than from age, sex, or race or from changes in marital status, work, or residence. They acknowledged that a large literature has reported that events like job loss, the death of a loved one, or divorce can have dramatic effects on well-being, but call attention to other studies (such as Palmore, Cleveland, Nowlin, Ramm, & Siegler, 1979) indicating that most people quickly adjust to such negative events. Moreover, as Brickman and Campbell (1971), Campbell, Converse, and Rodgers (1976), and others have shown, people adjust to improvements in their life circumstances even more rapidly.

There are limitations to the Costa et al. (1987) research. For example, it did not assess the effects of changes in health status on well-being, and its measure of well-being was so global that it could have missed more domain-specific effects of environmental change on well-being. And, in fact, there is evidence to suggest that well-being may be domain-specific—that is, residential well-being may be quite different from occupational well-being or marital well-being. Nevertheless, the possibility that a person's subjective sense of well-being may derive more from personal attributes than from the impact of his or her environment should not be rejected out of hand. There may be more than folk wisdom in the adage that "money can't buy happiness." Neither, perhaps, can changes in one's environment.

In conclusion, all of this speculation is intended as a cautionary note about the relationship between changes in objective standards of life and subjective well-being. Improving the quality of a person's life may increase his or her sense of well-being, or it may not. That remains an empirical question and a difficult one to answer. In my own view, it is likely that individuals differ greatly in their sensitivity to environmental effects. But let us suppose that the evidence I have summarized here is correct, and that features of a person's environment are less important in bringing about a sense of well-being than are aspects of that person's personality or temperament. If this finding were confirmed, what would that imply for our current and future efforts to ensure an improved quality of life for persons with mental retardation?

First, I believe that we must be prepared to uncouple objective standards of quality from the subjective experience of well-being. We should continue every effort to ensure that mentally retarded persons have access to better housing, health care, recreational activities, dignified employment, and everything else that an enlightened society can provide for its citizens. But we must never forget that all a society should do is provide options; however well-meaning, it should not impose standards. Nor should it imagine that all who accept its array of life-quality options will experience a greater sense of well-being than they did before, or that all who reject these options in favor of an alternative lifestyle will be less satisfied.

Because individual choice among available options is essential if there is to be any meaningful improvement in peoples' lives, we must assure that it is persons with mental retardation who choose what they want, not we who choose for them. And if their choices do not invariably bring them a greater sense of well-being, we should not then impose our choices on them. They, like the rest of us, should have the right to strive for satisfaction in life in their own way. And we must understand that some of them, like the rest of us, will be more successful than others.

REFERENCES

Bradburn, N. M. (1969). *The structure of psychological well-being*. Chicago: Aldine.
Brickman, P., & Campbell, D. T. (1971). Hedonic relativism and planning the good society. In M. H. Appley (Ed.), *Adaptation level theory: A symposium*. New York: Academic Press.

Bruininks, R. H., Meyers, C. E., Sigford, B. B., & Lakin, K. C. (Eds.). (1981). *Deinstitutionalization and community adjustment of mentally retarded people* (Monograph No. 4). Washington, DC: American Association of Mental Deficiency.

Campbell, A., Converse, P. E., & Rodgers, W. L. (1976). *The quality of American life: Perceptions, evaluations, and satisfactions*. New York: Russell Sage Foundation.

Cobb, H. (1972). *The forecast of fulfillment: A review of research on predictive assessment of the adult retarded for social and vocational adjustment*. New York: Teachers College Press.

Costa, P. T., Jr., McCrae, R. R., & Zonderman, A. B. (1987). Environmental and dispositional influences on well-being: Longitudinal follow-up of an American national sample. *British Journal of Psychology, 78*, 299–306.

Deutscher, I. (1966). Words and deeds: Social science and social policy. *Social Problems, 13*, 235–254.

Dupuy, H. J. (1978, October). Self-representations of general psychological well-being of American adults. Paper presented at a meeting of the American Public Health Association, Los Angeles, CA.

Edgerton, R. B. (1975). Issues relating to the quality of life among mentally retarded persons. In M. J. Begab & S. A. Richardson (Eds.), *The mentally retarded and society: A social science perspective*. Baltimore: University Park Press.

Edgerton, R. B. (1981). Crime, deviance and normalization: Reconsidered. In R. H. Bruininks, C. E. Meyers, B. B. Sigford, & K. C. Lakin (Eds.), *Deinstitutionalization and community adjustment of mentally retarded people* (Monograph No. 4), pp. 169–174. Washington, DC: American Association on Mental Deficiency.

Edgerton, R. B., & Langness, L. L. (1978). Observing mentally retarded persons in community settings: An anthropological perspective. In G. P. Sackett (Ed.), *Observing behavior: Vol. I; Theory and applications in mental retardation*, pp. 210–219. Baltimore: University Park Press.

George, L. K. (1979). The happiness syndrome: Methodological and substantive issues in the study of social psychological well-being in adulthood. *The Gerontologist, 19*, 210–216.

Heal, L. W., Sigelman, C. K., & Switzky, H. N. (1978). Research in community residential alternatives for the mentally retarded. In N. R. Ellis (Ed.), *International review of research in mental retardation (Vol. 9)*, pp. 89–101. New York: Academic Press.

Kaufman, S. (1984). Friendship, coping systems and community adjustment of mildly retarded adults. In R. B. Edgerton (Ed.), *Lives in process: Mildly retarded adults in a large city*, pp. 40–58. Washington, DC: American Association on Mental Deficiency.

Keogh, B. K., & Pullis, M. E. (1980). Temperament influences on the development of exceptional children. In B. K. Keogh (Ed.), *Advances in Special Education (Vol. 1)*, pp. 112–121. Greenwich, CT: JAI Press.

Koegel, P. (1982). Rethinking support systems: A qualitative investigation into the nature of social support. *Dissertation Abstracts International, 43*, 1214-A.

Koegel, P., & Edgerton, R. B. (1984). Black "six-hour retarded children" as young adults. In R. B. Edgerton (Ed.), *Lives in process: Mildly retarded adults in a large city*, pp. 60–69. Washington, DC: American Association on Mental Deficiency.

Landesman, S. (1986). Quality of life and personal life satisfaction: Definition and measurement issues. *Mental Retardation, 24*, 141–143.

Lazarus, R., & Lannier, R. (1979). Stress related transactions between person and environment. In L. Pervin & M. Lewis (Eds.), *Perspectives in international psychology*, pp. 142–156. New York: Plenum.

Maddox, G. I. (1968). Persistence of life style among the elderly: A longitudinal study of patterns of social activity in relation to life satisfaction. In B. I. Neugarten (Ed.), *Middle age and aging*, pp. 70–89. Chicago: University of Chicago Press.

McCarver, R. B., & Craig, E. M. (1974). Placement of the retarded in the community: Prognosis and outcome. In N. R. Ellis (Ed.), *International review of research in mental retardation*, pp. 146–159. New York: Academic Press.

Mitchell-Kernan, C., & Tucker, M. B. (1984). The social structures of mildly mentally retarded Afro-Americans: Gender comparisons. In R. B. Edgerton (Ed.), *Lives in process: Mildly retarded adults in a large city*, pp. 150–166. Washington, DC: American Association on Mental Deficiency.

Ormel, J. (1983). Neuroticism and well-being inventories: Measuring traits or states? *Psychological Medicine, 72,* 165–176.

Palmore, E. B., Cleveland, W. P., Jr., Nowlin, J. B., Ramm, D., & Siegler, I. D. (1979). Stress and adaptation in later life. *Journal of Gerontology, 34,* 841–851.

Ross, R. T., Begab, M. J., Dondis, E. H., Giampiccolo, J. S., Jr., & Meyers, C. E. (1985). *Lives of the mentally retarded: A forty year follow-up study.* Stanford: Stanford University Press.

Schneider, M. (1976). The quality of life in large American cities: Objective and subjective social indicators. *Social Indicators Research, 1,* 495–509.

Stones, J. J., & Kozma, A. (1986). Happiness and activities as propensities. *Journal of Gerontology, 41,* 85–90.

Thorndike, E. L. (1939). *Your city.* New York: Harcourt, Brace & Company.

Zautra, A., & Goodhart, D. (1979). Quality of life indicators: A review of the literature. *Community Mental Health Review, 4,* 1–10.

Zetlin, A. G., & Turner, J. L. (1984). Self-perspectives on being handicapped: Stigma and adjustment. In R. B. Edgerton (Ed.), *Lives in process: Mildly retarded adults in a large city,* pp. 180–194. Washington, DC: American Association on Mental Deficiency.

16
Methodological Issues in Measuring the Quality of Life of Individuals with Mental Retardation

Laird W. Heal
University of Illinois

Carol K. Sigelman
University of Arizona

Although everyone seems to understand at some broad level what is meant by *quality of life*, the meanings attached to this concept vary considerably. Moreover, the information investigators obtain about the quality of life of a population is intimately related to the way in which they conceptualize and measure it. We leave to others the formidable task of conceptualizing quality of life. Instead, we assume here that investigators know what they want to measure. In this chapter, we face another formidable challenge—that of deciding how to measure it. Our purposes in this chapter are to present some of the key methodological issues that arise in assessing quality of life and to offer some guidance about how to resolve them, drawing primarily on research that has systematically evaluated methodologies for interviewing individuals both with and without mental retardation.

FUNDAMENTAL METHODOLOGICAL DECISIONS

To set the stage, let us call attention to four major ways in which methodologies for assessing quality of life can differ. First, measures can be

Acknowledgments. This report was supported in part by the Office of Special Education and Rehabilitative Services, U.S. Department of Education, under a contract (300-85-0160) to the Secondary Transition Intervention Effectiveness Institute at the University of Illinois. The research done at the Texas Tech University Research and Training Center in Mental Retardation was in response to an initiative by the President's Committee on Mental Retardation and was supported in part by a grant from the Rehabilitation Services Administration, Department of Health, Education and Welfare.

objective or subjective. That is, they can focus on the objective circumstances of people's lives (their income, housing, patterns of behavior, and so on) or they can assess attitudinal phenomena such as perceived satisfaction with life in general or with specific life circumstances. Objective measures can presumably be verified externally; subjective measures cannot. Second, a measure can be absolute or relative; it can directly index people's quality of life or it can compare their quality of life to some standard such as what they would ideally want, what they experienced in the past, or what most other people experience. Third, quality of life can be reported directly by the subjects of study or it can be assessed by someone else (by an informant or proxy such as a relative or friend or by the investigators themselves, as when researchers record objective data or conduct behavioral observations). Finally, the measure can be authored or generated by the investigator or by the subjects of investigation. A subject-authored approach could entail using unstructured techniques such as participant observation to elucidate clients' own value systems and perspectives (e.g., Edgerton, 1975) or it could involve designing an instrument based on explicit input from subjects (as Flanagan, 1978, did after collecting data from some 3,000 people about specific critical incidents that had enhanced or worsened their lives).

Although this typology is by no means exhaustive, it serves to stimulate thinking about methodological choice points. Table 16.1 incorporates the four dimensions into a consideration of the what, who, and how of measuring quality of life. The *what* question concerns whether a measure assesses objective or subjective information and whether it assesses quality of life in an absolute or relative sense. The *who* question concerns whether mentally retarded individuals or other people author measures and provide data. The *how* column reflects the more specific information goals and types of items that researchers select once they have made the fundamental decisions incorporated in the taxonomy. Finally, the citations included in the table, drawn primarily but not exclusively from the mental retardation literature, offer a few examples of the approaches that have in fact been used by quality of life researchers.

One immediately notes that not all of the 16 cells have entries. Most commonly, investigators themselves assess quality of life by employing investigator-generated measures (as Newton et al., 1988, have done by objectively assessing the number and types of activities in which clients engage) or they interview either clients or their proxies using investigator-generated interview schedules (as with the objective and subjective quality of life items designed by Schalock, Keith, Hoffman, & Karan, 1989). Other logical possibilities such as client-authored objective measures—measures that assess the objective life circumstances judged by mentally retarded

Table 16.1   Methodology Taxonomy for Assessing Quality of Life

What?[a] General Method	Who? Respondent	Author	How?[b] Type of Instrument	Citation
Objective or Quasi-objective				
Absolute	Investigator	Investigator	Objective behavioral measures	Newton et al. (1988)
			Quality of life items	Schalock, Keith, Hoffman, & Karan (1989)
			Quality of life standards	Zingarelli et al. (1987)
Relative to some standard	Investigator	Investigator	Normalization relative to "cultural norms"	Wolfensberger & Thomas (1983)
Subjective				
Absolute	Proxy	Investigator	Quality of life	Schalock et al. (1989)
			Consumer satisfaction	Temple University DD Center and UAP (1988)
	Client	Investigator	Subjective well-being	Andrews & Withey (1976)
			Satisfaction with home and friends	Heal, Novak, & Chadsey-Rusch (1981)
			Quality of life	Seltzer (1981)
			General happiness and satisfaction	Sigelman et al. (1983)
		Client	Participant observation	Edgerton (1975)
			Evaluation of life's critical incidents	Flanagan (1978)
Relative to some standard	Proxy	Investigator	—	—
	Client	Investigator	Relative subjective well-being	Heal & Daniels (1986)
		Client	—	—

[a] The questions of "where" and "when" are also methodologically critical, but they are not addressed in the current paper. "Where" depends on the ecological validity (Bracht & Glass, 1968) requirements of the evaluation, and "when" depends upon the test-retest reliability requirements. [b] The type of instrument can also be classified by its item type: multiple choice, completion, open ended, open ended with examples, yes-no, Likert levels of agreement or disagreement, either-or—any of which can have pictures to make the question less dependent on language.

individuals to be most central to their well-being—might prove to be very credible quality of life indicators.

The decisions implied by the taxonomy presented in Table 16.1 can have substantial effects on the information obtained. For example, different subjective measures of quality of life seem to reflect a single quality that has been labeled *subjective well-being,* and they correlate more highly with one another than they do with objective indices of quality of life (Andrews, 1986; Andrews & Withey, 1976; Diener, 1984). In other words, method variance tends to dominate substantive variance in quality of life assessments. Moreover, many individuals seem to have difficulty responding to relative measures that require comparing current with past or future quality of life (Andrews & Withey, 1976). Indeed, Heal and Daniels (1986) developed such a relative quality of life measure for mentally retarded individuals but ultimately abandoned it because test-retest reliabilities were very low.

The issue of who serves as respondent or data provider is also significant, particularly in assessing the quality of life of mentally retarded individuals. For whatever reasons, answers provided by mentally retarded individuals and answers provided by their parents or attendants sometimes disagree considerably (Sigelman et al., 1983). And although we know very little about how findings based on investigator-authored and client-authored measures might differ, we can surmise that estimates of satisfaction with life circumstances could differ substantially, depending on whether investigators or clients generate the list of specific life circumstances to be evaluated.

In short, investigations of quality of life can potentially rely on a wide range of fundamental methodologies. In practice, however, many of them have involved interviewing either individuals or their proxies. Accordingly, we now turn to the more specific methodological decisions that researchers face when they interview either nonretarded or retarded individuals.

FACTORS AFFECTING RESPONSES IN SURVEY RESEARCH

In any research, validity of measurement must be established. In survey research, validity is diminished to the extent that "irrelevant" factors such as how a question is worded or who conducts the interview systematically alters the answers obtained. Those who would assess the quality of life of developmentally disabled individuals can learn much from the literature on systematic response effects or sources of error in survey research (see Belson, 1986; Converse & Presser, 1986; Schuman & Presser, 1981; Sudman & Bradburn, 1974, 1982; Turner, 1984). In a massive meta-analysis of such inadvertent response effects, Sudman and Bradburn (1974) reviewed and analyzed no less than 935 references to methodological studies from 95 social science journals as well as numerous dissertations, monographs, and books. They directed attention to three broad classes of variables that can potentially alter or distort either objective or subjective survey data: task variables (for example, face-to-face vs. self-administered surveys, alternate question wordings); interviewer roles and characteristics; and respondent roles and characteristics.

Task Variables

Much evidence suggests that responses can be systematically biased by question wording and question format or structure. For instance, Rugg (1941) asked these alternative questions: "Do you think the United States should allow public speeches against democracy?" and "Do you think the United States should forbid public speeches against democracy?" In response to the first question, 62% would not "allow" such speeches; in response to the second, only 46% would "forbid" such speeches. A seemingly minor difference in wording substantially altered responses.

Comparisons of closed-ended and open-ended questions reveal similar response effects associated with question format. Jenkins (1935) constructed an exhaustive checklist from all responses to a previously administered open-ended survey and found that this checklist (including an "all others" item) yielded response patterns closely comparable to those yielded by the open-ended survey. However, responses to an incomplete checklist, from which some of the popular answers had been removed, differed radically from responses to the open-ended question, suggesting that the specific make-up of a checklist, particularly its comprehensiveness, can greatly influence responding. When Belson and Duncan (1962) compared checklist and open-ended questions about TV programs watched and periodicals read by respondents during a specified time period, the checklist yielded higher claims of activity, leading Belson (1986; Belson & Duncan, 1962) to conclude that checklists are generally superior because they facilitate retrieval of information. However, a small fraction of respondents claimed to have watched programs included on the checklist that were not actually televised during the period of inquiry, suggesting that checklists can in some instances stimulate incorrect overreporting of behavior.

Survey researchers have also become sensitive to the fact that certain kinds of questions elicit systematic response biases. Questions that provide respondents with the opportunity to express agreement (by saying "yes," "true," "agree," and the like) may give rise to acquiescent responding. One strategy for detecting acquiescence is to ask content-free questions, as Gerjuoy and Winters (1966) did when they presented institutionalized mentally retarded adults with pairs of identical geometric figures and asked if one of the figures was larger (or smaller). Of all responses, 59.1% were "yes," a departure from chance that reflects acquiescence. A second means of assessing acquiescence is to ask questions for which the correct answers are known. Thus, Cronbach (1942) discovered that students taking true-false tests are inclined to guess "true" when they are in doubt. Finally, acquiescence has been detected through item-reversal techniques, in which a question and its opposite are asked and agreement with both questions indicates acquiescence. Using this approach in a study of children's cognitive development, Rothenberg (1969) discovered that fully 65% of the least cognitively mature children in the study contradicted themselves by saying that two sets of blocks had both the same number and a different number of blocks.

A related threat to validity is socially desirable responding, the tendency to present oneself in a favorable light (see DeMaio, 1984). Scores on personality scales often correlate highly with the independently rated social desirability of scale items (Edwards, 1957). Similarly, many people respond to survey items in ways that suggest that they are concerned with obtaining social approval and are hesitant to admit to undesirable behaviors, especially when items are subjective or attitudinal, when it is obvious which options are socially desirable or undesirable, and when questions are presented in face-to-face interviews rather than in self-administered questionnaires (Sudman & Bradburn, 1974). Both social desirability and acquiescence have proven to be significant problems in quality of life research, perhaps helping to explain why members of the general population typically rate the quality of their lives above the neutral point, regardless of how *neutral* is anchored or described (Andrews & Withey, 1976; Diener, 1984).

Three other messages about the effects of task variables on survey responses are worth mentioning. First, when respondents are asked to recall behavioral information, particularly about socially disapproved activities, their tendency to underreport behaviors increases as the length of the recall period lengthens (Sudman & Bradburn, 1974). Second, responses to particular questions can vary depending on the context in which they appear; for example, people report higher levels of general happiness when they have just been asked about their marital happiness than when they have just been asked about their finances (Turner, 1984). Finally, the ranges of such response effects or biases are larger for attitudinal (subjective) questions than for behavioral (objective) questions.

Interviewer Variables

Sudman and Bradburn (1974) concluded that response effects attributable to interviewer characteristics such as age, sex, race, and social class are generally less powerful than those attributable to task variables. When interviewer characteristics do matter, it is usually under highly specific conditions, such as the interviewer's race influencing responses when people are asked about their racial attitudes (Schuman & Converse, 1971).

Respondent Variables

Sudman and Bradburn (1974) concluded that the strength of response biases generally did not vary as a function of the sex, race, or age of the respondent. However, they did find that children with 8 years or less of school tended to be especially susceptible to many response effects. Moreover, respondent and task variables sometimes interact so that, for example, elementary school students are especially likely to overreport their behavior in response to closed-ended checklists and respondents with less than a high school education are especially likely to give different answers to long questions than to short questions. Although Sudman and Bradburn generally did not find level of education to be an influential factor within the adult population, Schuman and Presser (1977; 1981) have found that adults with limited education are especially susceptible to certain response effects. Specifically, compared with more educated adults, they are especially likely to acquiesce, to give discrepant answers to "allow" versus "forbid" question wordings, and to underreport on open-ended questions but overreport on closed-ended questions.

Implications for Interviewing Mentally Retarded Individuals

The response effects literature carries some sobering messages for those who would assess the quality of life of individuals with mental retardation. It clearly demonstrates that variations in such task factors as question wording, question structure or format, and the extent to which a question implies a socially desirable response can alter the answers provided by nonretarded individuals. Fortunately, this literature contains many practical guidelines about how to minimize response effects and write effective questions (see especially Andrews & Withey, 1976; Converse & Presser, 1986; Sudman & Bradburn, 1982). Tactics that increase validity of response in the general population (including individuals who serve as proxies for mentally retarded subjects) are also likely to increase validity of response in the mentally retarded population.

Unfortunately, this literature also implies that response effects that threaten the validity of survey data are especially likely to be evident among individuals who are cognitively immature and/or relatively uneducated. By implication, the literature on child language and communication development represents one fertile source of guidance for researchers who plan to interview individuals with mental retardation. Children and adults who are mentally retarded can generally be expected to acquire communication skills such as the ability to answer different types of questions in the same order that nonretarded children do, and to display levels of communication development roughly comparable to those displayed by nonretarded individuals of similar *mental* age (see Sigelman et al., 1983).

However, one must still expect that questioning mentally retarded respondents about their quality of life will raise some unique methodological problems. Thus, there is ultimately no substitute for systematic research on the ability of individuals with mental retardation to answer questions and to answer them meaningfully. We now turn to that research.

RESEARCH ON INTERVIEWING MENTALLY RETARDED RESPONDENTS

Most of the fairly small body of research on the methodology of interviewing mentally retarded individuals was conducted at the Research and Training Center in Mental Retardation at Texas Tech University (see Sigelman, Schoenrock, Winer et al., 1981; Sigelman et al., 1983, for overviews). The project involved administering 20- to 30-minute interviews containing alternative forms of questions to retarded individuals, presenting the same or alternative questions in repeated interviews approximately 1 week apart, and conducting parallel interviews with parents or direct care staff to determine the extent of agreement between retarded interviewees and informants speaking on their behalf. Each of three main samples—institutionalized children (ages 12 to 16), institutionalized adults, and community children (ages 12 to 16)—included males and females in three IQ ranges (severe, moderate, and mild retardation). A fourth sample, used to evaluate interview strategies especially designed for individuals with very limited verbal skills, consisted of members of the institution samples who had been largely but not entirely unresponsive when first interviewed.

Four standards were applied in judging which of various alternative questions were the most promising approaches to obtaining meaningful information directly from retarded persons: responsiveness (the proportion of interviewees who could answer a question, regardless of the truth or falsity of answers); test-retest reliability (correspondence between answers to the same questions on two occasions); consistency (correspondence between responses to questions whose wording or format differed but whose meaning remained the same); and agreement with informants or, in some instances, with objective fact.

Responsiveness

Much as one might want to interview mentally retarded individuals using well-established quality of life measures designed for the general population, national surveys typically use language "within the range of comprehension of high school graduates" (Converse & Schuman, 1984, p. 309). Obviously, questions are useful only to the extent that individuals with mental retardation can comprehend and answer them (e.g., can mention one of the two options in response to an either-or question).

Sigelman, Winer, and Schoenrock (1982) found that high proportions—generally over 80%—of their mentally retarded samples could provide answers to yes-no questions (e.g., "Do you set the table?") and to picture-choice questions (e.g., given four face drawings ranging from very happy to very sad, "Which picture shows how you like the food here?"). Yes-no questions about activities tended to be easier to answer than yes-no questions about subjective phenomena such as happiness. Verbal either-or questions were answerable by 66% to 72% of the three main samples, and verbal multiple choice questions and open-ended questions proved to be the most cognitively demanding, answerable by about half of the institutionalized respondents and 70% of the community children. Responsiveness to questions increased as IQ increased (Sigelman et al., 1980). Preliminary screening interviews established the obvious: most profoundly retarded persons cannot answer verbal questions. In the IQ range associated with severe mental retardation, responsiveness scores differed greatly from person to person; within the moderately and mildly retarded ranges, most individuals proved able to respond to simple questions of a variety of types.

Reliability

The test-retest reliability figures reported by Sigelman et al. (1983) are both gratifying and disappointing. For example, when institutionalized children were asked the same yes-no questions about their activities on two occasions about a week apart, their answers were consistent an average of 87% of the time. However, this estimate of reliability was inflated by the strong tendency to say "yes" to most questions. What may have been reliable was the tendency to acquiesce rather than the tendency to provide valid information. Four-option multiple-choice questions about activities, although answerable by relatively few individuals, yielded about 72% test-retest agreement, whereas the consistency of answers to multiple-choice questions presenting four levels of happy and sad faces and inquiring about satisfaction with living circumstances was a discouragingly low 46%. Open-ended questions about discrete facts were answered consistently about two-thirds of the time (e.g., 63% gave the same first and last names on both occasions when asked their name), but open-ended questions calling for enumerations of activities only rarely yielded mention of the same activity both times and had high reliability only in the sense that many activities were *not* mentioned both times. Although these reliability estimates suggest that one can usually get the same answer from retarded individuals on two occasions, they are difficult to interpret without determining whether the answers obtained also seem to be valid.

Consistency

Perhaps the most compelling criterion of the adequacy of a questioning approach is that it yield answers that are consistent with answers to alternative questions on the same topics and that are relatively free of systematic response bias. The Texas Tech data demonstrate that acquiescence in response to yes-no questions is a major source of response inconsistency (e.g., Sigelman, Budd, Spanhel, & Schoenrock, 1981b). In all three samples, the following oppositely worded questions were presented: Are you usually happy? versus Are you usually sad? and Are you usually by yourself? versus Are you usually with other people? The percentages of respondents who answered yes to both versions of the same question ranged from 39% to 51%. By comparison, 0% to 8% displayed a nay-saying bias, saying no to both forms of a question. For the happy versus sad questions, although not for the alone versus with other questions, the tendency to acquiescence increased as IQ decreased. In the difficult-to-interview sample of institutionalized children and adults, acquiescence was also revealed by incorrect answers to factual questions; for example, in response to yes-no questions, over 40% of these respondents claimed to be Chinese or to be school bus drivers.

There was one set of alternative yes-no questions for which nay-saying rates exceeded acquiescence rates (Budd, Sigelman, & Sigelman, 1981). Institutionalized adults were asked both "Are you allowed to . . ." and "Is it against the rules to . . ." questions about disapproved activities (hitting people, staying up late, calling people ugly names, and leaving without asking). On these items, an average of 38% of the responding adults contradicted themselves by saying no to both forms of a question, whereas a smaller percentage (17.5%) said yes to both. This finding suggests that a desire for social approval may underlie both acquiescence and nay-saying. That is, retarded respondents may say yes to many yes-no questions in order to be agreeable *and* may say no to questions that mention socially undesirable behaviors to deny any association with these taboos.

Although the problem of acquiescence in response to yes-no questions was particularly severe, either-or questions sometimes engendered a systematic response bias of their own (Sigelman, Budd, Spanhel, & Schoen-rock, 1981a). When asked parallel either-or questions in which only the order of options was altered (e.g., Are you usually happy or sad? versus Are you usually sad or happy?), respondents were more likely to contradict themselves by choosing the second option both times. This recency bias was fairly prevalent, characterizing an average of almost 21% of paired answers in three samples (versus about 9% reflecting a primacy bias and involving the choice of the first option both times).

Finally, open-ended questions were associated with the response bias of underreporting activities. As a result of both underreporting on open-ended questions and acquiescence on yes-no questions, respondents typically claimed to engage in far fewer activities when they were asked open-ended questions than when they were asked yes-no questions (Sigelman, Budd, Winer, Schoenrock, & Martin, 1982). Although Belson (1986) concluded that yes-no checklists are preferable to open-ended questions in surveys of the general population, either approach is suspect with the mentally retarded population.

Interestingly, just as practice in answering questions seems to improve responsiveness to questions (Sigelman et al., 1983), it may also improve consistency of response to alternative questions. Conroy and Bradley (1985) found that only 16 of 23 residents of an institution responded consistently to a yes-no question and a multiple-choice question with happy and sad faces about satisfaction with their living circumstances. Four years later, deinstitutionalized individuals responded with perfect consistency. While this increase in consistency may have been attributable more to the respondents' strong preference for remaining in the community than to their considerable experience in being interviewed, residents who remained in the institution also displayed substantial increases in response consistency on various satisfaction items over time.

Agreement with Informants or Factual Records

The final standard that was applied by Sigelman et al. (1983) in judging the quality of information received from mentally retarded interviewees was its agreement with information obtained from other sources. While one should not assume that disagreements between retarded individuals and their parents or direct care staff necessarily reflect invalid responding on the part of retarded individuals, one can be more confident of responses if two respondents agree. In one fairly representative analysis of resident-staff agreement, agreement was 52% for a yes-no checklist and 60% for an open-ended question about participation in various sports (Budd et al., 1981). Disagreements in response to the checklist most often involved the resident's saying "yes" but the caretaker's saying "no," whereas disagreements on the open-ended questions more often involved the resident's not mentioning an activity that the caretaker mentioned. This pattern of disagreements suggested that acquiescence and underreporting on the part of retarded individuals were largely, although not totally, responsible for discrepancies between their answers and the answers provided by care staff. At the same time, correlations between IQ and agreement, while significant in two of three samples, were weaker than one might expect (Sigelman et al., 1980), implying that agreement with informants is an imperfect indicator of response validity.

Yet the validity of answers obtained from mentally retarded individuals is often limited even when the standard of validity is known fact. Many such individuals have difficulty providing accurate responses to open-ended questions inquiring about their full names, birthdates, and addresses (Sigelman et al., 1983). Some cannot answer such questions, and about a third of those who do answer do not provide fully correct information.

Possible Solutions to Problems in Interviewing Mentally Retarded Individuals

Perhaps the main message of this research is that obtaining meaningful information about quality of life directly from individuals with mental retardation is problematic. Simply getting answers from individuals with limited verbal skills is only the first of the challenges. Response effects that jeopardize the validity of answers obtained from the general population seem to operate even more strongly in mentally retarded populations. Where does this leave researchers who wish to survey persons with mental retardation about their quality of life?

The solution adopted by the Texas Tech researchers was to identify optimally effective questioning techniques by pitting alternative questions against each other and determining which of them optimized responsiveness, reliability, self-consistency, and agreement with informants or known facts. By these criteria, either-or questions (or objective multiple-choice questions with three or four options)—particularly when accompanied by pictures—surfaced as the most promising questioning approach. Factual multiple-choice questions offering discrete options (ways to get to school or types of dwellings) worked well, much better than multiple-choice questions presenting happy and sad faces or quantitative options such as *a lot*, *sometimes*, *not much*, and *never* (Sigelman et al., 1983). Moreover, when Sigelman and Budd (1986) systematically compared questions with and without pictures, they found that pictures enhanced responsiveness to either-or and multiple-choice questions, only slightly reduced agreement with informants, and, particularly in the low-verbal sample, reduced the tendency to choose the second of the two options in either-or questions. Thus, instead of using a yes-no checklist to find out about participation in various activities, one might develop line drawings of these activities, a comparison drawing of a person doing nothing, and ask questions like this: "Some people cook their dinner on the stove. Other people don't cook their dinner on the stove. Which one is most like you? Point to the picture." Such questions, especially when they are objective rather than subjective, can be answered by most severely to mildly retarded persons and, more importantly, can yield relatively valid answers.

A second approach, adopted by Heal and Chadsey-Rusch (1985), is to interview mentally retarded individuals with whatever types of questions seem most natural and then statistically correct for response bias. In their 29-item *Lifestyle Satisfaction Scale*, Heal and Chadsey-Rusch (1985) included an acquiescence subscale, which consisted of paired questions for which responding yes to both would constitute self-contradiction and indicate acquiescence. Using multiple regression techniques, lifestyle satisfaction scores were then corrected for acquiescence (adjusted downward, because acquiescence predictably inflated estimates of satisfaction). This approach has considerable promise, and it could also be used to adjust either-or measures for the recency or second option response bias.

A third option is to concede that many mentally retarded persons cannot provide meaningful information in interviews, and to rely instead on data provided by informants or by the investigators themselves. A less extreme variant of this solution is to devise a screening interview that can be used to determine whether the individual or someone else should provide quality of life data. Such a screening interview might assess responsiveness to questions, determine the validity of responses to basic questions whose answers are known, and gauge susceptibility to response biases that might compromise the validity of answers to the full interview. The problem, of course, is that any resulting differences in quality of life between higher-ability and lower-ability individuals might be attributable more to the different research methods used than to true differences in the quality of their lives. Because profoundly retarded individuals are generally incapable of participating in verbal interviews, this problem exists already for those who seek to study the entire mentally retarded population.

Ultimately, researchers might be best off adopting a blend of these approaches. For example, they might rely on either-or or multiple-choice questions accompanied by pictures whenever feasible; build into their interview schedules checks for response bias that can later be used to adjust scores to remove the effects of response bias; and turn to information-gathering techniques other than client interviews when those alternative techniques are likely to yield the most valid data.

SUMMARY AND CONCLUSIONS

We began this chapter by presenting several fundamental methodological decisions that must be made in order to assess the quality of life of mentally retarded individuals, calling attention to potentially important distinctions between objective and subjective, absolute and relative, subject-completed and informant-completed, and subject-generated and investigator-generated measures. We then turned to some of the methodological problems that arise in interviewing members of the general population, particularly problems stemming from systematic response biases associated with question format and wording. The literature in this area clearly demonstrates that what one learns about the quality of life of non-retarded individuals can differ considerably depending on how questions are asked. This means, of course, that information obtained from individuals who serve as proxies for mentally retarded individuals cannot be assumed to be valid unless care is taken in designing survey instruments to reduce response effects.

The challenges of assessing quality of life through survey methods are only magnified when mentally retarded individuals serve as respondents, as documented by the systematic research on the methodology of interviewing mentally retarded individuals reviewed here. It seems challenging indeed to get answers to questions from many persons with mental retardation and, more importantly, to elicit responses that are reliable, consistent with responses to different questions on the same topic, and substantiated by information obtained from other sources. These rather discouraging findings may tempt researchers to forgo interviewing mentally retarded persons entirely. Thus, investigator-gathered behavioral observations of rates of smiling, laughing, frowning, and crying might be used in place of self-reports of subjective well-being.

Our own position is that multiple methodologies, each of them demonstrated to be reliable and valid, are needed in order to adequately assess the quality of life of mentally retarded individuals, and that interviews with such individuals should be one of these methodologies. There are compelling philosophical reasons for providing mentally retarded consumers with opportunities to tell us how they perceive their lives and how they would like their lives to change. Moreover, we have directed attention in this chapter to empirically based guidelines that can improve survey methodology and enable more mentally retarded individuals to speak for themselves. When interviews yield useless information, it is too often because researchers are not seeking information as effectively as they might. It is a disservice to individuals with mental retardation to "slap together" a measure and simply hope for the best. Developing *any* reliable and valid quality-of-life measure requires considerable effort, effort that promises to result in a fuller understanding of the lives of developmentally disabled citizens.

REFERENCES

Andrews, F. M. (Ed.). (1986). *Research on the quality of life.* Ann Arbor: University of Michigan.

Andrews, F. M., & Withey, S. B. (1976). *Social indicators of well-being: Americans' perceptions of life quality.* New York: Plenum.

Belson, W. A. (1986). *Validity in survey research.* Brookfield, VT: Gower Publishing.

Belson, W. A., & Duncan, J. A. (1962). A comparison of the checklist and the open response questioning systems. *Applied Statistics, 11,* 120–132.

Bracht, G. H., & Glass, G. V. (1968). The external validity of experiments. *American Educational Research Journal, 5,* 437–474.

Budd, E. C., Sigelman, C. K., & Sigelman, L. (1981). Exploring the outer limits of response bias. *Sociological Focus, 14,* 297–307.

Conroy, J. W., & Bradley, V. J. (1985). *The Pennhurst longitudinal study.* Philadelphia: Developmental Disabilities Center, Temple University.

Converse, J. M., & Presser, S. (1986). *Survey questions. Handcrafting the standardized questionnaire* (Sage University Paper Series, Quantitative Applications in the Social Sciences No. 07-063). Beverly Hills: Sage.

Converse, J. M., & Schuman, H. (1984). The manner of inquiry: An analysis of survey question form across organizations and over time. In C. F. Turner & E. Martin (Eds.), *Surveying subjective phenomena* (Vol. 2, pp. 283–316). New York: Russell Sage.

Cronbach, L. J. (1942). Studies of acquiescence as a factor in the true-false test. *Journal of Educational Psychology, 33,* 401–415.

DeMaio, T. J. (1984). Social desirability and survey measurement: A review. In C. F. Turner & E. Martin (Eds.), *Surveying subjective phenomena* (Vol. 2, pp. 257–282). New York: Russell Sage.

Diener, E. (1984). Subjective well-being. *Psychological Bulletin, 95*(3), 542–575.

Edgerton, R. B. (1975). Issues relating to the quality of life among mentally retarded persons: In M. J. Begab & S. A. Richardson (Eds.), *The mentally retarded and society: A social science perspective.* Baltimore: University Park Press.

Edwards, A. L. (1957). *The social desirability variable in personality assessment and research.* New York: Dryden Press.

Flanagan, J. C. (1978). A research approach to improving our quality of life. *American Psychologist, 33*(2), 138–147.

Gerjuoy, I., & Winters, J. J., Jr. (1966). Lateral preference for identical geometric forms: II. Retardates. *Perception & Psychophysics, 1,* 104–106.

Heal, L. W., & Chadsey-Rusch, J. (1985). The lifestyle satisfaction scale (LSS): Assessing individuals' satisfaction with residence, community setting, and associated services. *Applied Research in Mental Retardation, 6,* 475–490.

Heal, L. W., & Daniels, B. S. (1986). A cost-effectiveness analysis of residential alternatives for selected developmentally disabled citizens of three northern Wisconsin counties. *Mental Retardation Systems, 2,* 35–49.

Heal, L. W., Novak, A. R., & Chadsey-Rusch, J. (1981). *Lifestyle Satisfaction Scale.* Champaign: University of Illinois Department of Special Education.

Jenkins, J. (1935). *Psychology in business and industry.* New York: Wiley.

Newton, S., Bellamy, G. T., Boles, S. M., Stoner, S., Horner, R., LeBaron, N., Moskowitz, D., Romer, M., & Schlessinger, D. (1988). *Valued outcomes information system (VOIS) operations manual.* Eugene: Center on Human Development, University of Oregon.

Rothenberg, B. (1969). Conservation of number among four- and five-year old children: Some methodological considerations. *Child Development, 40,* 382–406.

Rugg, D. (1941). Experiments in wording questions: II. *Public Opinion Quarterly, 5,* 91–92.

Schalock, R. L., Keith, K. D., Hoffman, K., & Karan, O. C. (1989). Quality of life: Its measurement and use. *Mental Retardation, 27,* 25–31.

Schuman, H., & Converse, J. M. (1971). The effects of black and white interviewers on white respondents in 1968. *Public Opinion Quarterly, 35,* 44–68.

Schuman, H., & Presser, S. (1977). Question wording as an independent variable in survey analysis. *Sociological Methods and Research, 6,* 151–170.

Schuman, H., & Presser, S. (1981). *Questions and answers in attitude surveys: Experiments on question form, wording, and context.* New York: Academic.

Seltzer, G. B. (1981). Community residential adjustment: The relationship among environment, performance, and satisfaction. *American Journal of Mental Deficiency, 85,* 624–630.

Sigelman, C. K., & Budd, E. C. (1986). Pictures as an aid in questioning mentally retarded persons. *Rehabilitation Counseling Bulletin, 29,* 173–181.

Sigelman, C. K., Budd, E. C., Spanhel, C. L., & Schoenrock, C. J. (1981a). Asking questions of retarded persons: A comparison of yes-no and either-or formats. *Applied Research in Mental Retardation, 2,* 347–357.

Sigelman, C. K., Budd, E. C., Spanhel, C. L., & Schoenrock, C. J. (1981b). When in doubt, say yes: Acquiescence in interviews with mentally retarded persons. *Mental Retardation, 19,* 53–58.

Sigelman, C. K., Budd, E. C., Winer, J. W., Schoenrock, C. J., & Martin, P. W. (1982). Evaluating alternative techniques of questioning mentally retarded persons. *American Journal of Mental Deficiency, 86,* 511–518.

Sigelman, C. K., Schoenrock, C. J., Budd, E. C., Winer, J. L., Spanhel, C. L., Martin, P. W., Hromas, S., & Bensberg, G. J. (1983). *Communicating with mentally retarded persons: Asking questions and getting answers.* Lubbock: Research and Training Center in Mental Retardation, Texas Tech University.

Sigelman, C., Schoenrock, C., Spanhel, C., Hromas, S., Winer, J., Budd, E., & Martin, P. (1980). Surveying mentally retarded persons: Responsiveness and response validity in three samples. *American Journal of Mental Deficiency, 84,* 479–486.

Sigelman, C. K., Schoenrock, C. J., Winer, J. L., Spanhel, C. L., Hromas, S. G., Martin, P. W., Budd, E. C., & Bensberg, G. J. (1981). Issues in interviewing mentally retarded persons: An empirical study. In R. H. Bruininks, C. E. Meyers, B. B. Sigford, & K. C. Lakin (Eds.), *Deinstitutionalization and community adjustment of mentally retarded people.* Washington, DC: American Association on Mental Deficiency.

Sigelman, C. K., Winer, J. L., & Schoenrock, C. J. (1982). The responsiveness of mentally retarded persons to questions. *Education and Training of the Mentally Retarded, 17,* 120–124.

Sudman, S., & Bradburn, N. M. (1974). *Response effects in surveys: A review and synthesis.* Chicago: Aldine.

Sudman, S., & Bradburn, N. M. (1982). *Asking questions: A practical guide to questionnaire design.* San Francisco: Jossey-Bass.

Temple University Developmental Disabilities Center and University Affiliated Program (1988). *A national survey of consumers of services for individuals with developmental disabilities.* Philadelphia: Temple University.

Turner, C. F. (1984). Why do surveys disagree? Some preliminary hypotheses and some disagreeable examples. In C. F. Turner & E. Martin (Eds.), *Surveying subjective phenomena* (Vol. 2, pp. 159–214). New York: Russell Sage.

Wolfensberger, W., & Thomas, S. (1983). *PASSING (program analysis of service systems' implementation of normalization goals): Normalization criteria and ratings manual* (2nd Ed.). Toronto: National Institute on Mental Retardation.

Zingarelli, G., Cleveland, D., & Allen, W. (1987, May). *Indications of quality life after community placement of state developmental center residents.* Paper presented at Annual Conference of the American Association on Mental Deficiency, Los Angeles.

17
Quality of Life of Persons with Severe or Profound Mental Retardation

Sharon A. Borthwick-Duffy
University of California, Riverside

Until recently, quality of life was a term that was used frequently in reference to the life situations of persons with severe and profound levels of mental retardation, but it had neither been defined nor measured. Berkson and Landesman-Dwyer (1977) concluded from their review of the literature that the main impact of research on severe and profound mental retardation from 1955 to 1974 was the change in our perception of these people, from a very primitive and rather degrading view to one that acknowledges their cognitive and social potential. As a result of the change in emphasis from custodial care to habilitation, these individuals have become less isolated, more independent, and are more frequently included in programming and social activities that may well lead to an enhanced quality of life. Still, persons with profound mental retardation have been referred to as "the most misunderstood and under-researched human group" (Swartz, 1979, p. ix).

Differences in functional abilities between groups with severe and profound mental retardation have also been documented in the literature (O'Grady & Talkington, 1976), as well as differences within mental retardation levels (e.g., Cleland, Rago, & Mukherjee, 1978; Landesman-Dwyer & Sackett, 1978; Miller, 1976). However, although there is some validity to criticisms of researchers and professionals who lump severe and profound levels of mental retardation together (Cleland, 1979), the quality of life issues presented in this chapter should be relevant to persons found on the continuum from severe to profound retardation.

QUALITY OF LIFE MODELS AND DEVELOPMENTAL LEVELS

The origins of quality of life models are found in community psychology studies of the life quality of nonretarded adults (e.g., Flanagan, 1982;

Acknowledgments. Preparation of this manuscript was supported in part by Grants No. HD-21056 and HD-22953 from the National Institute of Child Health and Human Development.

McKennell & Andrews, 1983; Moos & Moos, 1983). Although operational definitions differ somewhat across models, the same four dimensions—residential environment, interpersonal relationships, activities/community involvement, and stability—seem adequate to describe the major aspects of a quality of life model, regardless of intelligence level (Borthwick-Duffy, 1989). Recently developed quality of life models for higher functioning mentally retarded adults (e.g., Schalock, 1986) closely resemble the community psychology models, although increased attention is given in the mental retardation constructs to the utilization of community resources and leisure activities. It may be because these activities do not occur as naturally among persons with mental retardation that this aspect of the normalization principle is of particular importance to professionals. The operational definitions of measured variables in studies of mild and moderately retarded groups can also be explained in terms of the above mentioned four dimensions.

As has been noted, the conceptual and measurement models that have emerged in the field of mental retardation in recent years reflect attempts to identify the salient dimensions of life quality, but have mostly focused on the lifestyles of moderately and mildly retarded adults who live with some independence in community settings (e.g., Cragg & Harrison, 1986; Donegan & Potts, 1988; Halpern, 1986; Keith, Schalock & Hoffman, 1986). In contrast, the study of quality of life issues as they relate to children and adults with severe and profound mental retardation has received less attention in the literature.

There may be questions as to why it is necessary to discuss quality of life separately for higher and lower functioning retarded groups of people. Clearly, we would wish for happiness, satisfaction, environmental comfort and harmony, and a general feeling of well-being for all people we care about, regardless of IQ or age. However, while it is reasonable to assume that the same general dimensions of life quality are meaningful for all levels of intelligence, the relevance of specific criteria used to define and measure those dimensions is likely to differ across disabilities and handicaps. Flanagan (1982) suggested that information should be obtained from persons with various types of disabilities in an effort to supplement his quality of life model and make it more sensitive to the lifestyles of persons whose disabilities limit their opportunities and experiences. It follows then, that within disability groups such as mental retardation, measurement of quality of life should also be modified by the degree of the disability.

To illustrate the point, consider the group of nonambulatory profoundly mentally retarded (NPMR) people described by Landesman-Dwyer and Sackett (1978) as incapable of moving about, even with assistance, lacking all adaptive behavior skills, and unresponsive to external stimulation. The NPMR individuals studied by these investigators spent nearly 21 hours per day in either sleep or low-level activity, falling asleep throughout the day and night. For detecting behavioral change, standardized developmental tests were determined to have little utility among this group of people whose average developmental level was similar to that of a nonretarded 21-month-old infant. An important finding of this study, though, was that an experimental condition that included upright positioning and provision of salient social and nonsocial stimuli did have considerable positive effects on the behavior and activity levels of these people. Moreover, it was concluded that changes in these important aspects of the individual's quality of life, including alertness, attentiveness, and response to stimuli, could be both monitored and measured.

Thus, quality of life should be evaluated differently for the group just described than, for example, mentally retarded people who are employed, live independently, and socialize at home and in the community with family and friends. For persons who have more severe levels of mental retardation, the measurement of quality of life, although spanning the same dimensions, may be very different than for nonretarded or mildly retarded groups. For example, a community involvement dimension could be judged by civic activities or athletic team participation for a nonretarded or mildly retarded person, while the same dimension might be measured by the frequency of visits to the shopping mall, park, or grocery store accompanied by a caregiver for a person who lacks the basic skills to function independently in these settings. Likewise, stability can be interpreted as length of time in a job, marriage, or educational program for a mildly retarded or nonretarded person. For people with severe or profound mental retardation, an important aspect of stability is the lack of frequent movement from placement to placement. These people have been described as being vulnerable to a "conditional belongingness" in their residential and educational settings (Evans, 1983; Keys, Boroskin & Ross, 1973; Willer & Intagliata, 1984).

The NPMR group represents an extreme level of disability. Most persons with severe and profound retardation have more abilities and fewer handicaps than the NPMRs. Nevertheless, it seems reasonable that life quality for people who are dependent on others for the majority of their daily needs should be considered apart from persons living more independently.

QUALITY OF LIFE VS. QUALITY OF CARE

Residential environments are frequently studied with regard to their influence on outcomes such as placement stability and changes in adaptive behavior (Eyman, Demaine, & Lei, 1979). However, the characteristics and quality of the care provided have also been acknowledged as reflecting quality of life (Hemming, Lavender, & Pill, 1981; Seltzer, Sherwood, Seltzer, & Sherwood, 1981), regardless of their effect on other outcomes.

The distinction between quality of care and quality of life is an important one and is discussed in more detail in other chapters. It is mentioned here because the role that quality of care plays in quality of life is of particular importance to persons who are severely or profoundly retarded and are dependent on families or caregivers for providing for their training and physical and emotional needs. For many persons with severe or profound mental retardation, the majority of their time is spent within the residential environment, no matter how dedicated the parent or caregiver is to community integration and normalization principles.

Rosen (1986) discussed quality of life in terms of Maslow's hierarchy of needs. This kind of conceptualization places quality of care (*e.g.*, providing for health, safety, and basic physical needs) at the bottom of a quality of life continuum, with the highest order needs being independence, freedom of choice, self-esteem, personality, and freedom from undue restraints. Rosen speculated that for some individuals with severe and profound cognitive handicaps, satisfaction of some higher order needs could place an individual at risk and jeopardize the fulfillment of lower level needs. This view suggests that for some individuals, quality of care and quality of life are inseparable. That is, for some the quality of care received as basic needs are met may define quality of life, while for others, quality of care provides only the foundation for what is interpreted as quality of life.

Quality of care is frequently associated with standards of care, and licensing and accreditation standards were developed to insure the best possible care. Riddle and Riddle (1982) argued, however, that the documentation associated with meeting standards and regulations has become a barrier to the happiness of persons who live in facilities that are overly concerned with certification. They further concluded that standards say little about happiness and that standards are being misinterpreted to the detriment of those they are intended to protect. They criticized standards that adhere so closely to normalization principles that they ignore the wishes of the person who is retarded, suggesting, for example, that disallowing an adult's choice of a Raggedy Ann doll because it is not age-appropriate is unfair to the individual and ignores his or her "joy quotient". Conroy and Bradley (1985) also concluded from their study of Pennhurst residents that accreditation standards were not related to developmental progress, although their findings must be interpreted within the design limitations of their study (Hemp & Braddock, 1988). Moreover, if quality of care is necessary but not sufficient for achieving other desired outcomes, then it might not be expected to produce changes in development.

On the other hand, because persons with severe and profound mental retardation are more likely than others to have secondary handicaps (e.g., vision, hearing, physical impairments), more health problems, and be at greater risk of an early death than persons with less severe degrees of retardation, the quality of health care provided, the attentiveness of direct care staff, and the cheerfulness of physical surroundings may each be critical to the quality of life of these people, and may reflect the very essence of it. Residential stability and opportunities to develop social relationships with peers have also been cited as important quality of life indicators that are related to quality of care. For some people these may even take priority over training programs and the goal of movement to less restrictive settings (Hemp & Braddock, 1988). In this regard, Seltzer et al. (1981) concluded that the extent to which normalization or other sociophysical aspects of a home enhance an individual's quality of life, regardless of their effect on other outcomes, environmental quality can be perceived of as a quality of life goal in itself. It might be fair to say, then, that although quality care cannot guarantee the highest quality of life, it could be considered at the very least as a necessary component for all individuals.

EDUCATIONAL ASPECTS OF QUALITY OF LIFE

The importance of involving mentally retarded people in community activities is well recognized and is reflected in the deinstitutionalization and normalization policies of recent years. There is still disagreement, however, over the appropriateness of various educational and employment programs for persons with mental retardation, and for those with severe and profound retardation in particular.

Public Law 94-142 guarantees an appropriate educational program for all persons ages 3 to 21, regardless of severity of handicap. For those with severe and profound mental retardation, though, the implementation of this mandate has not resulted in clearly agreed upon curricula or placement procedures. Some currently proposed policies that are intended to apply to all persons with mental retardation may be most relevant to higher functioning students, but are likely to have the greatest *impact* on severely handicapped students.

In principle, the placement of individuals with severe and profound levels of mental retardation in an integrated educational setting should enhance their quality of life. Students with the most severe handicaps have been traditionally placed in segregated school sites because it was believed that they would receive maximum benefit from specially trained teachers; modified physical environments including restrooms in classrooms, training kitchens, and vocational workshops; onsite therapists; and adaptive equipment for motor development. This method has been challenged in recent years by those who believe that the benefits of integration outweigh the advantages of specialized school sites.

Brown, Ford, Nisbet, Sweet, Donnellan, and Gruenewald (1983) presented some persuasive arguments for the educational placement of severely handicapped students in chronological age-appropriate regular schools that are closer to home, rather than in segregated schools. Decreased transportation time; closer proximity to special school activities; school peers, related services, and extracurricular activities; use of nonhandicapped volunteers to reduce "dead time" in class; increased variety of experiences and stimulation; more normal standards of behavior; and positive psychological and social working environments are among the proposed benefits of regular school placements for students who are currently segregated. Although the debate over whether or not students should be physically integrated is primarily a philosophical one that parallels earlier arguments for deinstitutionalization, it is still reasonable to question whether evaluation studies will bear out the promise of improved quality of life in integrated settings.

Reaching beyond the challenge to eliminate segregated school settings, the goal of the Regular Education Initiative (Reynolds, Wang, & Walberg, 1987; Will, 1986) is to establish an educational system that would place students with mild and moderate disabilities who are currently segregated in special education programs into regular education classes. Focusing on academic-related outcomes, this plan is intended to utilize the most effective teaching strategies from special and general education, thereby increasing regular education teachers' skills in dealing with students of different ability levels. The Association for Persons with Severe Handicaps has also adopted a resolution that calls for the education of students with severe and profound disabilities in regular education programs (Stainback, Stainback, & Bunch, 1989). Wang and Birch's (1988) Adaptive Learning Environments Model (ALEM) has been billed as a large-scale mainstreaming program that can accomplish the goals of the Regular Education Initiative and, although it is intended to be appropriate for persons of all levels of mental retardation, evaluations of the model have not focused on those in the severe and profound range. Even for the groups that have been studied, there is disagreement about the efficacy of the ALEM as it has been evaluated by its authors (Bryan & Bryan, 1988; Fuchs & Fuchs, 1988a, b).

Whereas the ALEM focuses on academic-related outcomes, the Integrated Critical Skills Model (ICSM) emphasizes teaching severely handicapped students in the context of functional life activities in naturalistic, real-life situations (Brown et al., 1983). Brown and his associates questioned the assumption that severely handicapped students are able to transfer skills learned in simulated settings in the classroom to natural environments and believed that curricula should not depend on the generalization of skills. The ICSM also focuses on skills that will be utilized in nonschool and postschool environments, preparing students to function as independently as possible outside the school setting.

The issues related to the selection of content and teaching method will not be easily resolved. With regard to the relationship between educational goals and an individual's quality of life, Sailor, Gee, Goetz, & Graham (1988) concluded that:

> Quantifying quality of life in a way that allows for measurement of outcomes of educational programs for persons with the most severe disabilities is one of the greatest challenges we face in the coming decade (p. 89).

Bricker and Filler (1985) concurred, noting that, because of the heterogeneity of this group, "precise statements about the content of an appropriate education are currently difficult to generate for the severely retarded population" (p. 6). It is clear that these issues regarding the educational aspects of quality of life have not yet been settled. For example, Clurman (1987) recently suggested a new perspective: that for some persons with severe and profound mental retardation, the benefit of education might not be to add to one's repertoire of abilities, but might only be the *maintenance* of status quo abilities and a stable quality of life.

EMPLOYMENT ASPECTS OF QUALITY OF LIFE

Brown et al. (1984) proposed an employment training model for persons with severe handicaps. Although there is support for the basic premise of the model, their suggestion that these people might volunteer or forego wages during extended training periods has been disputed (Bellamy et al., 1984). These authors argued that unpaid work unnecessarily sacrifices employment wages and benefits, promotes unequal treatment of persons with severe disabilities, and affects self-esteem and other quality of life indicators. They advocated a supported employment model that is designed to allow persons with severe handicaps to experience a combination of the benefits of normal job experience with support at the worksite. The outcome of this debate is another one that will have a particular impact on persons with severe and profound mental retardation, as these people are most likely to require extended training and are less likely to develop marketable skills.

LANGUAGE DELAYS AND QUALITY OF LIFE

Profound mental retardation is frequently characterized by the lack of intelligible speech; and, although persons with severe retardation manifest some meaningful speech, their ability to express themselves is also limited by low levels of cognitive development (Cleland, 1979). This lack of receptive and expressive language plays an important role in an individual's ability to make choices and to provide meaningful responses to inquiries about his or her life satisfaction.

Choices in Daily Living

If an individual cannot communicate his needs, desires, or preferences, this has serious implications with regard to his freedom of choice in matters of daily life. However, the evidence suggests that individuals lacking verbal or signing skills are nevertheless able to communicate many of their preferences. In a recent study of 48 people with severe or profound retardation living in a large public residential facility, direct care staff reported no differences in their ability to assess the preferences and needs of clients who had varying estimates of quality of life (Rocheleau, Spolar, & Yang, 1988). Cirrin and Rowland (1985) also found in a sample of persons with severe and profound levels of retardation that all subjects were capable of intentionally communicating through nonverbal means, and that great diversity existed in the types and frequency of communication styles used. Caregiving strategies such as paying careful attention, mechanisms such as computerized symbol boards, and directly teaching individuals to learn to use freedom of choice have been suggested to help create environments that foster communication and allow people more opportunities to gain control of their life situations and open doors to the outside world (Cirrin & Rowland, 1985; Kurzer, Mott, & Stamatelos, 1984; Riddle & Riddle, 1982). Further progress in this area would offer some promise to improving the quality of life of persons who lack traditional forms of communication.

Self-Report Measurement of Quality of Life

Obtaining the individual's own evaluation of his overall life circumstance is likely to be a greater challenge than determining his choices in daily living because it requires an ability to understand the questions asked, to realistically assess options, and to express feelings about his residence, relationships, integration, employment, and education. The work by Heal and Sigelman in this volume suggests a rather bleak picture: severely and profoundly retarded individuals may be unable to provide accurate judgments of their own life quality, and parents or other advocates may not be able to accurately represent their feelings for them. Nevertheless, we continue to be challenged to develop methods to help nonverbal persons to communicate and to utilize input from families and other advocates in the evaluation of the quality of life of these people (Heal & Chadsey-Rusch, 1985; Schalock & Heal, 1988).

MEASUREMENT OF QUALITY OF LIFE

In an attempt to quantify the abstract construct of life quality, measurement instruments have been developed that provide a quality of life "score" for persons with mental retardation. Two examples will be discussed in this section. The *Quality of Life Questionnaire* (Keith, Schalock, & Hoffman, 1986) elicits information about an individual's control over his environment and his satisfaction with various aspects of his life. Considerable attention has been given to establishing the psychometric properties of this instrument and it has been used to evaluate the match between an individual and his environment (Schalock & Jensen, 1986). The directions state that if a person is verbal, he/she should answer the questions honestly, and if the person is nonverbal, two staff persons should independently evaluate the individual and then average their scores. Thus an attempt is made to modify procedures to obtain information on nonverbal individuals. However, even though many of the questions can be answered by others for persons with severe retardation, a significant portion of the instrument emphasizes criteria that are most relevant for adults who are involved in some kind of employment, who are likely to invite friends over, plan meals, shop, select their own doctor, and so forth. Hence, even when responses are obtained, there is likely to be little variability among the scores of persons of varying ages who are either severely or profoundly mentally retarded and are uninvolved in any of these activities. Conversely, the level or types of activity that may be more appropriate for this group are absent from the survey. Rather than reflecting poorly on the instrument, this simply illustrates the necessity of operationalizing quality of life differently for persons with more severe handicaps.

The *Quality of Life Index* (Bonanno, Gibbs, & Twardzicki, 1982) is a survey that was designed to measure the ambience, friendship, and happiness of people with mental retardation, with the overall purpose of improving quality of life in day programs and residential centers. This instrument has been demonstrated to be useful for persons with severe and profound retardation (Rocheleau et al., 1988) and seems to be valid and reliable. It can also be utilized with higher functioning groups, although some of the important indicators for persons living more independently are not covered by this survey. Moreover, it does not elicit information from individuals who would be able to provide useful, meaningful responses about their own circumstances.

Scores on the *Quality of Life Index* are based on information obtained from residential service providers, day program leaders, observation of the individual and his environments, and written documentation in client files on service plans, progress notes, medical records, and social activities. Thus, although the individual is not a direct respondent to any of the questions on the survey, an effort is made to obtain information from a variety of sources.

The authors of the two instruments just described have made an attempt to quantify quality of life based on theoretical dimensions of life quality. The differences in the measures illustrate the range of operational definitions of quality of life that may be applied to persons at different levels of functioning. The kind of data provided by measures like these can be very useful, particularly in the evaluation of intraindividual changes over time. However, as the *Index* manual emphasizes, a survey of this type is only one kind of measurement and should always be used in conjunction with other information about the individual.

CONCLUSIONS

It has been the intent of this chapter to highlight some of the quality of life issues that may be unique to persons with severe and profound mental retardation. In some areas, the issue is the *impact* that general policies for persons with mental retardation are likely to have on this group of severely handicapped individuals. People with severe and profound mental retardation are unique in their limited expressive and receptive language abilities. They are more likely to have secondary handicapping conditions and health problems. Their levels of cognitive functioning may limit their opportunities to interact in the community and will certainly affect the degree of independence with which they can perform different activities. While this by no means suggests that their quality of life must be lower than those with fewer handicaps, it should mean that our evaluation, whether it be in the form of a score or a general impression, should take this into account before broad generalizations about what is good for all persons with mental retardation are made.

As we attempt to determine what will bring about the greatest improvement in quality of life for people who are limited in their ability to make choices regarding the direction of their own lives, we must continue to improve our ability to perceive their needs and to evaluate their overall happiness and life conditions. Certainly the evaluation and measurement of life quality must follow a clear delineation of the important dimensions of quality of life, keeping in mind that, regardless of intelligence level, individuals will differ in their preferences and their own perceptions of what constitutes a good quality of life.

REFERENCES

Bellamy, G. T., Rhodes, L. E., Wilcox, B., Albin, J. M., Mank, D. M., Boles, S. M., Horner, R. H., Collins, M., & Turner, J. (1984). Quality and equality in employment services for adults with severe disabilities. *Journal of the Association for Persons with Severe Handicaps, 9,* 270–277.

Berkson, G., & Landesman-Dwyer, S. (1977). Behavioral research on severe and profound mental retardation (1955–1974). *American Journal of Mental Deficiency, 81,* 428–454.

Bonanno, R., Gibbs, E. F., & Twardzicki, N. (1982). *The Quality of Life Index.* Boston: Wrentham State School, Children's Hospital.

Borthwick-Duffy, S. A. (1989). Quality of life: The residential environment. In W. E. Kiernan & R. L. Schalock (Eds.), *Economics, industry, and disability* (pp. 351–363). Baltimore: Paul H. Brooks.

Bricker, D., & Filler, J. (1985). The severely mentally retarded individual: Philosophical and Implementation dilemmas. In D. Bricker & J. Filler (Eds.), *Severe mental retardation: From theory to practice* (pp. 2–10). Lancaster, PA: Lancaster Press.

Brown, L., Ford, A., Nisbet, J., Sweet, M., Donnellan, A., & Gruenewald, L. (1983). Opportunities available when severely handicapped students attend chronological age appropriate regular schools. *Journal of the Association for Persons with Severe Handicaps, 8,* 16–23.

Brown, L., Shiraga, B., York, J., Kessler, K., Strohm, B., Rogan, P., Sweet, M., Zanella, K., VanDeventer, P., & Loomis, R. (1984). Integrated work opportunities for adults with severe handicaps: The extended training option. *Journal of the Association for Persons with Severe Handicaps, 9,* 262–269.

Bryan, J. H., & Bryan, T. H. (1988). *Where's the beef?* Paper presented at the annual conference of the Council for Exceptional Children. Washington, DC, March.

Cirrin, F. M., & Rowland, C. M. (1985). Communicative assessment of nonverbal youths with severe/profound mental retardation. *Mental Retardation, 23,* 52–62.

Cleland, C. C. (1979). *The profoundly mentally retarded.* Englewood Cliffs, NJ: Prentice-Hall.

Cleland, C. C., Rago, W. ., & Mukherjee, A. (1978). Tool use in profoundly retarded humans: A method of subgrouping. *Bulleting of the Psychonomic Society, 12,* 86–88.

Clurman, B. (1987). Fighting for education rights: Severely disabled children can benefit from education. *The Exceptional Parent, 17*(4), 48–56.

Conroy, J. W., & Bradley, V. J. (1985, March). *The five-year longitudinal study of the court-ordered deinstitutionalization of Pennhurst: A report of five years of research and analysis.* Philadelphia: Temple University.

Cragg, R., & Harrison, J. (1986). *A questionnaire of quality of life* (pilot version). West Midlands Campaign for People with a Mental Handicap, Wolverley, Kidderminster, Worcs., England.

Donegan, C., & Potts, M. (1988). People with mental handicap living alone in the community: A pilot study of their quality of life. *The British Journal of Mental Subnormality, 34*(1), 10–22.

Evans, D. P. (1983). *The lives of mentally retarded people.* Boulder, CO: Westview Press.

Eyman, R. L., Demaine, G. C., & Lei, T. (1979). Relationship between community environments and resident changes in adaptive behavior: A path model. *American Journal of Mental Deficiency, 83,* 330–338.

Flanagan, J. C. (1982). Measurement of quality of life: Current state of the art. *Archives of Physical and Medical Rehabilitation, 63,* 56–59.

Fuchs, D., & Fuchs, L. S. (1988a). Evaluation of the Adaptive Learning Environments Model. *Exceptional Children, 55,* 115–122.

Fuchs, D., & Fuchs, L. S. (1988b). Response to Wang and Walberg. *Exceptional Children, 55,* 138–146.

Halpern, A. (1986, May). *The dimensions of community adjustment.* Paper presented at the Annual Meeting of the American Association on Mental Deficiency, Denver, CO.

Heal, L. W., & Chadsey-Rusch, J. (1985). The lifestyle satisfaction scale (LSS): Assessing individual's satisfaction with residence, community setting, and associated services. *Applied Research in Mental Retardation, 6,* 475–490.

Hemming, H., Lavender, T., & Pill, R. (1981). Quality of life of mentally retarded adults transferred from large institutions to new small units. *American Journal of Mental Deficiency*, 86, 157–169.

Hemp, R., & Braddock, D. (1988). Accreditation of developmental disabilities programs. *Mental Retardation*, 26, 257–267.

Keith, K. D., Schalock, R. L., & Hoffman, K. (1986). *Quality of Life: Measurement and programmatic implications*. Lincoln, NE: Region V Mental Retardation Services.

Keys, V., Boroskin, A., & Ross, R. (1973). The revolving door in an MR hospital: A study of returns from leave. *Mental Retardation*, 11, 55–56.

Kurzer, J., Mott, D. W., & Stamatelos, T. (1984, May). Quality of life: Reemerging processes in the field of mental retardation. Paper presented at the annual meeting of the American Association on Mental Deficiency, Minneapolis, MN.

Landesman-Dwyer, S., & Sackett, G. P. (1978). Behavioral changes in nonambulatory, profoundly retarded individuals. In C. E. Meyers (Ed.), *Quality of life in severely and profoundly mentally retarded people: Research foundations for improvement* (pp. 55–144). Washington, DC: American Association on Mental Deficiency.

McKennell, A. C., & Andrews, F. M. (1983). Components of perceived life quality. *Journal of Community Psychology*, 11, 98–110.

Miller, C. (1976). Subtypes of the PMR: Implications for placement and progress. In C. C. Cleland, J. D. Swartz, & L. W. Talkington (Eds.), *The profoundly mentally retarded: Second annual conference proceedings* (pp. 57–61). Austin, TX: Western Research Conference and the Hogg Foundation.

Moos, R. H., & Moos, B. S. (1983). Adaptation and the quality of life in work and family settings. *Journal of Community Psychology*, 11, 158–170.

O'Grady, R. S., & Talkington, L. W. (1976). Selected behavioral concomitants of profound retardation. In C. C. Cleland, J. D. Swartz, & L. W. Talkington (Eds.), *The profoundly mentally retarded: Second annual conference proceedings* (pp. 70–85). Austin, TX: Western Research Conference and the Hogg Foundation.

Reynolds, M. C., Wang, M. C., & Walberg, H. J. (1987). The necessary restructuring of special and regular education. *Exceptional Children*, 53, 391–398.

Riddle, J. I., & Riddle, H. C. (1982). The "joy quotient": Observations on our need to prioritize pleasure in the lives of the severely handicapped. *An occasional paper of the National Association of Superintendents of Public Institutions for the Mentally Retarded*, #20, January, 1983.

Rocheleau, A., Spolar, P., & Yang, J. (1988). Quality of life measurement for institutionalized retarded individuals. In A. B. Silverstein (Ed.), *Pacific State Archives: Volume 13*, (pp. 95–103). Pomona, CA: UCLA Developmental Disabilities Immersion Program.

Rosen, M. (1986). Quality of life for persons with mental retardation: A question of entitlement. *Mental Retardation*, 24, 365–366.

Sailor, W., Gee, K., Goetz, L., & Graham, N. (1988). Progress in educating students with the most severe disabilities: Is there any? *Journal of the Association for Persons with Severe Handicaps*, 13, 87–99.

Schalock, R. L. (1986, May). *Current approaches to quality of life assessment*. Paper presented at the Annual Meeting of the American Association on Mental Deficiency, Denver, CO.

Schalock, R. L., & Heal, L. W. (1988). *Research in quality of life: Current status and policy recommendations*. Unpublished manuscript prepared for the Administration on Developmental Disabilities.

Schalock, R. L., & Jensen, C. M. (1986). Assessing the goodness-of-fit between persons and their environments. *Journal of the Association for Persons with Severe Handicaps*, 11, 103–109.

Seltzer, M. M., Sherwood, C. C., Seltzer, G. B., & Sherwood, S. (1981). Community adaptation and the impact of deinstitutionalization. In R. H. Bruininks, C. E. Meyers, B. B. Sigford, & K. C. Lakin (Eds.). *Deinstitutionalization and community adjustment of mentally retarded people* (pp. 82–88). Washington, DC: American Association on Mental Deficiency.

Stainback, W., Stainback, S. & Bunch, G. (1989). Introduction and historical background. In W. Stainback, S. Stainback, & M. Forest (Eds.), *Educating all students in the mainstream of regular education* (pp. 3–14). Baltimore: Paul H. Brookes.

Swartz, J. D. (1979). Foreword. In C. C. Cleland, *The profoundly mentally retarded*. Englewood Cliffs, NJ: Prentice-Hall.

Wang, M. C., & Birch, J. W. (1988). Effective special education in regular classes. *Exceptional Children, 50,* 391–398.

Will, M. (1986). *Educating students with learning problems: A shared responsibility.* Washington, DC: U.S. Department of Education, Office of Special Education and Rehabilitation Services.

Willer, B., & Intagliata, J. (1984). *Promises and realities for mentally retarded persons: Life in the community.* Baltimore: University Park Press.

PART IV
The Future of Quality of Life as a Concept and a Principle

The future of the Quality of Life movement raises a number of issues that are discussed in this final section. Rud Turnbull begins the section with a scholarly chapter addressing the issue of quality of life and public philosophy that should guide all citizens in their public and private conduct. Throughout the chapter, he sets out a political/philosophical conception of quality of life concluding with the notion that

> For all of us, as well as for the public philosophers, there is an underlying measure of quality of life. It is the measure that ascribes quality of life according to the extent to which people choose to be with each other, the ways in which they give form to their choices to be with each other, and the nature, extent, and duration of their relationships. Quality of life is indeed measured by relationships. (p. 207)

A unique but very significant perspective on quality of life is presented by Ruth Luckasson, who shares some of her concerns about the use of the quality of life concept from the perspective of a lawyer and a mental retardation professional. Despite the virtuousness and soothing seductiveness of the phrase *quality of life*, Dr. Luckasson asks us to consider carefully the use of the phrase as a global evaluation of the lives of persons with disabilities.

As mentioned frequently throughout this volume, the quality of life of persons with disabilities is influenced greatly by the quality of services they receive. It is to the issue of assessing and ensuring the quality of services to people with disabilities that Valerie Bradley directs our attention in Chapter 20. After critiquing current quality assurance systems, Ms. Bradley summarizes emerging quality assurance trends and outlines a number of recommendations about the design of quality assurance systems that reflect the quality of life experienced by service recipients.

This focus on quality services and their outcomes is continued in the chapter by Jim Conroy and Celia Feinstein. In their chapter, the authors suggest that in the future, we should not rely solely on standards of licensing—we must also concern ourselves with outcomes. The authors then discuss the important point that quality of life is not only a process, but also a desired and measurable outcome from habilitation services.

The final chapter by Bob Schalock suggests that an enhanced quality of life for persons with disabilities cannot be separated from the three major trends currently impacting our service delivery system: the natural environment, empowerment, and accountability. He goes on to discuss that if these trends are going to significantly enhance a person's quality of life, we must collectively pursue principles that will foster policy development, parameters that will guide research efforts, and procedures that will underlie service delivery.

18
Quality of Life and Public Philosophy

H. Rutherford Turnbull III and Gary L. Brunk
The University of Kansas

There are several ways of measuring or conceptualizing the quality of life of people with disabilities and their families. We will identify and briefly discuss seven of them, limiting the discussion to a simple statement of the nature of the measure; an overview is presented because other chapters in this book have reviewed each of them in detail. We then will offer a different perspective on quality of life than will be found elsewhere in this volume. We will argue that most current measures of quality of life, although necessary, are not sufficient unless they are linked to measures of quality of life for all of the nation's citizenry. In a sense, we advocate for the mainstreaming of measures of quality of life of people with disability into at least one of the major measures of quality of life for people who do not have disabilities. In making this argument, we wish to address the matter of the public philosophy that does or should guide all citizens, disabled or not, in their public and private conduct. In setting out a political/ philosophical measure of quality of life, we hope to add a new dimension to the measurement and discussion of quality of life.

A few introductory words are in order. First, we assume that readers will already be familiar with much of the literature on quality of life (QOL) and that, if they are not, this book itself will furnish such sufficient references that we may forego the abundance of citations that usually accompanies chapters in AAMR monographs and much of my other work.

Second, we owe Bob Williams a debt for pointing out a very important caveat. He has written (1989, personal correspondence) that, to him, the term *quality of life* has a "very hollow and antiseptic ring to it." He finds it "at one and the same time not very descriptive and extremely limiting. Perhaps, this is because Duff and Campbell (1973; 1976) have been so successful in defining QOL as a fixed, predetermined 'figure' which is inherently less than the true sum of all its parts." Williams added that, instead of referring to an individual's "QOL Quotient," it is more helpful to discuss the opportunities that someone with or without severe disabilities can have to "develop positive experiences, positive associations/relationships, and thus, a positive present and future outlook on life." These observations are important, coming as they do not just from a person with

**Table 18.1   Different Ways to Measure or Conceptualize the
Quality of Life of People with Disabilities and Their Families**

Quality of Life As:
1. Measured by science
2. Measured by rights
3. Direct democracy and citizen participation
4. Mutual accommodation
5. Value-driven policy
6. Determined by evaluation and accountability
7. Decisions on public philosophy and public policy

a severe disability, but from one whose very presence in our community is relevant to my argument in this chapter.

Finally, Bud Fredericks, the father of a young man with mental retardation, has commented that we should emphasize that quality of life depends in large part on the individual's ability to exercise "real choices within the capabilities of the individual and not the capabilities of the system" created to provide services (1989, personal correspondence). We certainly agree, as evidenced by Turnbull's concern with consent, choice, and decisionmaking for people with mental retardation (Hazel, Deshler, & Turnbull, 1987; Turnbull, A. P., & Turnbull, 1985, 1988; Turnbull, H. R., 1978, 1986; Turnbull, Knowlton, Backus, & Turnbull, 1988; Turnbull, H. R., & Turnbull, 1985). Nonetheless, we have chosen not to focus exclusively on choice as a component of quality of life, although we believe it is, but on a more general discussion of the seven ways summarized in Table 18.1 of measuring or conceptualizing the quality of life of people with disabilities and their families.

QUALITY OF LIFE AS MEASURED BY SCIENCE

Efforts to decide whether or not to provide medical treatment to newborns with birth defects have resulted in a formulation of quality of life for the newborn. This formulation asserts that quality of life is the function of the child's natural endowment multiplied by the sum of the contributions to the child that can be expected from the home or family and society. The normal expression of this approach is $QOL = NE \times (H + S)$ (Duff & Campbell, 1973, 1976).

This approach is the paradigm of the scientification of social and moral decisionmaking involving people with disabilities and their families. As in other attempts to use science to explain and justify behaviors that are or should be regarded as essentially moral and policy/political decisions

(Gliedman & Roth, 1980; Morse, 1978; Szasz, 1963, 1973; Turnbull & Wheat, 1983), and as in AAMR's own scientification of moral and policy issues as reflected in its standard texts on classification (Grossman, 1983), the scientific paradigm assumes that it is correct as a matter of both professional practice and the expression of moral philosophy to apply scientific models to a treatment or intervention decision. In connection with the treatment of newborns, this paradigm either intends or has been used to validate treatment decisions and thus to legitimatize decisions about the value of the child's life and the impact of that life on the child, the family, and society.

In many respects, the scientification of the medical treatment decision is not unlike the scientification of other intervention decisions, such as whether to use nonaversive or aversive behavioral interventions or to place students with disabilities in mainstream or least restrictive/most normal appropriate settings (Guess, Helmstetter, Turnbull, & Knowlton, 1986; Turnbull, 1986). In almost every debate about the proper way to intervene in the lives of people with mental retardation, the desired policy outcome— that is to say, the desired moral outcome—is defended on the ground of science.

There has been sufficient reaction against the scientification of quality of life indicators, including by AAMR's governing board's resolutions about rights to medical treatment and aversives, to somewhat discredit the scientification-alone approach. Thus, many people, ourselves included, who work in the field of mental retardation, including the unacknowledged workers and consumers who are typically called "family," argue that the prediction that is required by a QOL formula is difficult if not impossible to make. We also assert that in any event the moral decision, which is essentially whether the child's life has inherent value, should not be regulated to a mathematical approach. Likewise, many (ourselves included) also acknowledge that there is almost always an ethical or moral dimension to any decision that is grounded in science or in other interventions (Turnbull, 1988a).

Although we who see the (at least) bifurcated nature of intervention or other decisions do not eschew the value of science as a normally wholesome and almost always necessary component of quality of life, we are firm in rejecting the mathematical scientification of quality of life as the only measure. We take the position, as we hope most sophisticated students of mental retardation do, that there is a very real need for science. After all, science has several values. At the very least, it helps identify and thus predict the nature and extent of the person's disability and, inferentially, a possible impact of that disability on the person, family, professionals, and society. That is an important role.

But science alone, no matter how reliable its predictive powers about the nature and extent of disability and its inferential predictive powers about impact, cannot be relied on as a dominant measure of quality of life. Science is but one measure, and it must be taken into account, but only in connection with other measures.

QUALITY OF LIFE AS MEASURED BY RIGHTS

Some (including ourselves) measure and seek to improve quality of life by asserting that people with disabilities and their families have inherent minimum rights. In turn, we tend to measure the achievement of quality of life by the degree to which rights are either enacted or enforced.

In the case of the newborn with disabilities, for example, we assert the "sanctity of life" as a defense against the scientification, mathematical quality-of-life measure. Likewise, as an extension of the sanctity argument, we assert that there are certain enforceable claims to minimum rights (Rawls, 1971), that these claims are enforceable as a matter of constitutional law (Michelman, 1969), and that the inherent rights of the person with a disability create a duty on society to provide the means to obtain and enjoy those rights.

Thus, assertions that quality of life will be improved by the rights (e.g., to early education and intervention, subsequent appropriate education, treatment and habilitation, least drastic/restrictive environments and interventions, home-based or community-based services, supported work, and a minimum level of publicly provided financial support) are reflected in and have resulted in the creation of a plethora of laws creating entitlements to publicly funded services for people with disabilities and their families. These entitlements fundamentally reflect the belief that quality of life for the person and the person's family is ensured and can be improved when there are enforceable and funded rights to certain types of services. Moreover, these entitlements also mirror the fact that policymakers and advocates agree that there has been and probably always will be a failure of society, as it is presently constructed and operating, to respond to the quality of life claims of people with disabilities and their families unless there are certain *rights*. This predictable failure, which history abundantly documents, justifies the creation and enforcement of rights, which in turn become benchmarks of quality of life.

In short, the legal rights approach measures quality of life according to the absence or presence of enforceable and funded entitlements. It appeals basically to activist governmental intervention, not to "disinterested" mathematical scientification of measures of quality of life.

QUALITY OF LIFE AS DIRECT DEMOCRACY AND
CITIZEN PARTICIPATION

There is a great deal of discussion these days about "empowering" people with disabilities and their families. Such discussion seems to take the position that power, exercised with permission from society and policymakers by professionals or parents, has resulted in a diminished quality of life for people with disabilities and more often than not their families. It should come as no surprise, therefore, that the right to certain evaluations and procedural safeguards in education—voluntary admission to public or private residential facilities or other programs, involuntary commitment, treatment within settings and programs, proceedings to adjudicate a person to be incompetent, and medical treatment decisionmaking—is an often asserted right and a frequently provided one (Turnbull, 1990).

This right, it seems to us, underlies and reflects a belief that quality of life is enhanced when decisionmaking powers are shared—that is, when consumers (whether the people themselves, as in the self-advocacy conceptualization, or their families, as in the right-to-education formulation) and professionals participate jointly in evaluation, program development, implementation, and evaluation. As many of us recognize, however, shared decisionmaking is just one aspect of quality of life; what really counts is not the process of decisionmaking, however important that component is, but equal access to the same opportunities, including opportunities for the exercise of choice as enjoyed by people who do not have disabilities. As Fredericks (1989, personal correspondence) noted, "without access, opportunities and choices are not the same." Under the direct democracy approach, the measure of quality of life is *citizen participation*, also called *self-determination, shared decisionmaking*, and *rebalancing power relationships*. This approach to quality of life is related to the concept of *personal autonomy*, a value considered not only in public policy but also in psychology.

Quality of life, then, is a matter of fate control. Our political traditions of local government, the demands of the 1960s for local control/community control of public education and for maximum citizen participation in policy decisions, the Vietnam war demonstrations, Ralph Naderism/consumer protection, and even the biennial elections are the expressions of the view that the quality of life depends on and therefore should be measured by the degree to which an individual participates in decisions that directly or even indirectly affect that person's life.

In one respect, this measure of quality of life is paradoxical. One would think that the recapturing of autonomy in public and private lives would reject a role for government, because the deprivation of consumer participation has been attributed to huge and impersonal government. Yet, those of us who measure quality of life as autonomy and seek to give it expression under the rubric of consumer participation in decisionmaking processes seek to ensure it by creating a right to the opportunity for participation in education and other program decisions, interventions, and evaluations. Thus, those of us who seek to enhance the quality of life by increasing opportunities for participatory decisionmaking do so by turning to government, not by eschewing it. In so doing, we fundamentally affirm that quality of life is measured by the degree to which consumer participation is available, and we equally assert that there is or ought to be a right, guaranteed by public law and enforceable against the state's educators and other agents, to a certain quality of life, namely, that quality of life that can or will result when people who are directly affected by a decision have a right and exercise that right to participate in the decision affecting them. Shared decisionmaking is a deeply cherished value in America, and, it seems, one whose presence or absence is itself a measure of the quality of life.

QUALITY OF LIFE AS MUTUAL ACCOMMODATION

Another measure of the quality of life looks to the relationships between people with disabilities or their families and the society in which they live. It recognizes that all people and their families are members of communities and that their quality of life is a function of the ability not only to be present in their communities but also to participate in those communities. There is a difference between being "in" and being "of" a community (Turnbull & Turnbull, 1988). To accomplish not just desegregation and integration "in" but also participation "of," it is necessary for the person with a disability, that person's family, and society all to make mutual adjustments.

Thus, professionals and families make extensive efforts to enhance the capacities of people with disabilities. These attempts to secure a greater degree of human development are directed in large part toward the accommodation of the person and family to the existing society and its communities. In seeking to augment the inherent capacities of a person with a disability or the person's family through education, vocational rehabilitation, and other interventions, professionals and families address the person's capacities to function in society; the provision of free appropriate education, vocational rehabilitation services, and rights to other interventions or programs seek to change the person by ameliorating the effects of the person's disabilities on the person. These attempts are but one component of mutual accommodation. They focus on the individual or family.

There is, of course, another component. It is not directed, however, at improving the capacities of the person or the family. Instead, it is directed at creating rights against discrimination and toward accommodations by society to the person. These rights are claims that the person has against society. Stated in the alternative, they are duties that society has to the person. And, of course, they are devices that the person and others similarly situated may use to change the nature of society and the community. The duties of nondiscrimination impose on society and the community the obligation to change themselves. When the society and communities change, the opportunities for and likelihood of accommodation increase.

By two routes, then, the quality of life of the person and the family are augmented: first, by accommodating the person to society and the community, and second, by accommodating society and the community to the person. This approach to quality of life relies on science (the sciences of special education, vocational rehabilitation, rehabilitation engineering, etc.) and the creation of mutual rights and duties. It also acknowledges that participation in decisionmaking is a way of achieving mutual accommodations. Because it is related to these other measures of quality of life, it makes clear a significant point about quality of life—namely, that no single measure suffices.

QUALITY OF LIFE AS VALUE-DRIVEN POLICY

Still another measure of quality of life exists and it, too, is related to the other measures. Quality of life is determined by the congruences of public values and behavior. We therefore assert that measures of quality of life should be explicitly tied to values.

For example, today it is common to hear heated debates about deinstitutionalization, anti-institutionalization, defacilitation (movement away from workshops and large congregate living in the community), community-based education, community-referenced curricula, home- and community-based living, permanency planning and adoption, family support, supported employment, and nonaversive interventions. Although almost always couched in the language of *appropriate interventions, appropriate settings*, or *rights*, these concepts are fundamentally value based, where the values are equal treatment and equal opportunity. The common theme is that people with disabilities should not be treated differently than people who do not have disabilities; or, if they are treated differently, such treatment accomplishes the purpose of equal opportunities.

Thus, one can measure quality of life according to the degree that equal opportunities or equal treatment (that is, equal moral and ethical standing by people with disabilities) are reflected in and advanced or hindered by policies, professional practice, and family behaviors.

QUALITY OF LIFE AS DETERMINED BY EVALUATION
AND ACCOUNTABILITY

It is by now settled that almost all interventions with people with disabilities and their families should be evaluated. Typically, evaluation consists of input or outcome measures or both; and, typically, evaluation is either quantitative or qualitative in nature. More often than not, the argument for evaluation is predicated on the desire for accountability: the public's funds should not be spent without an assurance that the expenditures result in the outcomes desired by the policies underlying the funded programs.

Yet there seems to be more to the argument than meets the eye. Surely, there is a legitimate need to ensure that the funded services result in the desired outcomes. Accountability to the taxpayer (who is, after all, the overlooked consumer) demands no less. Moreover, the person who directly receives the services (nowadays called the *direct consumer* or *end user*), whether that person be the one who has a disability or that person's family member, and the professionals who provide the services (another overlooked consumer) are, themselves, said to be entitled to assurances that the means (the services) were consistent with the ends (the policies). The implicit understanding, and sometimes the explicit premise, in all evaluation is that the quality of any intervention, and thus the quality of life of the person(s) at whom the intervention is targeted, can and should be measured.

Those of us who demand evaluation as a way of ensuring accountability in the provision of services are making arguments related to quality of life. Quality of life, then, is determined by evaluation. Accreditation standards and procedures, for example, are attempts to ensure a certain quality of life; so, too, are standards and procedures for the provision of an appropriate education or vocational rehabilitation program. Measures of consumer satisfaction, or value-driven evaluation procedures such as Wolfensberger's PASS, likewise assert that the quality of life is a correlate of and can be determined by evaluation procedures. Quality of life is a matter that can be ensured when procedures and standards of evaluation reveal that services and interventions suit their purposes; likewise, quality of life consists of the setting of procedures and standards for services, and, after or as services are rendered, their evaluation.

QUALITY OF LIFE AS DECISIONS ON PUBLIC
PHILOSOPHY AND PUBLIC POLICY

Concerns about quality of life for people with disabilities and their families do not exist in a self-contained capsule, unassociated with general concerns about the quality of life of the citizenry as a whole. There are inevitable and wholesome connections between the debates about quality of life of people who have no disabilities and debates about the quality of life of those who have disabilities. These connections are not always apparent, but they nonetheless exist. Every one of us faces quality of life issues.

Currently in the disability field one hears a great deal of talk about informal supports or informal support systems. Researchers and service providers have begun to focus on the ways in which people with disabilities and their families create and use friendships as means for obtaining services or other necessary or desirable components of life. Wolfensberger's (Wolfensberger & Zauha, 1973) call for citizen advocacy, Edgerton's research (Edgerton, 1967; Edgerton & Bercovici, 1976; Edgerton, Bollinger, & Herr, 1984) on benefactors of people in communities, Turnbull and Turnbull's (1985) anthology of parents who speak out about life with a person with a disability, Kaufman's (1988) accounts of her daughter's transition from school to adulthood, Schwartz's creative leadership of the Pennsylvania Developmental Disabilities Planning Council and its use of discretionary funds, O'Brien's leadership in the renewal of the goals of community-based providers, the creation and sustaining of intentional communities such as L'Arche and Camphill, and the general call for the creation of systems of informal support—all of these point to the use of informal supports as essential to the quality of life of people with disabilities and their families.

Similarly, state legislatures have begun to create family support programs; currently, 28 states have such programs. But, as Braddock (1989, personal communication) has observed, only three or four (notably, Michigan) provide unrestricted direct cash assistance to families under the rubric of family support. Braddock added, and we concur, "We need to build greater public support for unrestricted cash assistance payments to families (i.e., to nurture informal supports as well), but few states have been willing to conceive and implement such programs." Perhaps the following observations will provide some theoretical justifications for more tolerant use of the public fiscal via unrestricted grants so that people with disabilities and their families will have the wherewithal to pay for the informal support— to afford "community"—that their quality of life so needs and deserves.

At the same time that the field of developmental disabilities began to recognize that informal and formal supports are essential for quality of life, critics (Bellah, 1982; Berger & Neuhaus, 1976; McIntyre, 1984; Rawls, 1971; Sullivan, 1982) of public policies related to nondisability issues were acknowledging that there are fundamental problems in the nature of public philosophy and the relationships of government to individuals. These problems bear heavily on the quality of life of the citizenry at large. They therefore affect people with disabilities and their families. For that reason alone, they warrant examination.

But because they also relate, albeit somewhat opaquely, to the issue of informal support, they are more than tangential to the issue of quality of life. Just as the field of developmental disabilities is examining the nature of informal support as an ingredient of quality of life, so too are various experts in public philosophy asking all of us to examine the ideas that drive public policy and its impact on our private lives.

Indeed, our major message in this chapter is this: the "right" and "left" or "conservative" and "liberal" critiques of America in the late 20th century are more than criticisms of the way in which we all live; they are, in unhappily large part, comments on the deterioration of the quality of life that all of us (disabled and not) experience or will experience. The political philosopher Sullivan (1982) is explicit about that fact:

> . . . A public philosophy develops out of the insight that the quality of personal life is grounded in social relationships, an insight that is embodied in the political art of integrating the various kinds of self-concern into an awareness of mutual interdependency (p. 208).

It was Hobbes who, many years earlier, observed that we are social beings not by choice but by necessity. That is, in order for each person to prosper emotionally, physically, spiritually, and materially, each needs the other—we need to be in relationship to each other. Among other things, this means that in order to have liberty in our individual lives we must restrain some of our own liberties and those of others. The human condition of liberty requires the human ability to be less than full free. Accordingly, the public philosophers' critiques are fundamentally relevant to the lives of people with disabilities, their families, professionals, service providers, and policymakers; and they provide one of the most useful comments on the issue of quality of life of people with disabilities and their families. Indeed, we are willing to go so far as to say that we probably can learn as much about issues of quality of life of people with disabilities and their families by attending to the new criticisms of America as a whole as we can by continuing to focus only on disability-specific QOL concerns.

There are two major public philosophies in America. One is *philosophic liberalism*; the other is *civic republicanism*. They are not mutually exclusive, although they are in their cores contradictory. Indeed, Americans have practiced them simultaneously, although we have shifted our loyalties between them from time to time and have witnessed heated debate over their merits and the application of their principles to our private and public lives. These ideas rely on different perceptions of the nature of the individual and the role of others and the body politic in regard to the individual. We will briefly describe each of these two philosophies and attempt to show their relationships to the quality of life issue, especially in its concern with informal supports.

Philosophic Liberalism

The tenets of philosophic liberalism are expressed commonly in such familiar terms as rugged individualism, laissez-faire capitalism, centralized economic planning, self-determination, or individual autonomy. Its central focus is the liberty of the individual to pursue economic advantage; it is characterized by self-interest and private advantage, often at the expense of the public welfare.

Although philosophic liberalism did not forswear a role for the central government, that role was to be distinctly limited. The role was to create economic conditions and a governmental role in which the pursuit of private advantage was encouraged and therefore protected. In part, this was to be accomplished by centralized administration of certain components of the national economy. The purpose of centralization was to ensure the soundness of the currency, the protection of the sources and means of capital production, and the regulation, albeit mostly by relatively light-handed means, of the conflicts between economic forces.

In his treatise *Reconstructing Public Philosophy*, Sullivan (1982) made the following observation:

> Philosophic liberalism, the set of beliefs common to the Liberal and Conservative tendencies of post-New Deal American politics, is deeply anti-public in its fundamental premises. Conceiving of human beings as exclusively and unchangeably self-regarding, liberal philosophy has viewed human association as a kind of necessary evil and politics in an area in which the clashes of individual and group politics can be more or less civilly accommodated. As a philosophy of government and social life, liberalism exalts both the supremacy of private self-interest and the development of institutional means for pursuing those interests. In its extreme forms, this philosophy denies meaning and value to even the notion of common purpose, or politics in its classic sense (p. xii).

Sullivan also noted:

> . . . The liberal conception drew a firm distinction between public and private realms, thereby gaining autonomy for religion and intellectual as well as economic pursuits. But this reduced the public realm to formal institutions in which the conflicts among the 'interests' of civil society were umpired and negotiated, draining public life of intrinsic morality and significance. The philosophical basis of these developments was the liberal conception of life as essentially a business of individual self-interest, a notion highly compatible with

a fundamentally economic and strategic view of human action (1982, p. 13).

Although it may not be readily apparent, there is a direct connection between classic, individualistic philosophic liberalism and the developmental disability field's concern with quality of life. The connection is this: the tenets of philosophic liberalism undergird the disability field's emphasis on the ideologies of independence, consent, choice, empowerment, client participation, equal opportunities, integration, normalization, and social role valorization.

After all, the overarching purpose of these ideologies has been basically to chip away at the restrictions that public and private values, social and legal norms and forms, and laws and funding streams have placed on people with disabilities, and to create new rights of participation in education, employment, residential, and other typical (i.e., community) activities.

In chipping away at restrictions and creating rights, these ideologies and the public policies they have generated have asserted that people with disabilities, like those who do not have disabilities, have inherent rights to equal treatment and equal opportunity. The right to equal treatment and equal opportunity is more than a constitutional matter, although it surely is that; it is also a matter of creating programs that result in a more independent person. In this sense, the development of an independent person is an assertion that independence is a valued goal in and of itself, particularly in the context of individualistic liberalism.

The historical context for the rights revolution is especially apposite. It is, of course, conventional wisdom that the history of racial segregation and the legal and policy precedents that attempts at integration spawned were harbingers of the rights revolution. But there was more to that revolution. The lessons of Social Darwinism were well learned by advocates for people with disabilities. These lessons were that less able does equate with less worthy and that less worthy means segregation from the norm, vastly inferior treatment, and, in turn, vastly inferior opportunities to survive in the mainstream of society dominated by individualistic liberalism.

If philosophic liberalism, with its distinctively individualistic cast, meant anything, it was that people must compete for their place in the world. If the place in the world that Social Darwinism assigned to people with disabilities was unacceptable, then they had valid claims to opportunity for education, habilitation, and rehabilitation in order to equip them to compete. In short, the belief that people with disabilities should have a place in the mainstream, in a society that is dominated by individualistic, economically oriented philosophic liberalism, became the public philosophy rationale for the plethora of rights that federal and state laws now create.

Civic Republicanism

The second dominant theme of public philosophy in America has been civic republicanism (Bellah, 1982, cited in Sullivan, 1982). Shorthand phrases that describe civic republicanism are *cooperation* and *volunteerism*. According to Sullivan (1982),

> . . . Civic republicanism denies the liberal notion that individuality exists outside of or prior to social relationships. Instead, the republican tradition has taught that there is an ineluctably participatory aspect to political understanding that develops only through the moral maturation of mutual responsibility. Civic republicanism does not share the liberal idea that individuals are atoms of will essentially uninfluenced by their web of interrelationships, or the concomitant notion that all values are finally manifestations of the power to control. On the contrary, freedom is ultimately the ability to realize a responsible selfhood, which is necessarily a cooperative project. For republicanism, there are qualities of social relations, such as mutual concern and respect, that transcend utility and that can be learned only in practice. One reason republicanism has proved tenacious in a liberal America is this very embodied quality of its knowledge, although it requires explication to realize its own development.

> [Additionally] . . . the most valuable message of the republican tradition follows directly from this understanding. It is that the protection of human dignity depends upon the moral quality of social relationships, and that this is finally a public and political concern. Civic life is essential for individual security and integrity, but the ascendancy of liberalism has made it difficult to conceive those critical practices of mutual concern upon which liberal moral autonomy depends. The civic republican understanding of citizenship as shared initiative and responsibility among persons committed to mutual care provides the basis for a more mature public philosophy. But today that insight needs to be brought into explicit connection with large-scale governmental and economic institutions seeking to develop an effective citizenship in the areas of life controlled by those organizations (p. 21).

Again, the public philosopher's concern with the absence of civic republicanism and the means for revitalizing it are directly related to the developmental disabilities field, which is concerned with informal support, friendships, intentional communities, and rights to association between people with and without disabilities.

The common criticism of philosophic liberalism, from deTocqueville forward, said Sullivan (1982), is that its emphasis on utilitarian individualism is ultimately corrupting of individual and community life. Neither will be optimal as long as pure independence in action and motive is the driving force of our individual and collective behavior. What is needed, wrote Sullivan, is a reconceptualization of public philosophy and a reformation of private and public behavior and policies that is nothing more than the notion of civic association. And that is a tradition that is peculiarly, if not uniquely, American. DeTocqueville, wrote Sullivan (1982), saw that the "heart of American democracy was active civic association" (p. 216). The citizen can be an active member of any number of associations—whether churches or synagogues, professional (e.g., AAMR), or community benevolent (e.g., Rotary) groups—and thereby has the means to be free.

More than that, these intermediate structures can enable individuals to become citizens and to thereby acquire a sense of personal connection and significance unavailable to the depoliticized, purely private person. The role of classic politics and policy is to provide

> . . . a public framework of law and search for equity [whereby] moral relationships of trust and mutual aid are built up which come to transform the individual into a citizen. Politics in the genuinely associational sense is, then, more than pursuit of self-interest, since it involves sharing responsibility for acts that create a quality of life different from the mere sum of individual satisfactions (Sullivan, 1982, p. 218).

Sullivan's observations are directly relevant to quality of life for people with disabilities and reflect the disability field's concern for informal supports and friendships, for not just presence but participation in communities, for going beyond antidiscrimination and even beyond equal opportunities to full citizenship. Thus,

> . . . our present danger does not come from government as such, or from the entrepreneurial spirit either, for that matter. The danger to our democratic institutions comes, rather, from the declining effectiveness of just those intervening structures, the civic associations for all sorts that service to mediate between individual and state (Sullivan, 1982, p. 222).

CONCLUSIONS

Now, allow us to conclude by making our argument in the most forceful way possible. There is a new language and, with it, renewed values. These are values that many of us in the disability field share with the political philosophers. Many of us advocate for civic associations and intentional communities such as Camphill and for value-based mini-communities such as L'Arche. In short, we advocate for different manifestations of civic association.

To advance our interests in civic association, we also advocate for the development of informal supports and the financial means to sustain them. But we fear that typically overbearing governmental regulation will stifle these forms of civic association. And, in our worst-case scenarios, we fear that government regulation will even create the conditions that will cause publicly supported informal supports to become institutionalized, to become "just another program." We fear that result because we see that our efforts to create community-based programs sometimes have gone awry: too many of those programs that we wanted not to be mini-institutions have become just that. The individual is increasingly isolated from the nondisabled world and increasingly turned into an autonom, a person for whom there are individualized plans of all kinds but very little personalized consideration or communal association.

We have been arguing that there is a natural connection between the concerns for the quality of life of all Americans and the quality of life of Americans with disabilities. This connection is revealed in the new language that we, like the public philosophers, use. They share our vocabulary, language that is laden with such terms as *quality of life, cooperation, fellowship, community as relationship, building community, fraternity* (as distinguished from liberty and equality), and *intentional associations.* There is an underlying common measure of life for the public philosophers and for those of us in the disabilities field.

It is not unique to observe that the genius of American life is the simultaneous development of liberty (philosophic liberalism), equality, and fraternity. What is different—and this, of course, is the thrust of the argument—is how people in the developmental disabilities field respond to that native genius (Turnbull, 1988b).

Some respond by emphasizing fraternity (that is, civic republicanism). Some see the underlying measure of quality of life to be relational—grounded in civic association and thus quintessentially American and, within American life, universal. Who are those people, and how do they behave? Some seek to develop associations or informal supports by such innovative means as are used by the Pennsylvania Developmental Disabilities Planning Council. Others emphasize the development and nurturance of such European originated means as Camphill and L'Arche communities. Still others approach the issue of civic association by such means as peer relationships in schools and mentor systems at worksites or in communities.

For all of us, as well as for the public philosophers, there is an underlying measure of quality of life. It is the measure that ascribes quality of life according to the extent to which people choose to be with each other, the ways in which they give form to their choices to be with each other, and the nature, extent, and duration of their relationships. Quality of life is indeed measured by relationships. The development of the means to create, sustain, and enhance those relationships under a constitutional form of government that is intrinsically capitalistic and democratic is, as it always has been, the central issue of lives affected by disability. It is, of course, a matter of public philosophy and of existentialism.

REFERENCES

Bellah, R. N. (1982). Foreword. In W. M. Sullivan, *Reconstructing public philosophy* (page i). Berkeley: University of California Press.

Berger, P., & Newhaus, R. (1976). *To empower people: The role of mediating structures in public policy*. Washington, DC: American Enterprise Institute for Public Policy Research.

Duff, R., & Campbell, A. G. M. (1973). Moral and ethical dilemnas in the special-care nursery. *New England Journal of Medicine, 289,* 890–895.

Duff, R., & Campbell, A. G. M. (1976). On deciding the care of severely handicapped or dying persons: With particular reference to infants. *Pediatrics, 57,* 488–495.

Edgerton, R. B. (1967). *The cloak of competence*. Berkeley: University of California Press.

Edgerton, R. B., & Bercovici, S. M. (1976). The cloak of competence: Years later. *American Journal of Mental Deficiency, 80,* 485–497.

Edgerton, R. B., Bollinger, M., & Herr, B. (1984). The cloak of competence: After two decades. *American Journal of Mental Deficiency, 88,* 345–351.

Gliedman, J., & Roth, W. (1980). *The unexpected minority: Handicapped children in America.* New York: Harcourt Brace Jovanovich.

Grossman, H. J. (1983). *Classification in Mental Retardation.* Washington, DC: American Association on Mental Deficiency.

Guess, D., Helmstetter, E., Turnbull, H., & Knowlton, E. (1986). *Use of aversive procedures with persons who are disabled: An historical review and critical analysis.* Seattle: The Association for Persons with Severe Handicaps.

Hazel, S., Deshler, D., & Turnbull, H. (1987). *Research into self-advocacy as a technique for transition.* Lawrence, KS: University of Kansas, Institute for Research and Learning Disabilities.

Kaufman, S. Z. (1988). *Retarded isn't stupid, mom.* Baltimore: Paul H. Brookes.

McIntyre, A. (1984). *After virtues* (2nd Ed.). Notre Dame, IN: University of Notre Dame Press.

Michelman, F. I. (1969). Foreword: On protecting the poor through the fourteenth amendment, *Harvard Law Review, 9,* 83–90.

Morse, S. (1978). Crazy behavior. *Southern California Law Review, 51,* 528–532.

Rawls, J. (1971). *A theory of justice.* Cambridge, MA: Harvard University Press.

Sullivan, W. M. (1982). *Reconstructing public philosophy.* Berkeley: University of California Press.

Szasz, T. (1963). *Law, liberty, and psychiatry.* New York: MacMillan.

Szasz, T. (1973). *Psychiatric slavery.* New York: MacMillan.

Turnbull, A., Knowlton, E., Backus, L., & Turnbull, H. (1988). Letting go: Consent and the "yes, but . . .." problem in transition. In B. Ludlow, A. Turnbull, & R. Luckasson, (Eds.), *Transitions to adult life for people with mental retardation: Principles and practices.* Baltimore: Paul H. Brookes.

Turnbull, A. P., & Turnbull, H. R. (1985). Developing independence. *Journal of Adolescent Health Care, 6*(2), 108–119.

Turnbull, A. P., & Turnbull, H. R. (1988). *Families and community integration.* Lawrence, KS: University of Kansas, Beach Center on Families and Disability.

Turnbull, H. R. (Ed.). (1978). *Consent handbook* (Special Publication No. 3). Washington, DC: American Association on Mental Deficiency.

Turnbull, H. R. (1986). Presidential address. *Mental Retardation, 24,* 265–275.

Turnbull, H. R. (1988a). Fifteen questions: Ethical inquiries in mental retardation. In J. Stark, F. Menolascino, M. Albarelli, & V. Gray (Eds.), *Mental retardation and mental health* (pp. 368–378). Washington, DC: President's Committee on Mental Retardation.

Turnbull, H. R. (1988b). Response to Burt. In L. Kane, P. Brown, & J. Cohen (Eds.), *The legal rights of citizens with mental retardation*. Lanham, MD: University Press of America.

Turnbull, H. R. (1990). *Free appropriate public education: Law and education of children with disabilities* (3rd Ed.). Denver: Love Publishing.

Turnbull, H. R., & Turnbull, A. P. (Eds.) (1985). *Parents speak out: Then and now*. Columbus, OH: Charles E. Merrill.

Turnbull, H. R., & Wheat, M. J. (1983). Legal responses to classification of people as mentally retarded. In J. Mulick & J. Matson (Eds.), *A handbook of mental retardation*, pp. 157–169. New York: Pergamon Press.

Wolfensberger, W., & Zauha, H. (1973). *Citizen advocacy and protective services for the impaired and handicapped*. Toronto: National Institute on Mental Retardation.

19
A Lawyer's Perspective on Quality of Life

Ruth Luckasson
The University of New Mexico

My perspective on the phrase *quality of life* reflects my own efforts as a lawyer and a mental retardation professional. Experiences in this dual working life lead me to conclude reluctantly that the dangers of the phrase potentially outweigh whatever usefulness it may have. I urge the disability community to reject the use of the phrase *quality of life* as a global evaluation of the life of the person with mental retardation.

Many of the chapters in this volume challenge common assumptions about the quality of life (or lack of it) in people with mental retardation. I find myself agreeing with my colleagues as they attempt to formulate sensitive definitions that begin from the actual perceptions of people with disabilities themselves, and as they attempt to incorporate important dimensions of the lives of people with disabilities into their analyses. But even as I find great merit in their efforts, my fears about the unintended consequences of legitimizing the phrase *quality of life* are unassuaged. The chapters by consumers of mental retardation services and their family members provide an essential perspective to the efforts to develop the idea of "quality of life" in a manner that enhances its ability to contain human dignity and worth. But in my opinion, no amount of refinement by the disability community can salvage the phrase.

The best efforts to define "quality of life" in a way that is compatible with the principles of normalization, integration, and the worth of all human beings cannot change the risk that continued use of the phrase remains, at its core, too dangerous and places the lives and futures of people with disabilities in peril. The disability community's best efforts to define it in the way that we think best will fall to the idiosyncratic definitions of individuals outside the disability community. The risk is that the phrase will, in individual cases, be used as a shorthand calculation of the overall condition and worth of a person with mental retardation.

My greatest concern is that a legitimization of the phrase *quality of life* within the disability profession will lead to a certain tolerance, or even preference, for the phrase and result in its increased use as a shorthand justification for denial of rights to people with disabilities. The worry is that we will be lulled by the phrase's familiarity and soothing tone of

211

rightminded concern to the point that we fail to resist its use in pernicious ways. The stereotypes and prejudices that for years formed the justification for discriminatory actions against people with disabilities, and that have only slowly, after tremendous effort, begun to fall away, will reappear under a superficially more sympathetic guise. Negative, damaging judgments about people with disabilities that are no longer tolerated by enlightened citizens will reappear, sanitized under the rubric *quality of life*.

Only a few years ago it was common to hear statements such as "The mentally retarded don't feel pain," "The mentally retarded can't work," "A mentally retarded person is a vegetable," or even "A Down's is not a person." All of these statements reflected judgments about the quality of life of a person with mental retardation. The candor of the words, however, exposed the true character of the sentiment. Today, there remain very few environments in which statements such as the examples above would go unchallenged. It has been a hard fought battle. The disability community has expended considerable human and political resources to eliminate statements such as these from public and private discourse about disability.

One of the premises for the efforts eliminating such language has been that eliminating prejudice and stereotyping from language will go hand-in-hand with eliminating it from attitudes. In large part, this seems to have proved correct. Public attitudes toward people with disabilities do seem improved. This is demonstrated in polling data, the landmark legislation passed by Congress and the states in the last 20 years, and everyday experiences in the lives of people with disabilities.

Attitudes may be improved, but they have no guarantee of permanence. Much work remains to be done. Fears, prejudice, stereotyping, and discrimination continue to lurk beneath the surface. Will the phrase *quality of life* provide the vehicle for reemergence and tolerance of unfounded prejudice? The very words in the phrase are soothingly seductive. *Quality* is such a virtuous-sounding word. Who would object that, especially in the 1990s, everything (and everyone) ought to be *quality*? And *life* sounds similarly high minded. The phrase has an almost religious tone to it.

But I suggest that the phrase will prove irresistible as a vehicle for fears and prejudice about people with disabilities. Ignorance and discriminatory treatment that would not be tolerated in their plain language will routinely be accepted if the speaker is able to couch the comments with sincerity and sympathy and more socially acceptable references to quality of life. For example, a hospital that announced a policy that it would not provide organ transplants for individuals with disabilities because "mentally retarded people lack the capacity to appreciate life" or "deaf people would be better off dead" would surely be punished in a variety of ways. On the other hand, if the same hospital announced that it would make transplant decisions on the basis of quality of life (thereby disguising their prejudices), they would likely make identical decisions but immunize those decisions from criticism.

Courts frequently reflect the prejudices of the broader society. Judges are not immune from harmful stereotypes about people with disabilities. Judges may be able to weigh and analyze fairly cases in which the evidence is expressed in understandable language about abilities, disabilities, health status, research, and other factors about an individual. But if professional testimony is couched in terms of quality of life, some judges may be tempted to accept the conclusion as somehow *scientific* and thus beyond the scope of normal judicial inquiry. The judicial system will be tempted to remove itself from such "messy" cases, to defer to the judgment of quality of life "experts" and effectively remove judicial protections from what are actually legal issues of discrimination based on handicap. The so-called evidence in the case was, in fact, merely conclusions likely to be based on the witness's own biases, fears, prejudices, and stereotypes about the lives of people with disabilities. By acquiescing in the legitimization of the phrase *quality of life*, the disability community is allowing witnesses to use the shorthand phrase and giving judges the invitation to deny basic human rights to people with disabilities on the basis of pseudoscientific predictions or estimations of an individual's quality of life.

Some hints of the uses to which judgments of quality of life might be put in the future can be found around us. For example, at least one state has already prepared a written list of medical procedures, ranked according to how likely they are to improve quality of life for the most people, by which it intends to ration health care for those whose care is paid for by the state. At a midwestern college, a group of seminar students and their professor recently drafted model euthanasia legislation that would allow the quality of life determination of *intolerable dependence* in normal living activities as a justification for euthanasia. In a recent case, an insurance company denied funds for a child's organ transplant, arguing that the quality of life of a child with brain damage would not be worth the transplant. Similar justifications have been used to attempt to deny special education, related education services, habilitation, and social services to children and adults with disabilities.

If global judgments about an individual's quality of life become the calculus when health care is rationed, services allocated, financial support distributed, or decisions of life and death made, stereotypes and prejudices about individuals with mental retardation will discriminate against them. Another example illustrates the risk. The Baby Doe case was heard by the U.S. Supreme Court in 1985 (Bowen *v.* American Hospital Association, 479 U.S. 610, 1986). The question was whether the discriminatory denial of lifesaving medical care to infants with handicaps solely on the basis of their handicaps was prohibited under Section 504 of the Rehabilitation Act of

1973. While the Court ultimately ruled that the Baby Doe regulations were beyond the scope of Section 504, the Court made no ruling on the Constitutional rights of the infants. The American Association on Mental Retardation, along with The Association for Persons with Severe Handicaps, the American Association of University Affiliated Programs for the Developmentally Disabled, and the National Rehabilitation Association, filed one of the *amicus curiae* (friend of the Court) briefs in the case. Debate about the denial of necessary medical care to infants with handicaps almost invariably turns to discussion of the prospect for the baby's quality of life.

In summary, I have serious reservations about using the phrase *quality of life* as a global evaluation of the lives of people with mental retardation. My experiences as a lawyer and mental retardation professional lead me reluctantly to conclude that the dangers of the phrase *quality of life* outweigh whatever usefulness it may have.

20
Quality Assurance: Challenges in a Decentralized System

Valerie J. Bradley

Human Services Research Institute

As mentioned frequently throughout this book, the quality of life of persons with disabilities is influenced greatly by the quality of services they receive. Assessing and ensuring the quality of services to people with mental retardation is a fairly recent phenomenon. According to Scheerenberger (1983), the American Association on Mental Deficiency (AAMD) took the first recorded steps when it decided to address the issue of staffing for institutional programs in 1942. By 1953, Scheerenberger adds, the concern for standards led the AAMD to develop "Standards for Public Training Schools" that included programmatic and administrative prescriptions as well as numerical staffing requirements. These initial forays seem rudimentary compared with the complexity of issues faced by today's program overseers and policymakers.

This increasing complexity is a product of the decentralized character of services to people with mental retardation, changes in program philosophy, and the presence of a multilayered bureaucratic superstructure that has grown up around mental retardation service systems. Quality assurance now takes place at multiple levels of government and is conducted by a range of agencies with various public health, safety, and programmatic mandates. The field is about to become even more complicated as system change continues and as programmatic expectations and assumptions become more conceptual and less schematic. This chapter will address the challenges faced by those vested with quality assurance responsibilities and will cover the following issues:

- Critique of current quality assurance activities
- Quality assurance principles and purposes
- Emerging trends in the conduct of services to persons with mental retardation
- Ideological and programmatic changes that pose new questions for designers of quality assurance systems
- Realities of the current system that should be taken into account in quality assurance approaches

- Recommendations regarding the future design of quality assurance standards and procedures

CRITIQUE OF CURRENT QUALITY ASSURANCE SYSTEMS

Current quality assurance systems have not kept up with the pace of service development and reflect, in many states, an incoherent pattern of monitoring and protective mechanisms that were originally designed for a more homogeneous and less numerous system of providers. The following critique summarizes some of the limitations of contemporary quality assurance techniques.

Minimum Standards

The standards used to judge services for persons with mental retardation tend to perpetuate mediocrity because they represent minimal compliance thresholds. Clearly, there are basic requirements that all services should meet and that are unlikely to change over time, including minimum health and safety standards. Standards, however, should not mark only minimal achievement, but instead should contribute to the dynamic character of a system by constantly exhorting providers to higher levels of attainment. Outstanding providers are neither challenged by existing compliance levels nor can they expect any rewards for their exemplary performance.

Burden of Documentation

As services have proliferated and become more decentralized, quality assurance has become a more time-consuming and difficult task. As a result, many public agencies have increasingly used paper proxies for quality. As the task has grown, it has become easier to monitor those things that can be counted or observed easily. Staff are inadequate in many agencies and their ability to spend time getting to know programs first hand has diminished.

Reactive Versus Positive

Traditional quality assurance systems use techniques that are more reactive than positive. Reactive mechanisms address service quality problems post facto and are generally negative and targeted to past practice. Positive monitoring mechanisms assist service providers in order to improve practice and to prevent potential problems before they develop. Clearly, ferreting out abuses in service delivery is an important activity in any quality assurance system. The problem arises when the system becomes dominated by negative oversight and sanctions. When this happens, providers begin to see the public monitors as adversaries concerned only with finding fault. As a result, the mutual support and cooperation necessary for service quality are undermined.

Implications

The result of these structural problems in quality assurance systems is that the communication of policy or a vision of what the service system should be is blocked both by the adversary nature of the process and by its narrow focus. The solution is a better balance between the aims of quality regulation (e.g., auditing and licensing) and quality enhancement (e.g., technical assistance and self-assessment).

PRINCIPLES AND PURPOSES

Before proceeding with the discussion of challenges in the area of quality assurance, it is important to pause and review the purposes and objectives that should govern any quality assurance system. Concern about quality is the result of a desire for standards that yield a product whose performance is reliable and predictable. These are criteria that should be part of the expectations for services to persons with mental retardation. The added dimension in human services is the desire to determine whether the service that is delivered has the intended effect. In other words, quality is the promise that is made to the client and quality assurance is necessary to ensure that the promise is kept.

In addition to keeping that promise, there are several other reasons why the development and refinement of quality assurance mechanisms are important endeavors:

- To protect the rights of persons with severe disabilities who are now and who will be living and working in community settings.
- To maintain and live up to the trust that parents of individuals with mental retardation have put in the concept of community living for their family members.
- To provide feedback to providers of service in order to assist them in improving and enhancing their programs.
- To respond to pressure from funders, such as state legislators, to justify and defend the efficacy of community programs.

- To embody, in quality standards, the most recent developments in service technology and service provision and, as a result, to provide programmatic leadership and vision.
- To ensure the maintenance of programmatic excellence over time.

This rationale leads to a set of objectives that are generally agreed to underpin the design of quality assurance systems (Bradley, Ashbaugh, & Harder, 1984) including assurance that:

1. Providers of human services have the capability to provide an acceptable level of service.
2. Client services are provided consistent with accepted beliefs about what constitutes good practice.
3. A commitment of resources produces a reasonable level of service.
4. The services that are provided have the intended effect.
5. The limited supply of services is provided to those clients most in need.
6. The legal and human rights of people with mental retardation are protected.

EMERGING TRENDS

Several changes are taking place in services to persons with mental retardation that will have a direct bearing on our conceptions of quality assurance. As recently as 10 years ago, most persons with developmental disabilities who required residential placement were admitted to a publicly managed and funded facility. Though approximately 100,000 persons with mental retardation and other developmental disabilities still reside in public facilities (White, Lakin, Hill, Wright, & Bruininks, 1986), the number of people living in privately run community residences is well over 115,000 (Hill, Bruininks, Lakin, Hauber, & McQuire, 1985). Many of the individuals placed in private community residences over the past several years are certainly as disabled as are their counterparts in public facilities (Conroy & Bradley, 1985). In addition, the size of residential programs continues to decrease. According to the University of Minnesota survey of residential settings in 1982, most of the residences (99.6%) that had opened since the 1977 survey were small, with a median size of four residents.

Quality assurance activities over the past two decades have been further complicated by major advances in service delivery, such as the separation of day programs from residential settings. Whereas early quality monitoring activities could be carried out in discrete locations where large numbers of people lived and received services, today people are spread over vast geographic areas and almost all leave their homes during the days to participate in some form of day activity. More recently the notion of a "day program" is undergoing substantial change with the development of supported work and enclave settings that essentially function "without walls" and without conventional staffing patterns.

The proliferation of residential and day settings has been accompanied by a geometric expansion of quality assurance entities at the local, state, and federal levels. Providers of service must contend with numerous public agencies and private accreditation agencies, whose requirements and regulatory structures vary and whose standards and expectations rarely coincide. This picture of quality assurance may become even more complex if the federal government steps up its enforcement activities.

There is every reason to assume that trends toward smaller residential settings and more normal work environments will persist. Litigation in several states continues to direct the energies of policymakers toward phasing down institutions and creating community programs for class members. Pressure continues to be brought at the federal level to change the current incentives in the Medicaid program to favor smaller, more integrated community programs. Finally, there is a growing realization that developing "beds" and "slots" may not be sufficient to realize the promise of truly individualized programs.

The implications of these trends for quality assurance revolve primarily around the difficulties in mounting a multiple-sites, statewide monitoring strategy that is sufficiently flexible to accommodate a range of service approaches and that protects the well-being of people with more severe disabilities. No one mechanism for assuring quality can be successful given the trends noted. Multiple means must be sought to meet the complex and multifaceted needs for quality assurance.

IDEOLOGICAL CONSIDERATIONS

The field of mental retardation and developmental disabilities, perhaps more than any other, is guided in large measure by a set of values and ideological principles. Recent reforms in the system have been driven by norms such as normalization and rights of due process and protection from harm. To be relevant, then, quality assurance practices must be cognizant of these values and must, to the extent possible, reflect such values and be capable of translating them into operational standards.

Until recently, the operating norms had to do with concerns like least restrictive setting and maximization of individual potential. More contemporary ideological trends pose different and more complicated challenges for those concerned about quality assurance. Three of these trends are discussed below.

Community Integration

One of the more compelling values that is increasingly influencing the critique of services to people with mental retardation is the norm of community integration. If the work of the 1970s and '80s has been to build the foundation for a service system in the community, then the frontier of the '90s is to ensure that people with mental retardation and other developmental disabilities are visible and active members of our communities. To ensure that the promise of community integration—a full life in the mainstream of the world of work and leisure—is kept, quality assurance systems must be available that both monitor the fulfillment of the integration goal and assist in facilitating the implementation of the concept. Such notions as community integration are not self-implementing—they must be nurtured and supported. The field of mental retardation and developmental disabilities is fairly good at housing and training people with mental retardation, but the skills needed to encourage integration are not necessarily taught in our professional schools.

Individualization

The notion of individualization has been part of the fabric of mental retardation services for some time, but has recently been refined and reexamined in light of our notions of the concept of continuum (Taylor, 1988). This new way of approaching an old norm involves an assertion that the focus of services should be on the unique needs of an individual rather than on the creation of a set of services through which or into which people can move. The ultimate realization of this norm is the development of services tailored to individual needs and the incorporation of supports from the surrounding community that are available to all of us.

Functionality

A final value that has begun to pervade the field is the notion that teaching and instruction should be directly relevant to the life experiences of persons with mental retardation. Like the notion of individualization, functionality suggests that teaching incremental skills with no application in the individual's world is to subject persons with disabilities to a series of hurdles that prevent them from learning those skills that will be more instrumental in the lives. The notion of functionality is also consistent with the aggressive use of adaptive devices to assist people in carrying out daily activities—devices that compensate for either physical or cognitive limitations.

Quality Assurance Issues

These three ideological trends pose a variety of questions to quality assurers. First, how do you design a quality assurance system that protects the well-being of clients but that is not intrusive into people's homes and jobsites? It's one thing to have Health Care Finance Administration monitors trooping through a large institution, but it's quite another to have monitors show up at a person's job or home. Second, how do you ensure that people with disabilities are involved in the process of setting standards and monitoring programs? Third, how do you develop a quality assurance system that is capable of assessing a constellation of specialized and generic services rather than discrete facilities and programs? Finally, how do you assess whether or not people are receiving services that are truly meeting their functional needs? These are difficult questions and they point out that notions of quality are not unidimensional and that multiple perspectives are necessary to assess and apply quality standards—most importantly the views of those who receive services.

REALITIES OF THE CURRENT SERVICE SYSTEM

In addition to the problems posed by changes in programmatic and ideological conceptions, there are also practical problems faced by the service system that quality assurance system designers must take into consideration. A major issue has to do with concerns for the long-term stability of privately run, dispersed, and highly individualized service systems and the extent to which current quality assurance techniques can minimize client dislocation.

To study this issue in detail, the Human Services Research Institute recently completed a study of the dynamic of change in residential services (Bradley & Allard, 1988). Several data-gathering activities were conducted in order to develop an initial picture of the stability of community residential programs. A literature search was conducted, state mental retardation directors were canvassed, state site visits were mounted, and a sample of residential providers in 20 states was surveyed. In order to describe the phenomenon of stability with some precision, the term *changed* was substituted and was defined as *moved, changed ownership, discontinued services* to persons with developmental disabilities, or *ceased operations*.

Initial Survey

Of the residences surveyed, approximately 25% had changed since the University of Minnesota survey of 1982 (Hill et al., 1985). The greatest amount of change, 34.9%, was in the size category of 1 to 6 persons. The least amount of change, approximately 17%, occurred in the 7- to 15-person residences. It should be noted that the overall percent of change in residences serving persons with developmental disabilities is lower than the rate of movement in the general population calculated over the 5-year period from 1975 to 1980.

With respect to changed facilities, not many residences went out of business (11.72%), but a substantial number either moved (39.9%) or experienced a change in ownership (44.2%)—the latter occurring most frequently among large, 16- to 63-person residences. At the same time, at least half of the small, 1- to 6-person residences, that indicated a change had moved during the most recent 4 years.

Commissioner Survey

The survey of state mental retardation commissioners elicited information on some general trends that relate to the dynamics of change in residential services. One interesting fact was that approximately one-half of the residences in the 34 states reporting were operated by nonprofit organizations and at least 35% were operated by individual partners or families. Another interesting finding is that commissioners reported that very few providers operated more than 10 residential programs and that the vast majority of providers are small.

With respect to monitoring activities, very few states indicated that they had revoked or suspended any residential program licenses in 1985. Indeed, 31 states had no suspensions and 24 had no revocations. Ten states noted that they had revoked fewer than 10 licenses. Although 23 states said that they had formal quality assurance processes other than licensing, only 17 indicated that such processes were linked to fiscal review or a reimbursement process. With respect to client movement, only 16 states provided estimates regarding clients who were moved/released/transferred because of changes in their health, behaviors, or skill acquisition, or changes attributable to organization instability.

Insofar as the overall assessment of system stability, nine state commissioners indicated that they considered the stability of their community residential systems to be a problem. Several other states believed that their residential systems were basically stable but that certain parts were having difficulties or that their knowledge of stability was limited. For example, one state considered its family care programs to be unstable but not its other community residential programs.

Among the reasons given by state commissioners for stable residential systems were (in order of frequency): adequate reimbursement and/or financing, including additional funds for hard-to-place clients; strong commitment and/or a close relationship to the service provider system, including a history of stable and mature providers; presence of a good case management and monitoring system; influence of local economic factors (e.g., in rural areas, residential programs are more successful at recruiting, given depressed economies); commitment to developing a strong community system, including involvement of legislature, advocacy groups, and so forth; a locally based management system; training and technical assistance available to providers; and a focus on the development of small living arrangements.

Indepth Provider Survey

The indepth provider survey also yielded some provocative results. The findings are based on 180 responses—57 residences that had undergone some change and 123 that had not changed since 1982. Among those residences that underwent some change, most of the change was in a positive or at least a neutral direction (e.g., residences were downsized, agencies found better locations for houses, providers retired, etc.). On the negative side, very few providers noted that they had received any form of technical assistance, either programmatic or administrative. Further, some of the providers that had not undergone change noted that their agencies were on the edge economically. Finally, small providers in particular mentioned that they had difficulty managing cash flow and complex funding streams.

Implications

Regardless of protestations to the contrary, the system of residential services is still made up of small providers. Given the philosophical trends noted earlier, small, family-like residences will be the order of the day in the future. Such programs require support in the form of technical assistance on programmatic quality of life and financial issues. The research cited above suggests that such assistance is rarely available. The study also underscores the importance of a strong case management system capable of providing monitoring continuity in a system characterized by a certain amount of flux. Finally, the findings highlight the importance of a client tracking mechanism capable of monitoring movement to ensure that people with mental retardation are not subject to undue dislocation of their homes and social relationships.

RECOMMENDATIONS ABOUT THE DESIGN OF QUALITY ASSURANCE SYSTEMS

Based on the systemic, programmatic, and ideological trends noted above, there are several recommendations that should govern the creation of a quality assurance system including:

1. Participants in the design of quality assurance systems must develop a coherent vision of the service system that best meets contextual as well as programmatic needs. This vision must be supported by a system of technical assistance and support in order to ensure that the vision is accomplished and maintained over time. Without training and technical assistance, standards will end up as hollow exhortations.
2. In mounting training and technical assistance efforts, designers must support the development of those skills that will be most useful in a truly individualized service system, including community organization, empowerment and the facilitation of choice making, creation of community networks, identification of appropriate adaptations, and community relations.
3. Standards at all levels of the service system must be continually revised and updated to reflect changes in ideology and the state of the art.
4. Multiple perspectives regarding the quality of services must be taken into account—most particularly that of the person receiving services. Such input is necessary to truly understand the extent to which norms such as integration, functionality, and individualization are being realized.
5. Case managers should be the front line program monitors and should be trained in the use of quality assurance techniques. They should also be placed in organizational positions that are maximally independent of service provision.
6. Quality assurance mechanisms should include ongoing assessment of client progress and well-being. A quality assurance system that does not have as its prime focus the day-to-day well-being of clients is doomed to fail.
7. Quality assurance systems should ensure that placement and movement decisions take into account client choice and individual preferences and that they maximize the individual's social network.
8. Standard setting should be a collective process involving administrators, providers, and consumers. Such collaboration is necessary

to ensure that multiple viewpoints are reflected and to maximize trust and collegiality.

9. Advocacy services and grievance procedures are as much a part of quality assurance systems as licensing and other traditional functions.

CONCLUSION

This brief review of the issues to be confronted in the design of quality assurance mechanisms stresses the inherent tension between the immutability of quality assurance standards and procedures as currently employed and the fluidity and dynamism of a system that is constantly moving to a less and less conventional approach to service delivery. It is incumbent on policymakers to respond to these challenges by diversifying assessment mechanisms, retooling assessment procedures so that they are more relevant to day-to-day quality of life issues, and involving a wider spectrum of participants in the monitoring process. The discussion further points out the inherent tension between our desire to make the lives of people with mental retardation more normal and our responsibility to ensure that the "withering away of the system" does not result in abuse and exploitation out of our view.

REFERENCES

Bradley, V. J., & Allard, M. A. (1988). *The dynamics of change in residential services for people with developmental disabilities: An exploratory analysis.* Cambridge, MA: Human Services Research Institute.

Bradley, V. J., Ashbaugh, J. W., & Harder, P. (1984). *Assessing and enhancing the quality of services: A guide for the human services field.* Boston, MA: Human Services Research Institute.

Conroy, J., & Bradley, V. J. (1985). *The Pennhurst longitudinal study: A report of five years of research and analysis.* Philadelphia: Temple University Developmental Disabilities Center.

Hill, B. K., Bruininks, R. H., Lakin, K. C., Hauber, F. A., & McGuire, S. P. (1985). Stability of residential facilities for people who are mentally retarded: 1977–1982. *Mental Retardation, 23,* 108–144.

Scheerenberger, R. S. (1983). *A history of mental retardation.* Baltimore: Paul H. Brookes.

Taylor, S. J. (1988). Caught in the continuum: A critical analysis of the principle of least restrictive environment. *Journal of the Association for Persons with Severe Handicaps, 13,* 41–53.

White, C. C., Lakin, K. C., Hill, B., Wright, E., & Bruininks, R. (1986). *Persons with mental retardation in state-operated residential facilities: Year ending June 30, 1986 with longitudinal trends from 1950 to 1986 (Report No. 24).* Minneapolis: University of Minnesota, Department of Educational Psychology.

21
Measuring Quality Of Life: Where Have We Been?
Where Are We Going?

James W. Conroy and Celia S. Feinstein
Temple University

This chapter proposes that the future measurement of quality of life should include an outcome orientation. Although there is nothing particularly new about an outcome orientation, it has some very strong advantages that will be discussed in this chapter.

The outcome orientation has driven our own work in evaluating deinstitutionalization and community living over the past decade (Conroy & Bradley, 1985; Conroy, Walsh, & Feinstein, 1987). The central idea of this orientation is simply that we can best judge the quality of any service by measuring the benefits experienced by consumers of that service. This approach is therefore concerned primarily with individual consumers. The vast majority of conclusions about services must arise from aggregation of the life experiences of the individuals receiving the services.

The outcome orientation stands in contrast to the process orientations of licensing, standards, and accreditation. These process orientations aim at assuring that certain aspects of the intervention process are in place. It is assumed that if the processes are in place, then the experiences of the consumers of services will be of high quality; the next extension of the assumption is that outcomes will be good. Interestingly, these assumptions about the link between processes and outcomes have seldom if ever been tested for process standards.

The process approach demands that each person have a certain amount of space, that certain staffing ratios are met, that certain life safety concerns be addressed, and that there is a great deal of paper-based accountability for individual plans, services, management techniques, and unusual incidents. The process approach must be designed so that a team of reviewers can determine whether compliance with the standards is adequate, and this determination must be feasible within a reasonably short visit.

In general, the items in these process-oriented checklists arise from expert opinion. Knowledgeable professionals brainstorm about what they believe to be the characteristics of quality services. The long lists of such characteristics are shortened slightly by exploration of consensus and dissent, eliminating items about which there is little or no consensus. The remaining items possess the feature of face validity, which means that they *look* reasonable (at least to viewers with characteristics and values similar to those of the developers). However, there is no assurance that they actually represent the features that will guarantee that a service is high quality with measurable, desirable outcomes. In fact, many persons have had the experience of visiting a certified or accredited or licensed service setting, and yet have left with the feeling that the service was of low quality.

However, based on the evidence summarized in previous chapters, we do know how to measure a variety of outcomes that are generally believed to be related to quality of life. Therefore, in the remainder of this chapter, we will present some future-oriented general principles and examples of the utility of the outcome oriented approach to measuring quality of life.

QUALITY ASSESSMENT AND QUALITY ASSISTANCE

Why is it important to measure quality? The terms *qualitative* and *quantitative* seem, superficially at least, to represent very different interests. *Quantitative* implies measurement, while *qualitative* implies subjective impressions. However, in the present context, we contend that quality of life can and should be approached quantitatively as well as qualitatively.

The terms *quality assurance* and *quality enhancement* are very closely related to the terms *monitoring* and *program evaluation*. Whatever terms are used, the general purpose of any such activity is to assess the quality of services in order continually to enhance the quality of services. In systems theory, or cybernetics, this concept is viewed as the most elementary: without accurate feedback about the status of the system, the system cannot change in a consistently positive direction (Miller, Galanter, & Pribram, 1960; Wiener, 1948). Thus, it is useful to think of a quality enhancement loop as an elementary feedback system.

If the measurement process is not accurate, the system will fail to improve over time and we will not even know it. Certainly, that is not a desirable situation. The idea of a quality feedback loop is that the quality assessment (measurement) gives the necessary information to conduct quality assistance (providing whatever is needed to make the service better). The conceptualization of a quality enhancement loop is represented in Figure 21.1.

The quality enhancement loop shown in the figure consists of assessment and assistance. Naturally, before we take any kind of remedial action in a service system, we must have information about the state of the system. This should be provided primarily from the outcome perspective, but should

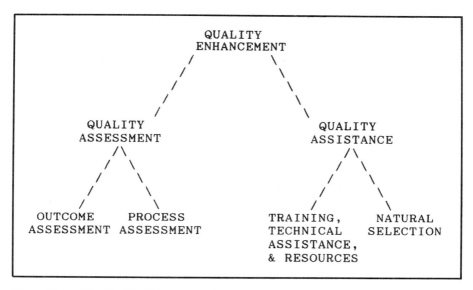

Figure 21.1. The Quality Enhancement Loop

also include the process perspective. Then it is possible to design interventions, of which there are two general categories. Remedies include
provision of training, technical assistance, and resources; an alternative
intervention might result in the occasional necessary removal of irretriev-
ably poor services.

A GROWING NATIONAL COMMITMENT TO THE
ASSESSMENT OF OUTCOMES

Our own expertise is heavily weighted toward creation of systems that
assess individual outcomes and then aggregate those outcomes to assess
the quality of the service system. The consumer's life experiences are the
ultimate unit of accountability. We believe that if we can quantitatively and
reliably measure that people are generally becoming more independent,
that they are as productive as possible, that they are as socially integrated
as possible, and that they are generally satisfied with the services they are
receiving, then we can conclude that they are receiving quality services
and, by inference, an enhanced quality of life.

An example of this kind of outcome approach may be found in the
national effort to survey individuals with developmental disabilities. The
Developmental Disabilities Assistance and Bill of Rights Act Amendments
of 1987 (P.L. 100-146) states:

> Each State Planning council shall conduct a comprehensive review and

analysis of the eligibility for services provided, and the extent, scope, and effectiveness of services provided and functions performed by, all State agencies (including agencies which provide public assistance) which affect or which potentially affect the ability of persons with developmental disabilities to achieve the goals of independence, productivity, and integration into the community, including persons with developmental disabilities attributable to physical impairments, mental impairments, or a combination of physical and mental impairments.

To assist in designing, completing and analyzing the required summary data, the University Affiliated Program at Temple University was consulted by the National Association of Developmental Disabilities Planning Councils (NADDC). This effort is expected to result in more than 13,000 completed interviews with people who meet the functional definition of *developmental disabilities*. Although the survey instrument was not designed primarily to provide insight into quality of life, a large number of items were taken from quality of life instruments that have been used with the general population, such as *The Quality of American Life* (Campbell & Converse, 1978). A great deal of information about quality and outcome issues, including quality of life, will soon be available.

GENERAL PRINCIPLES FOR FUTURE QUALITY ASSESSMENT EFFORTS

Given our proposed outcome orientation, we now outline 10 principles regarding future quality assessment efforts.

1. Quality enhancement does not assure quality. No quality enhancement system can really assure that high quality services are always delivered to every person. By itself, no such system is sufficient; there are other factors that are necessary. For example, in a system in which the average case manager's caseload is 100 individuals, or in which there is little or no value-based training, no quality enhancement system can guarantee what the term implies.

Within that limitation, however, it is still necessary to design a system to monitor the well-being of people in the service system. Once again, without accurate and continued feedback about the status of the system, it is impossible for the system to change consistently in the direction of increasing quality. In order that the system improve over time, quality enhancement is therefore necessary but not sufficient.

2. Quality enhancement occurs at multiple levels. Quality enhancement occurs at many levels of the service system. Part of what case managers do is quality enhancement, as are licensing regulations. Any statewide initiative in this area must select a clear and limited focus. Otherwise, the initiative is likely to dissipate in an effort to satisfy everyone's needs at all levels.

3. Emphasize a scientific approach. The quality enhancement activity must be presented and operated as a scientific endeavor; this will inevitably increase the credibility of the process. It is a given that no two observers can completely agree on the definition of quality in a community program; it follows that we are engaged in a continual process or collecting information that will teach us about what factors contribute to a quality program, and how best to measure those factors. Unless the simple precepts of the scientific method are used, we will fail to learn as we go.

4. Reliability is essential. If a monitor visits a residential setting on one day and finds deficiencies A, B, and C, and another monitor goes in two days later and finds deficiencies A, D, and E, then the provider is certain to become cynical about the quality enhancement activity. Because of poor interrater reliability, the provider comes to view such unreliable monitoring as being completely unrelated to the quality of the setting or its outcomes.

5. Focus on individuals. While we have already stated that quality enhancement occurs at multiple levels of the service system, it is important to point out that the most important level is that of the individual. The quality enhancement approaches that involve direct contact with the individuals being served are the ones that we value most. Emphasizing this kind of approach ensures that the individual is the ultimate unit of accountability. Quality enhancement must maximize the involvement and input from both primary and secondary (family member) consumers.

It is also important to point out that individually oriented monitoring of community systems is feasible and cost effective. The idea of evaluating every person's situation every year might seem to be prohibitively costly, but we have found this not to be the case. In Pennsylvania, for example, we collect environmental assessments, family surveys, plus individual quantitative data on behavior, services, health, and day programs, and our costs have never exceeded $250 per person per year. This has held true in other states as well.

6. Use outcome orientation. In the field of disabilities, we tend to emphasize the fact that all people can grow and learn; we believe the central goal of our efforts is to maximize individual potential. Changes in adaptive behavior and in the expression of challenging behavior can be measured effectively and reliably, and we believe that no quality enhancement system is complete until it can be demonstrated that individuals are showing measurable gains.

The notion of outcomes, however, is not limited to growth. Outcomes include the outcome of individual happiness, the outcome of family satisfaction, the outcome of increasing productivity, and the outcome of increased acceptance, status, and integration within our society. All of these outcomes must be measured. If they cannot be measured, then they must be subjected to attempts to measure, so that someday it can be scientifically determined whether changes have occurred. These concrete changes in individual lives should be the ultimate unit of accountability.

7. Keep assessment and assistance separate. The collection of reliable information about the quality of peoples' lives is only half of the quality enhancement loop. The second half involves doing something about what is found. We believe that the enhancement function (also called *quality assistance*, or, in punitive systems such as litigation, *compliance* or *enforcement*) should be kept separate from the assessment function. Assessors should seek the facts and report them, and enhancement/assistance personnel should verify the reports and decide how best to remedy situations of poor quality. Keeping these two functions separate enables the assessors to remain objective.

8. Keep assessment independent. Ideally, the assessment function should be free of vested interests and biases. Assessors should be interested in ascertaining the truth about people's situations. This leads to the conclusion that the quality assessment function is best located within an independent third party that has no "ax to grind."

9. The enhancement/assistance function needs clout. While we believe that the assessment activity should be carried out by an independent third party, the enhancement/assistance activity is best performed by an entity with clout. In order to require that a situation be corrected, or that a service provider accept training and technical assistance to improve performance, or to reward a program for doing an exceptional job, the enhancement entity must have power. In the developmental disabilities service system, this generally means control of, or influence on, funding.

10. Enhancement includes rewards. We maintain that the ideal quality enhancement system will not only deliver training, technical assistance, and penalties, but will also reward good performance. Rewards may be fiscal (for workers, bonuses, money to take college courses; for providers, increased per diem or permission to open more facilities) or may be less tangible (special recognition, certificates of commendation, annual social events, direct phone calls of congratulations from upper echelon officials). Any complete quality enhancement system must recognize the importance of and learn how to deliver and encourage the delivery of rewards all the way down to the direct service level.

CONCLUSION

Having called attention to the focus of our own perspective, it bears repeating that we contend that a good quality enhancement system must combine outcome and process assessment. One of the most serious short-comings of outcome-oriented quality of life assessment is that, if the outcomes are poor, then process investigation may be needed to determine exactly where the problems are. In this situation, it would be beneficial if both outcomes and processes are monitored regularly.

Nevertheless, our outcome orientation is such that we might conclude that a service is high quality even if that service shows poor compliance with generally accepted standards. For example, if consumers in a given agency were showing positive outcomes, but the agency could not pass accreditation standards or received very low ratings on PASS-3 (a measure of normalization; Wolfensberger & Glenn, 1975), we would tend to trust the outcomes and might infer that the process measures were not measuring true quality. Conversely, we believe it is quite possible that a facility that is fully accredited by national standards might produce poor outcomes and unpleasant life situations.

We hope that in the future growing interest in and commitment to quality of life will be balanced. By balance, we mean that systems designed to assess the quality of life of people with developmental disabilities should include both process and the outcome orientations and should also provide a continual and dignified mechanism for consumers to influence the system.

REFERENCES

Campbell, A., & Converse, P. (1978). *The quality of American life.* Ann Arbor: Center for Political Studies, University of Michigan.

Conroy, J. W., & Bradley, V. J. (1985). *The Pennhurst longitudinal study: A report of five years of research and analysis* (Pennhurst Study Report PC-85-1). Philadelphia: Temple University Developmental Disabilities Center.

Conroy, J., Walsh, R., & Feinstein, C. (1987). Consumer satisfaction: People with mental retardation moving from institutions to the community. In S. Bruening & R. Gable (Eds.), *Advances in mental retardation and developmental disabilities, Volume 3* (pp. 135–150). Greenwich, CT: JAI Press.

Miller, G. A., Galanter, E., & Pribram, K. H. (1960). *Plans and the structure of behavior.* New York: Holt, Rinehart & Winston.

Wiener, N. (1948). *Cybernetics.* Cambridge: Technology Press.

Wolfensberger, W., & Glenn, L. (1975). *Program analysis of service systems 3: A method for the quantitative evaluation of human services.* Toronto: National Institute on Mental Retardation.

22
Where Do We Go From Here?

Robert L. Schalock

*Hastings College and Mid-Nebraska Mental Retardation
Services, Inc.*

An enhanced quality of life for persons with disabilities cannot be separated from the three major trends that are currently impacting our service delivery system. In their simplest form, the trends include living, learning, and working in integrated environments; empowering persons with disabilities to choose and make decisions regarding their welfare and future; and holding service providers accountable for person-referenced outcomes that reflect an enhanced independence, productivity, community integration and quality of life.

However, if these trends are going to significantly enhance a person's quality of life, we need collectively to pursue a number of principles, parameters, and procedures that include:

- Principles that will foster policy development
- Parameters that will guide research efforts
- Procedures that will underlie service delivery

The purpose of this final chapter is to synthesize the material presented here around these three factors so that we can continue forming consensus and agenda for quality of life policy, research, and service delivery.

PRINCIPLES AND POLICY DEVELOPMENT

Throughout this book, numerous authors have suggested that the quality of life (QOL) concept can serve as the basis for a more coherent and unified disability policy, because QOL captures a broad array of issues and concerns that are important to persons with disabilities, their families, professionals, and governmental officials who administer programs and set policy. Because QOL is a generic concept, enhanced QOL outcomes for persons with and without disabilities are the same. Thus, a QOL-oriented disability policy would be based on the same social expectations and goals that society holds for nondisabled citizens.

However, such a coherent, QOL-oriented disability policy must be based

Table 22.1   Fundamental Quality of Life Principles Upon Which to Base QOL-Oriented Policy

1. QUALITY OF LIFE for persons with disabilities is composed of those same factors and relationships that are important to persons without disabilities.
2. QUALITY OF LIFE is experienced when a person's basic needs are met and when he or she has the same opportunity as anyone else to pursue and achieve goals in the major life settings of home, community, and work.
3. QUALITY OF LIFE factors vary over the life span of a person.
4. QUALITY OF LIFE is based on a set of values that emphasize consumer and family strengths.
5. QUALITY OF LIFE is determined by the congruence of public values and behavior.
6. QUALITY OF LIFE is a concept that can be consensually validated by a wide range of persons representing a variety of viewpoints of consumers and their families, advocates, professionals, and providers.

on a number of fundamental principles that will guide all aspects of policy formulation and implementation. Table 22.1 summarizes six of these principles as gleaned from the preceding chapters. Common to these principles is a quest for insuring a high life of quality, not only for specific individuals, but for society as a whole.

PARAMETERS TO GUIDE RESEARCH EFFORTS

A consideration of QOL variables should occupy a prominent role in both research and program evaluation activities. As with policy development and implementation, a set of QOL principles should guide these efforts. Six of these principles are listed in Table 22.2.

It seems to this writer that the issue of quality of life measurement will

Table 22.2   QOL Principles to Guide Research Efforts

1. The study of QOL requires an indepth knowledge of people and their perspectives.
2. The study of QOL for people labeled *mentally retarded* or *disabled* requires that the label be set aside.
3. The measurement of QOL should be tied to values and linked to measures of QOL for all the nation's citizenry.
4. The measurement of QOL requires multiple methodologies.
5. Family assessments that are driven by family choices and that are flexible, nonjudgmental, and emphasize the development of family strengths must be developed.
6. The application of QOL data is important in developing resources and supports for persons with disabilities and their families.

Table 22.3   Quality of Life (QOL) Taxonomy[a]

QOL Areas	Home	Community	Work (Production)[b]
		Environments (Integration)[b]	
Self-esteem— Social	Affection Recognition	Warm personal integration	Respect Recognition Production
Self-esteem— Beauty	Attractive physical appearance	Attractive physical appearance	Attractive physical appearance
Self-direction (Independence)[b]	Freedom of choice	Freedom of choice	Job matched to problemsolving ability Career ladder choices
Social relations	Family	Friends	Co-workers
Environmental comfort and convenience	Pleasant home	Pleasant community Convenient and effective generic services and resources	Pleasant workplace
Safety and security	Food Shelter	Safe community	Safe workplace Sufficient income

[a] Adapted from Schalock, R. L., and Heal, L. W. (1988). Research in quality of life. In D. Goode (Ed.), *Proceedings from quality of life for persons with disabilities*. Valhalla, New York: Mental Retardation Institute University Affiliated Facility.

[b] P.L. 100-146 implies that Quality of Life for developmentally disabled individuals is to be reflected in their *integration* into the generic community, their *independence* to pursue the services in that community, and remunerative *production* that contributes meaningfully to themselves and the community.

be an important part of the current and future QOL agenda. In that regard, I feel that there are at least the following five important tasks that must be addressed.

1. Develop taxonomies of QOL areas for a minimum of three age groups (school, adult, and elderly) that identify the features of the lifespace that best reflect the quality of life. An inductive approach should be used in which persons with disabilities are asked what factors are important to them and thereby reflect their subjective QOL. An example of how this might be done is presented in Table 22.3.

2. Operationalize the features of persons' lives (from the previous step) that best reflect their subjective QOL and then develop assessment instruments including:
   a. objective, public indices
   b. verbal, subjective lifestyle satisfaction
   c. nonverbal, subjective lifestyle satisfaction

3. Determine the weighting given to each QOL area by different individuals.
4. Assess the degree of QOL of each individual in each QOL area.
5. Pursue the following four important research issues:
   a. Correlate objective and subjective QOL measures.
   b. Evaluate interventions that improve both objective and subjective
      QOL scores.
   c. Determine whether improvements in one area effect improve-
      ments in another. For example, is a person's QOL improved
      through empowerment, employment, and/or least restrictive al-
      ternatives?
   d. Determine which models of QOL for disabled persons apply to
      other populations.

PROCEDURES THAT UNDERLIE SERVICE DELIVERY

The success of this book and the QOL agenda will ultimately be determined on the basis of improved QOL-oriented services to persons with
disabilities. To that end, this section of the chapter discusses a number of
principles and procedures that are consistent with the proposed QOL-
oriented policy changes and the anticipated results from the research efforts
discussed in the preceding sections.

QOL-Oriented Service Delivery Principles

As with the previously discussed policy and research areas, service delivery should also be based on a number of fundamental principles that
have been discussed throughout this volume. Six of the principles are listed
in Table 22.4.

QOL-Oriented Service Delivery Patterns

An enhanced quality of life for persons with disabilities is not likely to
be achieved without a values-based reorientation of the current service
delivery system. Although certainly not definitive, the following suggestions for service delivery change are worth considering:

- Shift the logic underlying service delivery from one of *preparation* for
  normal adult living to one of *support* in normal adult living.
- Focus program development, monitoring, and evaluation efforts on
  the lifestyle benefits or outcomes that service recipients receive.
- Shift the focus of program placement decisions to such variables as
  personal preference for living situation, proximity to family, presence

Table 22.4 QOL Principles to Guide Service Delivery

1. QUALITY OF LIFE is enhanced by satisfying basic needs and fulfilling responsibilities in regular life settings.
2. QUALITY OF LIFE is enhanced by empowering persons with disabilities and their families to participate in decisions that affect their lives.
3. QUALITY OF LIFE for any given individual is intrinsically related to the quality of life of persons in his or her environment.
4. QUALITY OF LIFE is enhanced by the acceptance and full integration of persons with disabilities and their families into their local communities.
5. QUALITY OF LIFE has both objective and subjective components, but it is primarily the subjective view of the individual that determines the QUALITY OF LIFE he or she experiences.
6. QUALITY OF LIFE variables should occupy a prominent role in overall program evaluation.

of friends in the neighborhood, and commuting demands for employment.

- Focus on both being *in* and *of* the community.
- Develop staff training and enrichment programs where necessary to recognize that the quality of life for any person is intrinsically related to the quality of life of other persons in the same environment.
- Develop and implement a consumer choice, QOL-oriented Individual Program Plan process.
- Sustain and enhance family and other relationships that impact the lives of persons with disabilities.
- Enhance the ability of consumers and their families to make decisions and choices that directly affect their lives and the delivery of services to them.
- Develop and implement community programs to increase networking among persons with disabilities and persons without disabilities and to improve community awareness about social and physical factors in the environment that impact the quality of life for all persons.
- Increase the emphasis placed on quality of life in overall program evaluation.

In conclusion, one cannot separate the quest for enhancing the quality of life of persons with disabilities from our own search for the same. What I have attempted to do in this final chapter is to suggest that an enhanced quality of life—or a life of quality, if you will—is built on a firm foundation of fundamental principles, supported by research parameters and service-related procedures.

No one among us feels that our quest will be easy. But our efforts and their results are of value to persons that each of us value very highly. As stated by Justin Dart in *A Life Of Quality For Americans with Disabilities* (*Report To The President: President's Committee on Mental Retardation*; May, 1986) ". . . we all know that there is a long hard road to travel to the just society of our dreams." Mr. Dart goes on to say,

> We must use all educational, social, political, legal and public communication systems to incorporate into the cultural consciousness the concepts that the existence and dignity of each human life is sacred and inviolable; that disability is a normal, predictable characteristic of the human process; that disabled people have the same rights and the same responsibilities as other persons; and that the fundamental right and obligation of all human beings is to fulfill their potential to exercise independent control over their own lives, to be as productive and self-sufficient as possible, to participate equitably in the mainstream of society, and to preserve and maximize the quality of life for themselves, for their families, for their communities, for their nations and for all people. (p. 12)